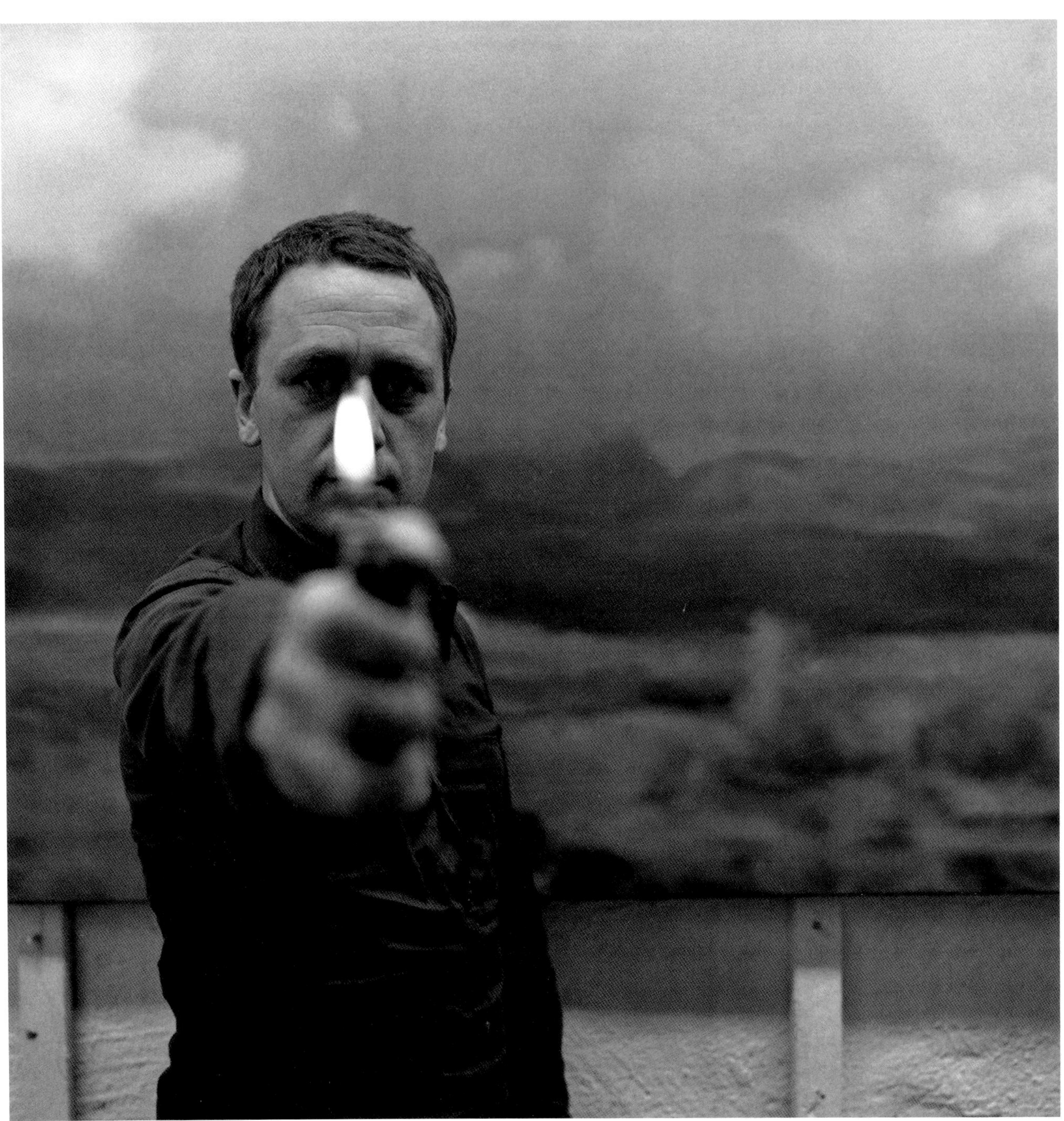

Klaus Honnef

Gerhard Richter

TASCHEN

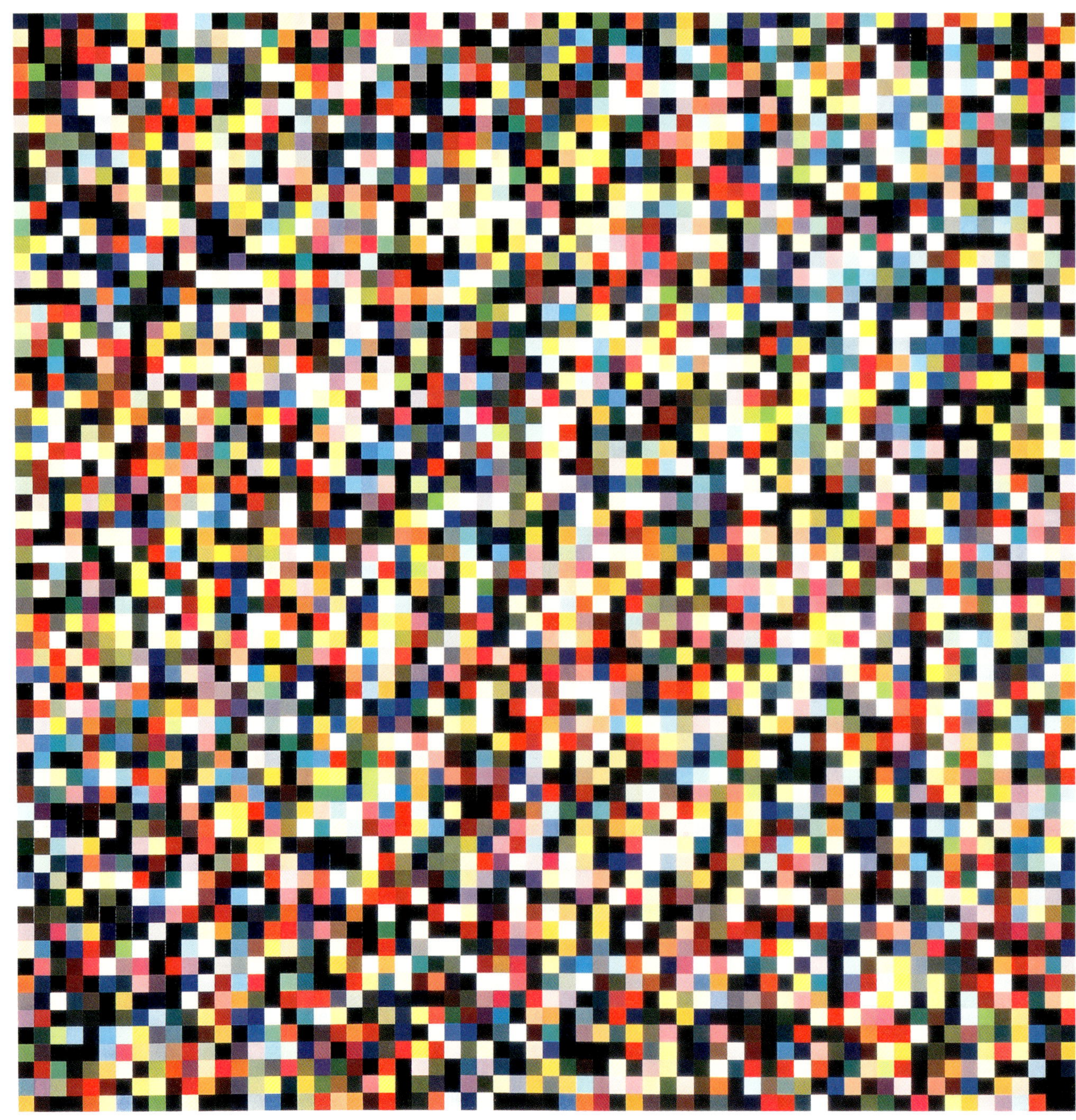

Contents

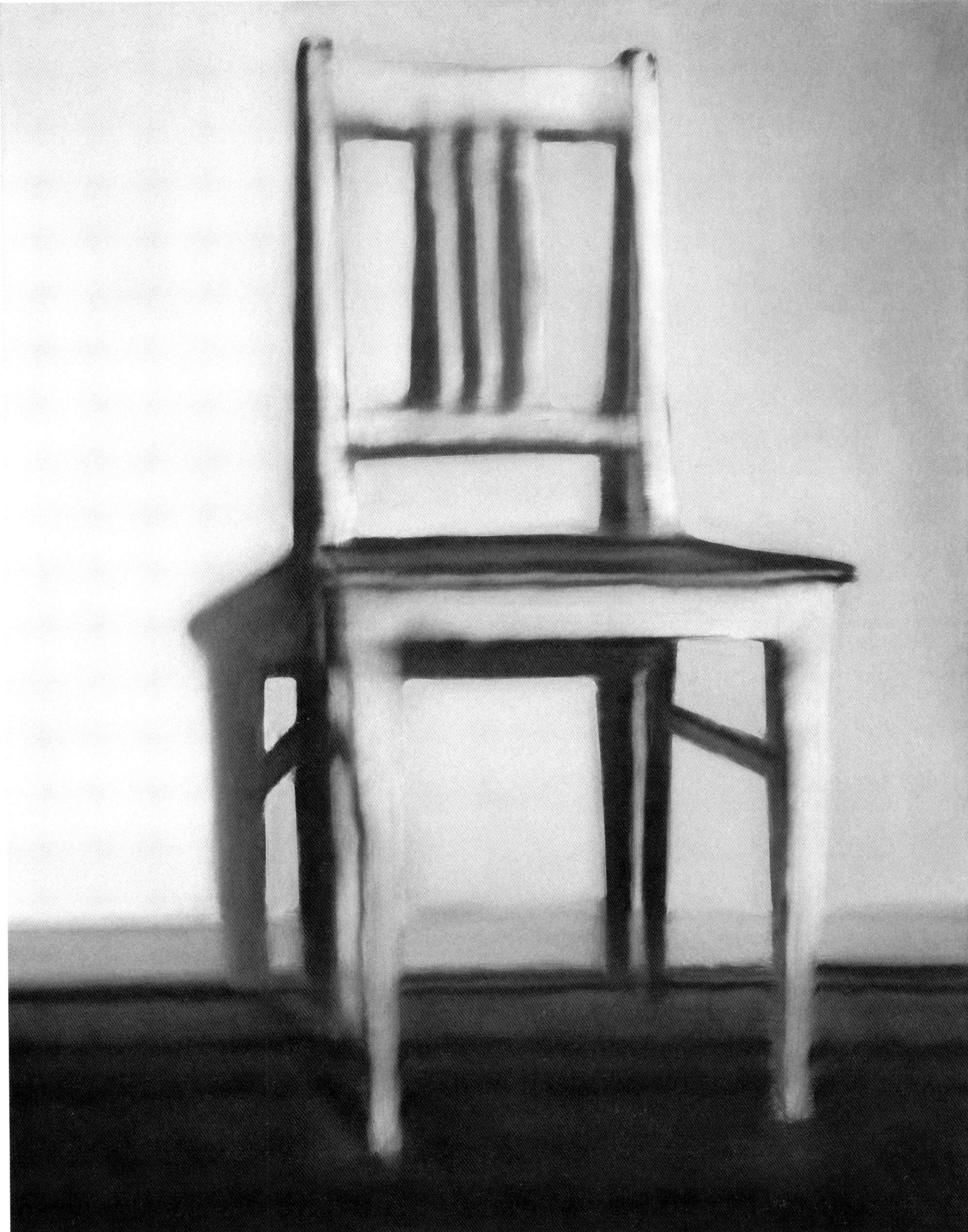

"In painting thinking is painting."[1]

While preparing a major retrospective of Gerhard Richter's paintings at the Museum of Modern Art in 2002, curator Robert Storr asked the artist a contentious question: "I wonder if art history had special importance for you?" The question's provocative core becomes evident only when we consider art's self-understanding after the dawn of modernism. Its sting is revealed against the turbulent background of 20th-century art because, in retrospect, modernist art is a symbolic revolution that sharply and unremittingly rejected all that preceded it. Belief in relentless progress fueled its engine. Key artistic trends, ideas, principles, and attitudes changed at breakneck speeds. Even anti-art initiatives resulted in new art forms, and these, in turn, in newer ones. Aesthetic criteria and convictions wore out faster than disposable gloves and, as a consequence, artists considered the history of art to be, at most, a supermarket for arbitrary citations. It ceased to provide binding aesthetic standards.

Richter's unambiguous answer is therefore all the more astonishing: "I am definitely inside of art history; it's my domain, my home."[2] Prompted to clarify, he specifies: "In the art, the painters' culture."[3] Although the response seems self-evident, it wasn't so for Richter. From the start, Richter's artistic path to the "art, the painters' culture" was paved with doubt and uncertainties. On the surface, therefore, a detour would seem a more appropriate metaphor. But what appears to the superficial gaze as a complicated tangle is in fact the absolute precondition for an artistic practice that derives its own outcomes from the practice itself, from the continuous ping-ponging of trial and error, from both productive and unproductive accidents, and from sustained intermissions. A practice that does not obey any preestablished intention or doctrine but instead focuses only on the actions performed on each canvas. Each brushstroke provokes a reaction that has a more or less significant effect on the painted picture's overall structure. Idiosyncrasy manifests itself in painting. "Painting has nothing to do with thinking, because in painting thinking is painting,"[4] Richter noted in one of his early pointed aphorisms.

That statement offers a key to Richter's art. The apodictic assertion relativizes and highlights an observation by the sociologist Pierre Bourdieu: "And yet, every stroke of the brush is both free and structured."[5] On the one hand, it is unmistakably the brushstroke of an artistic subject; on the other, structured by a variety of stimuli, experiences, techniques, and attitudes that artists

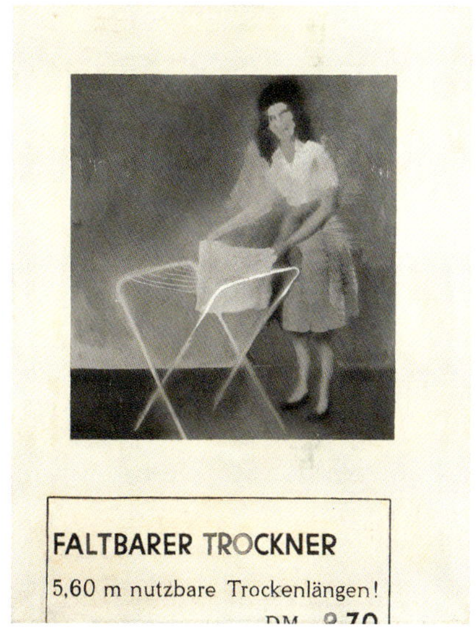

Folding Dryer, 1962 (CR 4)
Oil on canvas, 99.3 x 78.6 cm (39 x 31 in.)
Stuttgart, Froehlich Collection

PAGE 2
Gerhard Richter, 1970
Photo: Gerhard Richter, courtesy of Gerhard Richter Archive, Dresden

PAGE 4
4096 Colors, 1974 (CR 359)
Lacquer on canvas, 254 x 254 cm (100 x 100 in.)
Private collection

Kitchen Chair, 1965 (CR 97)
Oil on canvas, 100 x 80 cm (39⅜ x 31½ in.)
Recklinghausen, Kunsthalle

unconsciously or consciously acquire over the course of their lives. Acquired through a "system of constraints … which defines the margin of manoeuvre and the limits of free play."[6] Stimuli from a variety of sources—a mixture of lifeworld, cultural, and aesthetic—flow spontaneously into artistic attitude. They modulate both perception and aesthetic judgement. They feed on social structures and institutional conditions and are condensed in the artist's attitude.

Those who ignore these complex and sometimes contentious factors miss the artistic essence of Richter's paintings: their quiet, subversive power and their radical effect on more recent art as well as their subtle references. Subversively, they act against art's prevailing trends and intelligently undermine their sporadic authority, while their aesthetic references illuminate the artistic fields in which he releases stimulatory signals. Richter is a symbolic revolutionary. This is documented by his practice of painting: invisible to outsiders, visible only in artistic result. His exhibitions trigger a high level of irritation that dogged Richter's work and found expression in art criticism and the public's reaction. The art world has now become used to the pole reversal to which his images point, so that its true radicalism has eroded and become standard.

Richter did not reinvent painting. Nor did he revamp worn models after painting had been frequently and confidently declared dead by both artists and art critics. He did, however, liberate it from the uncontrolled growth of an ideology that reduced it to the depiction of visible facts. Richter renewed painting from the ground up, drawing it back to the elemental conditions of its potential. He stressed paintings' material foundation, and their material qualities became decisive linguistic devices. By lending them a reflexive moment and visualizing it, Richter added an unexpected freshness to old forms and categories that were exhausted and damaged by doctrinal use.

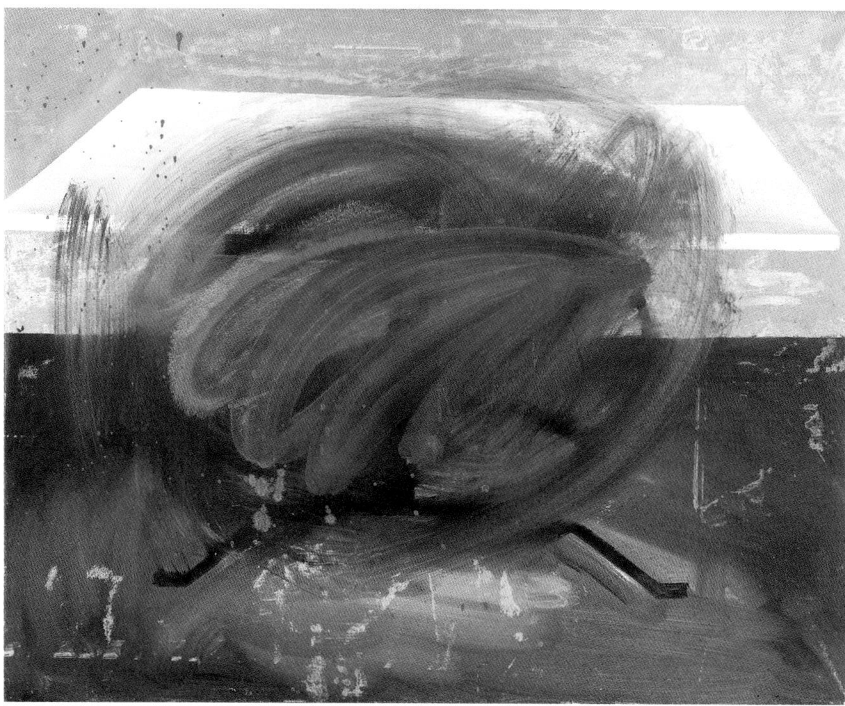

Table, 1962 (CR 1)
Oil on canvas, 90 x 113 cm (35½ x 44½ in.)
Cambridge, Busch-Reisinger Museum
Harvard Art Museum (loan from a private collection)

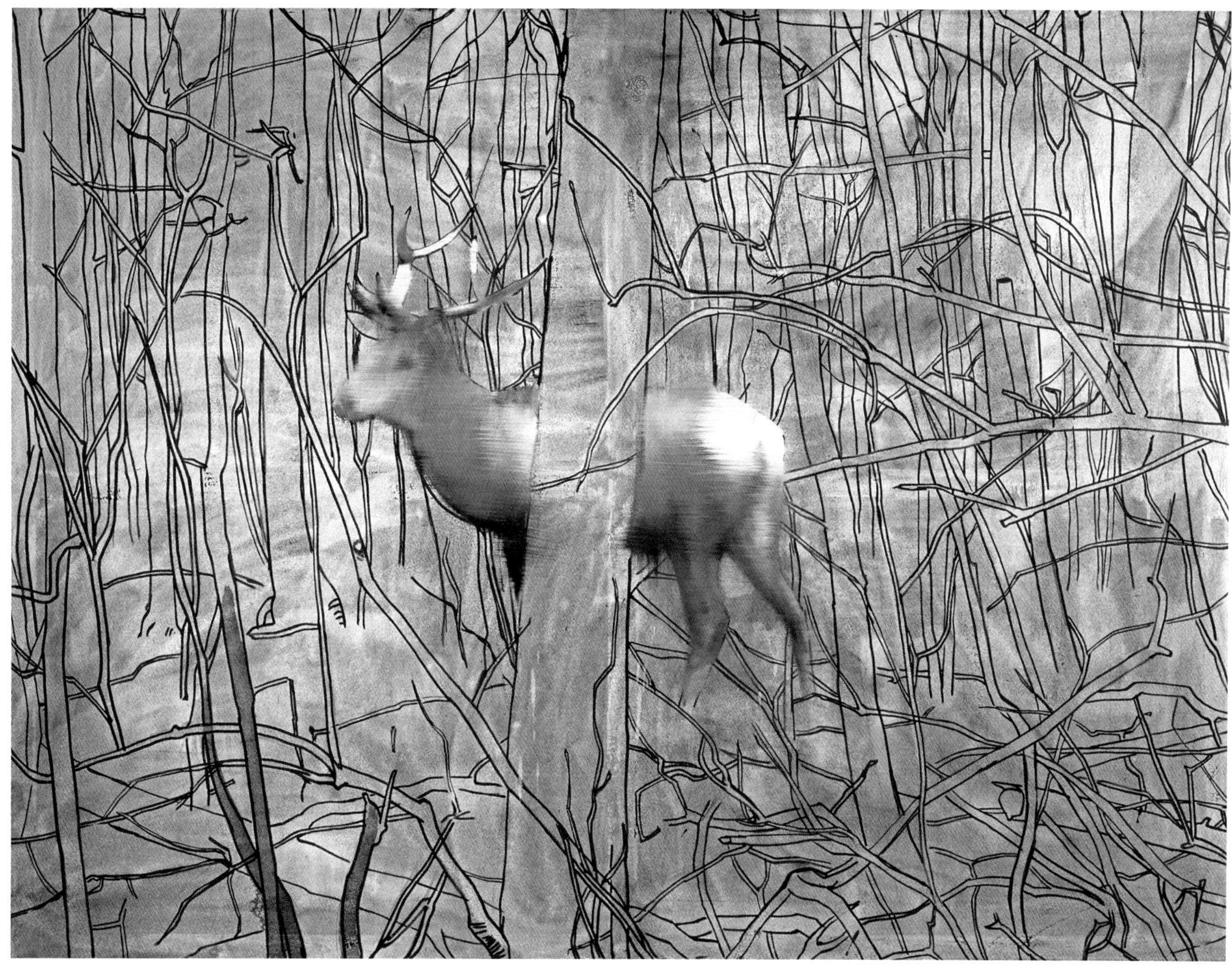

Deer, 1963 (CR 7)
Oil on canvas, 150 x 200 cm (59 x 78¾ in.)
Paris, Fondation Louis Vuitton

Nonetheless, the relationship between artist and painting reveals itself to be highly differentiated and by no means free of contradiction. There is a comparatively distant relationship, underlined by a strangely cool and detached unemotional passion. Richter's artistic attitude contains echoes of the "death of the author" idea put forward by Roland Barthes and Michel Foucault in France. One motif is particularly poignant: "I always want my paintings to tell something. That is why I refer to my work as pictures rather than paintings."[7] He is concerned with more than terminology. His choice draws a clear boundary against any form of expressive, indeed subjectively primed, painting. Richter draws a line against the paintings of author-artists who, in Roland Barthes's words, "feed" the work, "that is, he pre-exists it, thinks, suffers, lives for it."[8]

Richter denounced conventional ideas about the artist as a godlike creative genius. As an artist, his notion corresponds to Bourdieu's concept of the "agent" as the "actor" of dispositions either acquired through learning and experience, or unconsciously collected and internalized during the course of his or her life. This expresses the modernity of Richter's artistic attitude, despite his statement that "In every respect, my work has more to do with traditional art than with anything else."[9] The artist bears a dislike of exclusively self-referential painting. As early as 1962, Richter noted that his painting was driven by a "need to

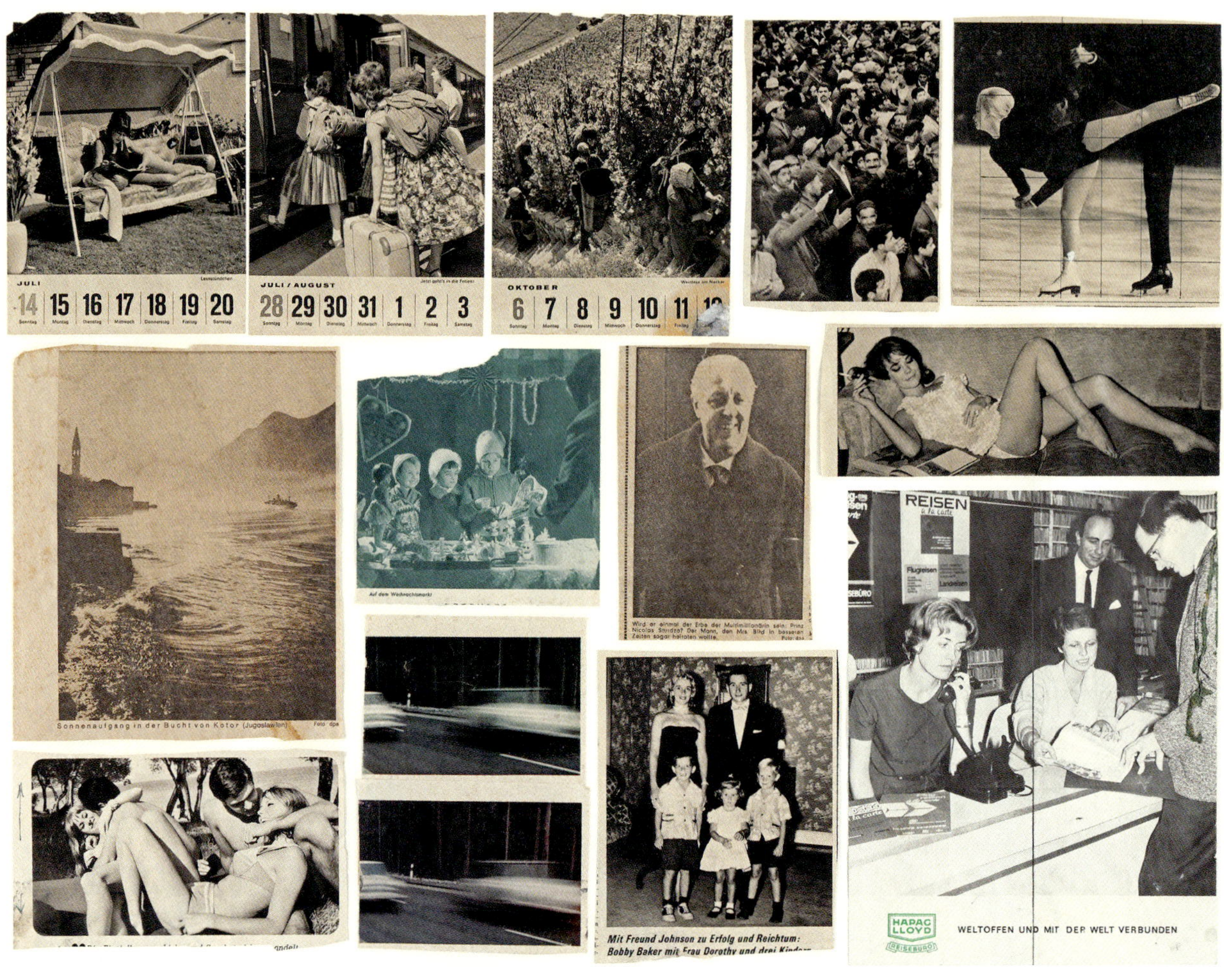

Newspaper photos, 1962 (Atlas Sheet: 7)
2 color, 12 b/w photographs,
3 calendar pages mounted on cardboard,
51.7 x 66.7 cm (20⅜ x 26¾ in.)
Munich, Städtische Galerie im Lenbachhaus und Kunstbau

communicate."[10] An explanatory supplement appears almost programmatic: "The effort to fix one's own vision, to deal with appearances (which are alien and must be given names and meanings)."[11]

It is not by chance that Richter's relationship with painting wavered in his early years. These were the decades after the mid-20th century, when an unprecedented furor raged in the Western art scene, leaving no stone unturned. Not even Dada, which emerged after World War I, was driven by such a tabula rasa mentality. Painters slashed canvases, packed *merde d'artiste* in cans, and printed newspaper photographs on primed canvases. Richter developed a surprisingly lively interest in the unusual artistic pursuits of anti-form and anti-art; in Fluxus, Pop Art, happenings, performance art, process art, and conceptual art.

Although deeply unsettling, these relatively anti-artistic tendencies made an impression on Richter, who sees uncertainty as painful but not necessarily negative. In a statement for Coosje van Bruggen in May 1985, Richter summarized his complex relationship to the artistic protests of the time: "It was all very cynical and destructive. It was a signal for us, and we became cynical and cocky and told ourselves that art is bull and Cézanne is stupid etc., and … I'll paint a photo! Fluxus was the catalyst."[12]

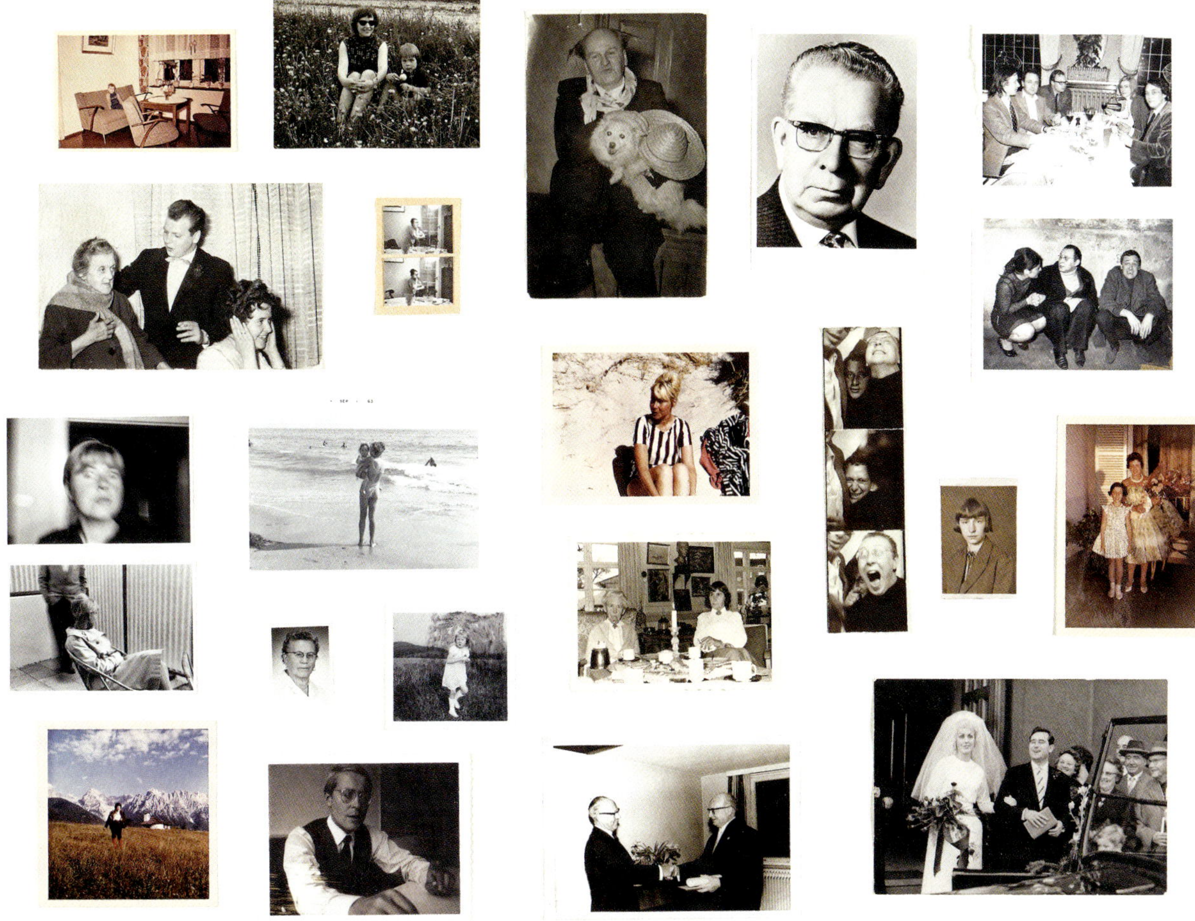

Album photos, 1962 (ATLAS SHEET: 6)
4 color, 21 b/w photographs mounted on cardboard, 51.7 x 66.7 cm (20⅜ x 26⅜ in.)
Munich, Städtische Galerie im Lenbachhaus und Kunstbau

Richter was a witness to the turbulent happenings, actions, and all the other artistic interventions of the time. He experienced close up the attacks on traditional aesthetic models and principles as well as the upheavals in the art scene. The cultural hurricane's epicenters were located in some of the smaller towns of North Rhine-Westphalia, the most populous state in the Federal Republic of Germany, as well as its capital, Düsseldorf. Many of these places had embraced avant-garde art before the Nazi era.

Richter and his wife Ema settled in Düsseldorf after his escape from the German Democratic Republic on March 1, 1961. Munich had originally been his destination. Fortuitous? If it was a coincidence, it was an intriguing one.

Born on February 9, 1932, in Dresden, where he studied mural painting at the city's Academy of Fine Arts, Richter registered the upheavals in the West German art scene with astonishing open-mindedness and curiosity. Perhaps he experienced them as a reflection of the artistic freedom he desired for himself and his art, one that he hoped to achieve by escaping. Richter was not, however, entirely unprepared for the events that he would encounter when he eventually did make it to West Germany. An aunt in the West had supplied him with books, catalogs, and cultural magazines. This information was supplemented by conversations with artist friends who had their own news sources in the West. Thanks to a day trip to Kassel for *documenta 2*, journeys to Hamburg and Munich, as well as a sojourn in Paris that lasted several days, Richter was adequately apprised of the main trends in Western Germany, having witnessed them himself.

After completing his studies, Richter gained a modest reputation and some prosperity in the GDR as a freelance painter. Commissions even allowed him to purchase a car. There were no political problems, although he painstakingly avoided causing a stir. Nevertheless, his artistic endeavors kept coming up against ideological lines, which ultimately left him no choice but to flee to the West. He longed to execute his artistic ideas free from state influence—and not just at night. Richter has repeatedly stressed his fundamental, almost physical aversion to ideologies of whatever hue. Ideological constraints are likely to have made him more sensitive to artistic tendencies that defied convention, even sometimes using artistic freedom to the point of excess.

In Düsseldorf, Richter embarked on a second course of study at the city's famous art academy, which would also come to distinguish itself as a hotbed of the avant-garde. He met Konrad Lueg and Sigmar Polke at a painting class taught by Karl Otto Götz, a leading representative of German Art Informel, and they became fellow travelers. Later, they were joined by Blinky Palermo. As Richter studied, he worked his way through and assimilated

Coffin Bearers, 1962 (CR 5)
Oil on canvas, 135 x 180 cm (53¼ x 70⅞ in.)
Munich, Bayerische Staatsgemäldesammlungen, Pinakothek der Moderne

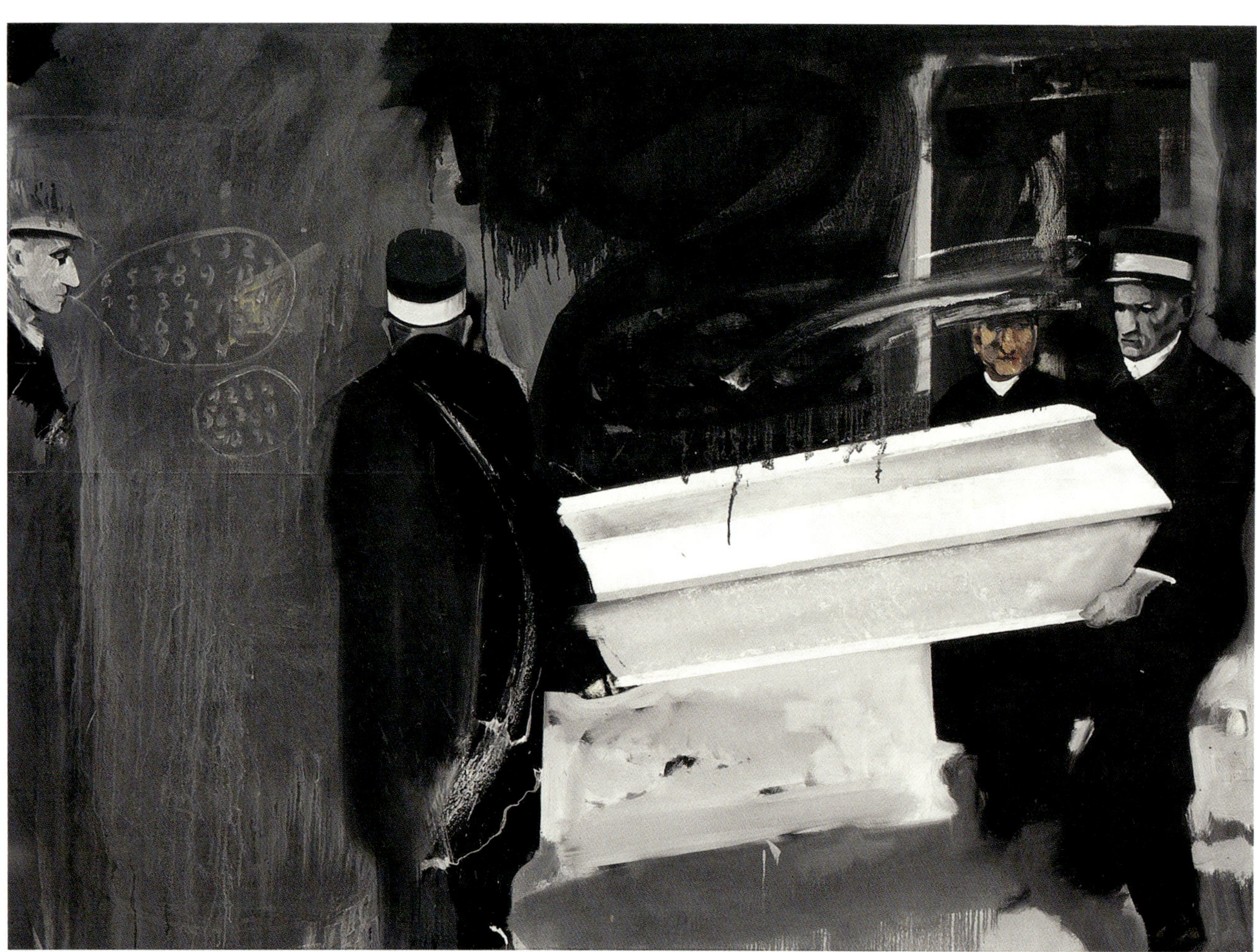

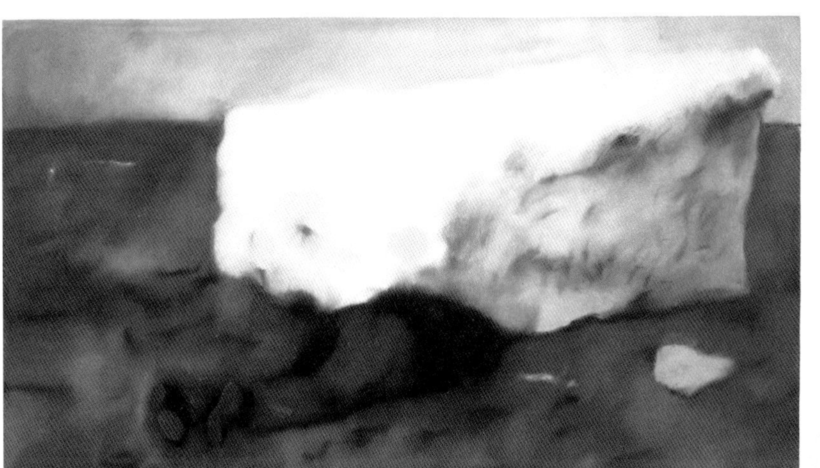

Dead, 1963 (CR 9)
Oil on canvas, 100 x 150 cm (39⅜ x 59 in.)
New York, The Museum of Modern Art

with the prevailing Western art forms, from Art Informel to Constructivism to Color Field Painting. However, this did not stop him from improving his economic situation by joining Lueg and Polke in designing carnival floats for Düsseldorf's traditional parade.

The political, social, and cultural fluidity of the time also had a major influence on his artistic attitude. The younger generation's growing dislike of the social structures under Konrad Adenauer's conservative regime, a subliminal fear of possible nuclear war, and a mistrust of the West's increasingly dubious slogans about freedom, were exacerbated by the escalation in the Vietnam War. This was compounded by the psychosocial aftermath of the Frankfurt Auschwitz trials, which finally brought the collectively suppressed crimes of National Socialism to public light. The global context was provided by a worldwide protest movement against the traditional institutional and personal authorities, which, in the eyes of the generation born during the war, had lost their legitimacy. These street-level protests dominated the mass media, which had initially backed the powers that be.

The art of the time was charged with obscuring political and social grievances, as well as the crimes of past decades and the social contradictions of the present, as a result of contemporary art's demonstrative insistence on self-reference. Under this pressure, the idea that art would stave off any further attempts at exploitation by National Socialism or Communism by pos-tulating its autonomy, lost its inviolable validity. Many of the younger artists and the art critics who sympathized with them—most of them born shortly before the war and not actively involved in it—had no wish to interpret the world. They wanted to change it.

Concrete reality offered material for numerous artistic actions. It also tended to be their subject. Pop Art focused on the phenomena of urban civilization and absorbed them: cinema, television, advertising, fashion, magazines, photography, and comics. Whereas the British version of Pop Art had a critical undertone, the Americans' was affirmative. Pop Art made a radical break with the elitism of art, opening it to visual stimuli provided by the mass media. Land artists turned the vast spaces outside the United States' urban conurbations into "canvases," which they and their companions captured on film and in photographs for posterity. When, despite strong opposition, Action Art and anti-art found their places in contemporary art, "documentary photography"—which had created visibility—automatically conquered the art world. Piggybacking, so to speak. Another, longer-lasting consequence of anti-art's success was the inevitable decline of traditional aesthetic criteria and categories.

Richter discovered photography as an adolescent when, in 1945, his mother gave him a small cassette camera. A musician herself, she steered him into the sphere of culture, music, and literature. He learned to develop film and print photographs in a darkroom set up by a friend of his father's. He photographed extensively and with great enthusiasm.

The bulk of his photographs was later published in *Atlas*[13], a pictorial compendium of his art in book form. The literature on Richter disregards that he was part of Germany's first generation whose "image of the world"—a term often used by the artist—was above all derived from photographic images in books, magazines, and private photo albums. Additionally, when he saw his first works of art, they were not originals but reproductions in books about art. There has been little investigation into the way and extent to which photographic images influence individual and collective ways of seeing. There is no doubt, however, that Richter—more than any other artist—thought about and worked intensively and extensively with the aesthetic challenges posed by photography.

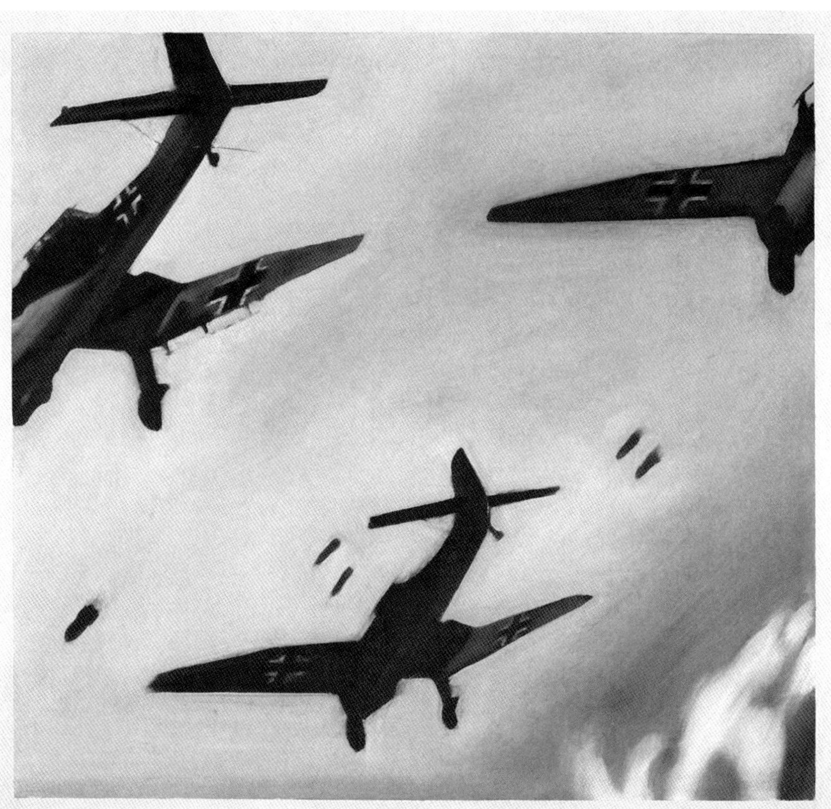

Stukas, 1964 (CR 18-1)
Oil on canvas, 80 x 80 cm (31½ x 31½ in.)
Munich, Bayerische Staatsgemäldesammlungen
Pinakothek der Moderne (loan from the Wittelsbacher Ausgleichsfond Collection)

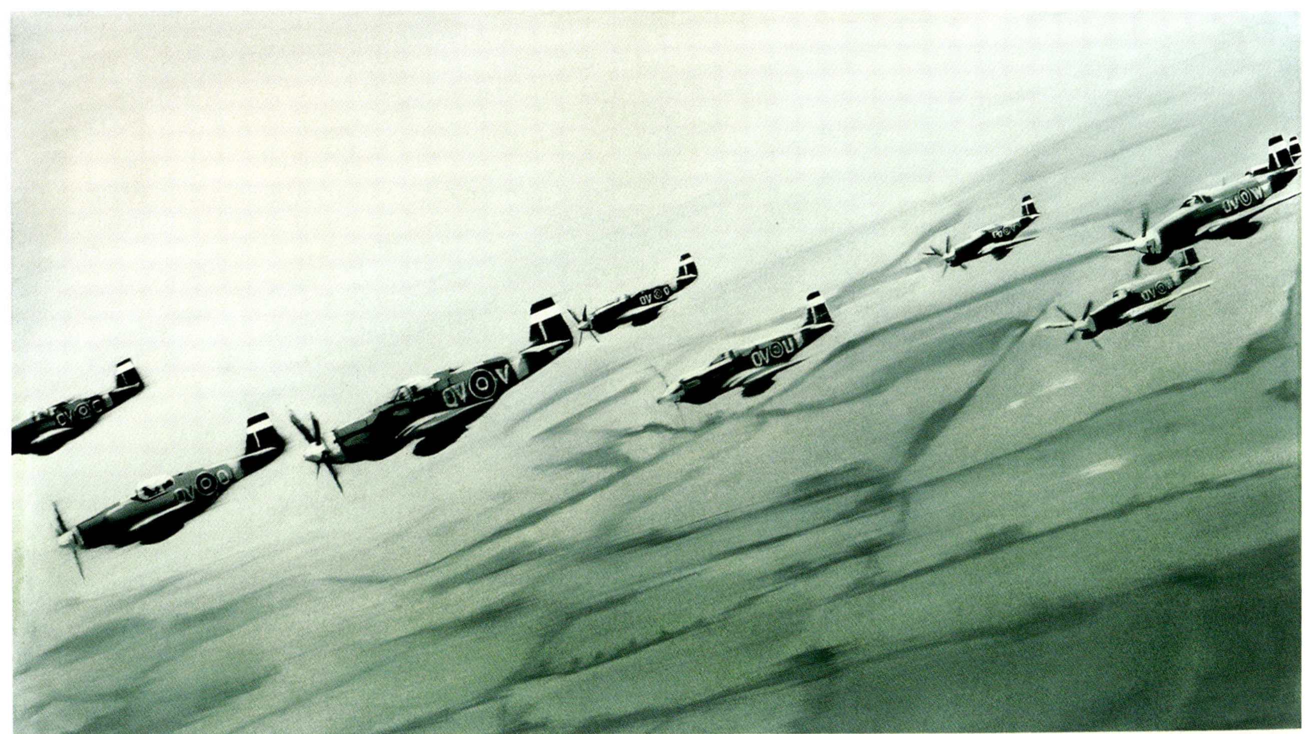

Mustang Squadron, 1964 (CR 19)
Oil on canvas, 88 x 150 cm (34¾ x 59 in.)
Dresden, Gerhard Richter Archive, Staatliche Kunstsammlungen Dresden (loan from a private collection)

Richter began to make photo paintings in 1962. Photo paintings? Undeniably, he owed his visual objects to photographic images. But, unlike Pop Art and related art movements, he did not produce like-for-like reproductions of photographic subjects or use them as reference material. In fact, in the process of continuous copying, Richter systematically worked his way up to the aesthetic core of the technical medium which, if nothing else, is located in the metaphysical or, at least, in the hallucinatory zone. The absence of that which it represents and what is actually only present as a shadow in the photographic image is determined by the photograph.

Richter's statement that "I'm not trying to imitate a photograph; I'm trying to make one,"[14] emphasizes that what he has in mind is the photographic image's unique aesthetic as well as the image itself. His written observations on photography also establish that his artistic endeavors are not just about photography—it is visual perception that interests Richter the most. This aligns him with all of modern art since Manet, Seurat, and Cézanne, the first artists to make paintings against the backdrop of the all-conquering mass medium of photography.

Richter's texts on photography reveal that he was steeped in theory. A typical note from 1964/65 distinguishes between seeing and knowing and illustrates the difference by making an insightful comparison between photography and painting: "Photographs show objects in a different way to painted pictures because the camera does not recognize objects but sees them. Freehand drawing recognizes the object in its parts, dimensions, proportions, and geometric figures. These parts are noted as ciphers and read coherently. It's an abstraction that deforms reality and promotes a specific stylization. By following contours with the help of a projector, you bypass this cumbersome cognitive process.

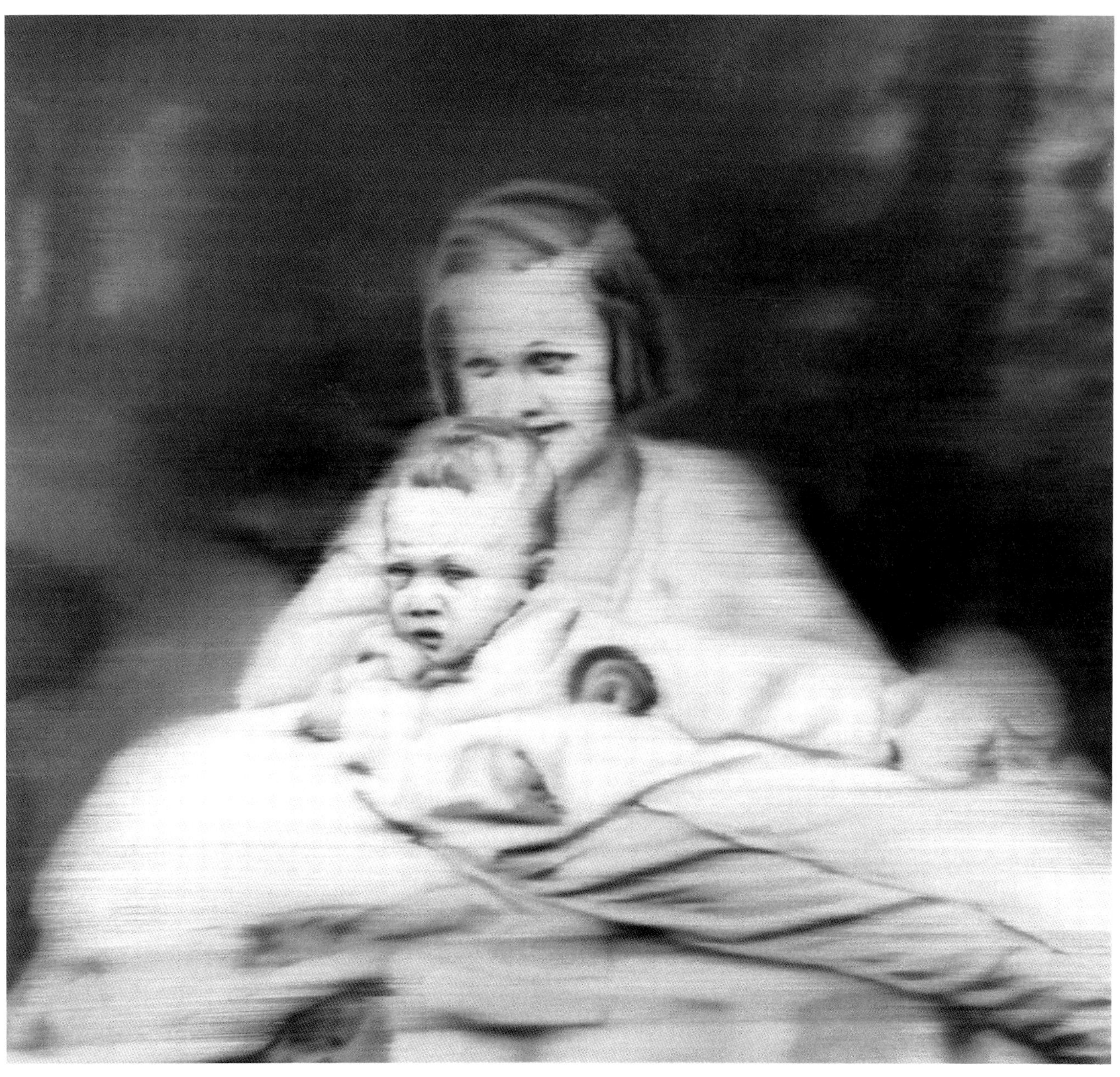

Aunt Marianne, 1965 (CR 87)
Oil on canvas, 100 x 115 cm (39⅜ x 45⅜ in.)
Taipei, The Yageo Foundation

Uncle Rudi, 1965 (CR 85)
Oil on canvas, 87 x 50 cm (34⅜ x 19¾ in.)
Czech Republic, Lidice Collection

We cease to recognize, and instead see and make what we did not recognize (informal)."[15]

With his photo paintings, the artist physically appropriated the camera's gaze just as he had appropriated variations of modern painting. He painted as a camera sees. As photography fixes its image in a heartbeat, Richter accepted the photographic image as real. He avoided all artifice such as composition, style, and subjectivity in the technical transfer of the images, be it by means of a projector or by tracing, with which painters had once rejected photography's claim to being art.

Although Richter applied the structural framework of the photographic model precisely to his photo paintings, they changed noticeably as soon as he enlarged the picture, which caused the formal relationships to become

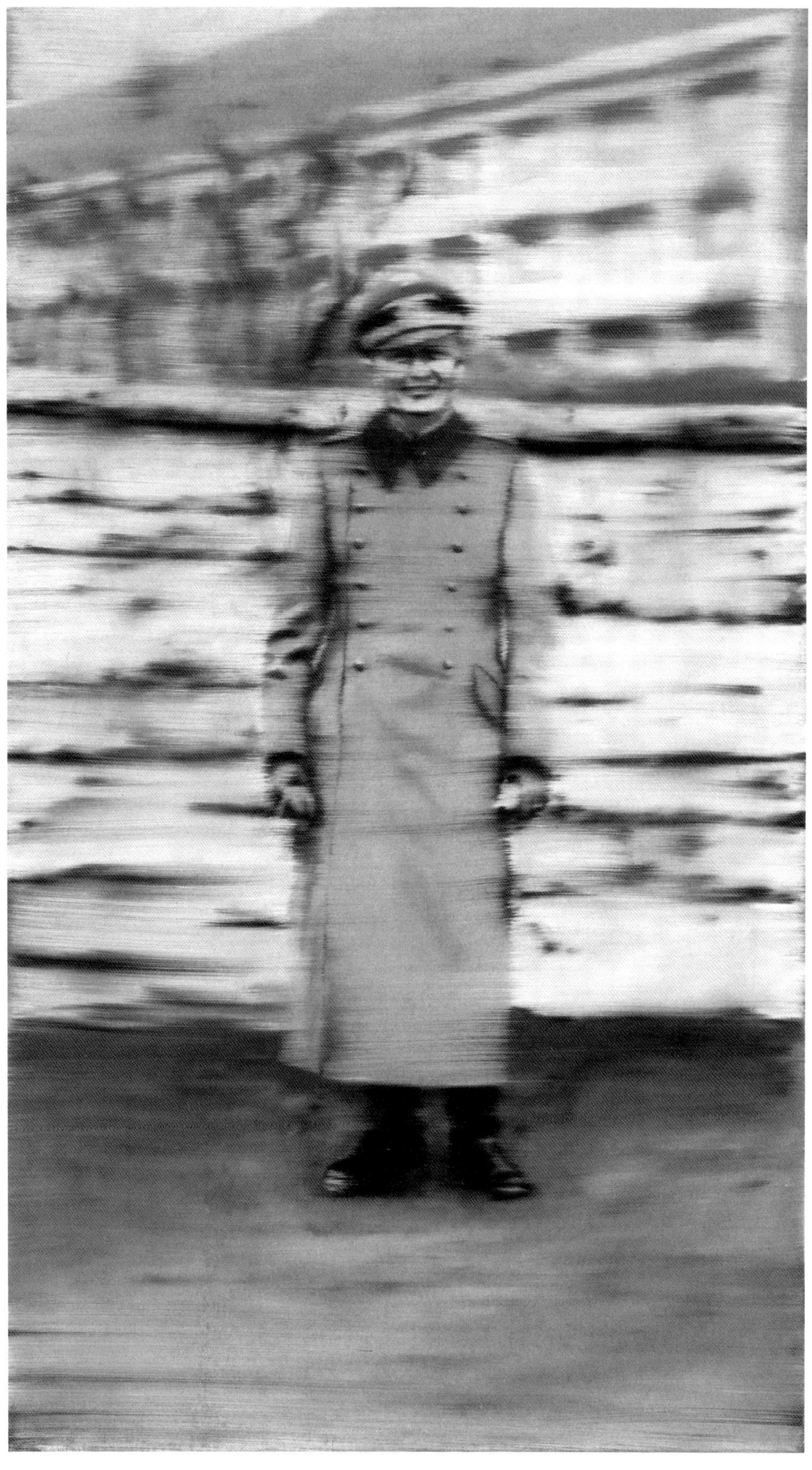

disproportional. A second decision therefore corrected possible visual irregularities. The artist used a soft paintbrush or other suitable tool such as a brush or squeegee to blur contours and eliminate a variety of inconsistencies and distortions. "I blur to make everything the same. Everything equally important and equally unimportant."[16] This created an almost homogeneous image surface, sometimes with clearly visible horizontal wipe tracks. Their photographic origin remains apparent, even if the artist erased the original's graphically constructed depth.

The painted photo fulfills the demand of modernism for dimensionality and anti-illusionism. In addition, Richter thwarted the putative "naturalness" of photographic representation by emphasizing its artificiality. He had recognized that the pictorial character of a photograph is largely ignored in the course of perception, so that the photographed object asserts itself as "reality" in relation to its depiction. The image as an image falls below the threshold of perception.

In photography, the depicted triumphs over the depiction. As a result, the actual photograph of "Uncle Rudi" is not perceived as an image, but as the depicted person: "This is Uncle Rudi!—or: This is a Wehrmacht officer!" It is as if the image in the photographic representation disappears in favor of the sitter. In the photographic image of *Uncle Rudi* (1965), the artist reversed the now ingrained photographic mechanism of optical perception—as with all photographic images—and thus heightened the image as an image by blurring its details.

The consequences of the reversal go beyond a mere reference to the character of the image itself. Richter also sabotaged the fleeting gaze with

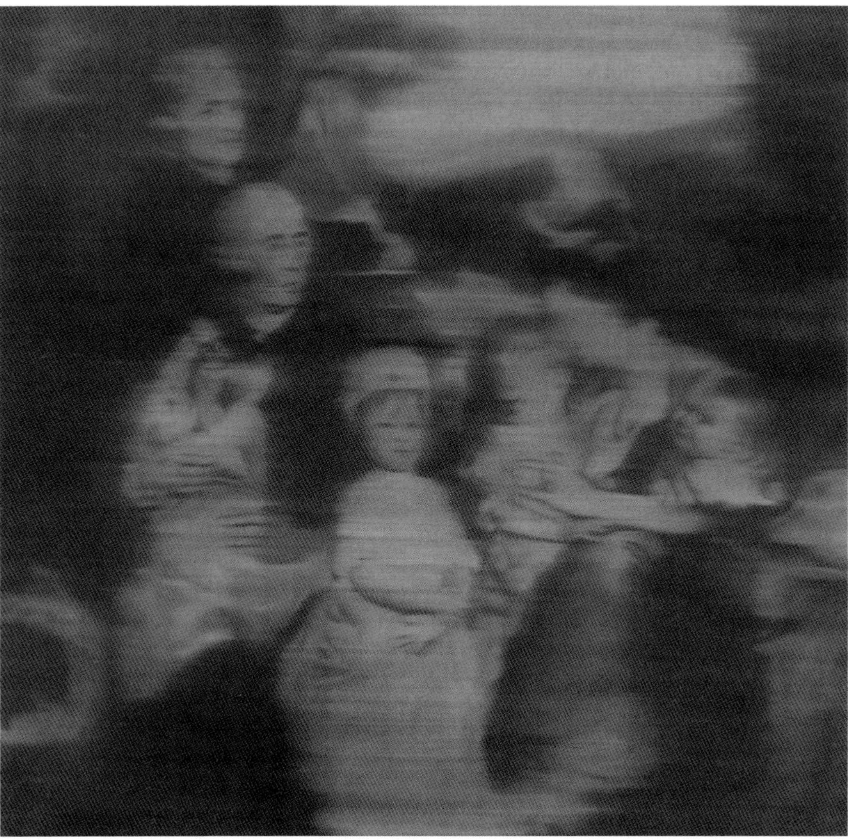

Family after Old Master, 1965 (CR 26)
Oil on canvas, 147 x 155 cm (57⅞ x 61 in.)
Munich, Museum Brandhorst
(Udo and Anette Brandhorst Collection)

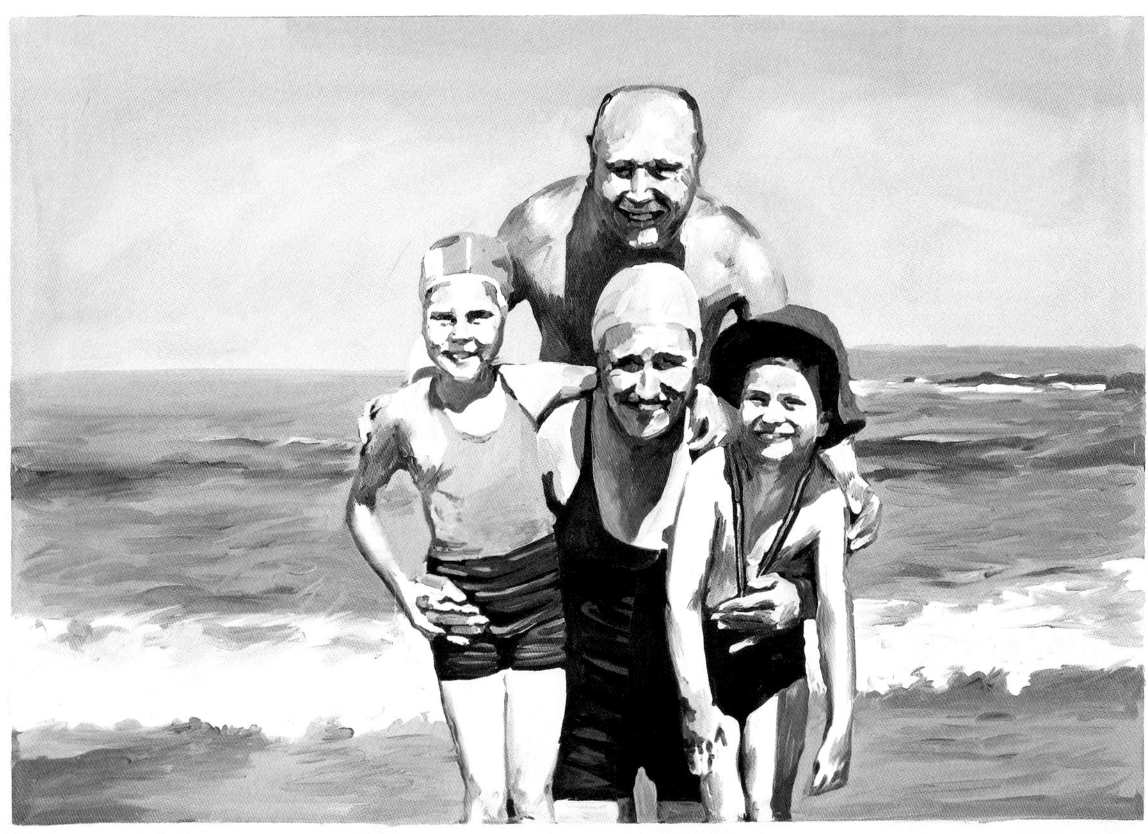

Family at the Seaside, 1964 (CR 35)
Oil on canvas, 150 x 200 cm (59 x 78¾ in.)
Duisburg, MKM Museum Küppersmühle für Moderne Kunst (Sylvia and Ulrich Ströher Collection)

which modernist images are usually seen, and stimulated the viewer's attention with his interventions. Almost casually, but most evocatively, he entices them to risk a second, a third look, and to take the step from seeing to recognizing. The smudged blur awakens curiosity and activates visual perception. The blurring also adds the appearance of movement to the pictures. Richter accentuated the arbitrariness depicted by each photographic detail of the visible, by shooting his "content" in the imagination beyond the image boundaries by means of the dynamics of the act of painting.

Behind Wehrmacht officer "Uncle Rudi," the solid structure of the house, including the wall in front of it, is a blur. The photo paintings force viewers to move. They stimulate them to move back and forth as they seek to set and recognize the paintings' objects. Neither image nor viewer is static. Both free themselves from the shackles of the central perspective order of the traditional image during contemplation. While photography irrevocably sends what it has visually captured into the past as soon as the camera shutter is released, the painted photographic image retains its presence as the product of a painterly act. "The painted picture, even when entirely illusionistic, always retains a reality as a hand-made and traditionally defined as image (= painting). In contrast, a photograph loses its own reality the

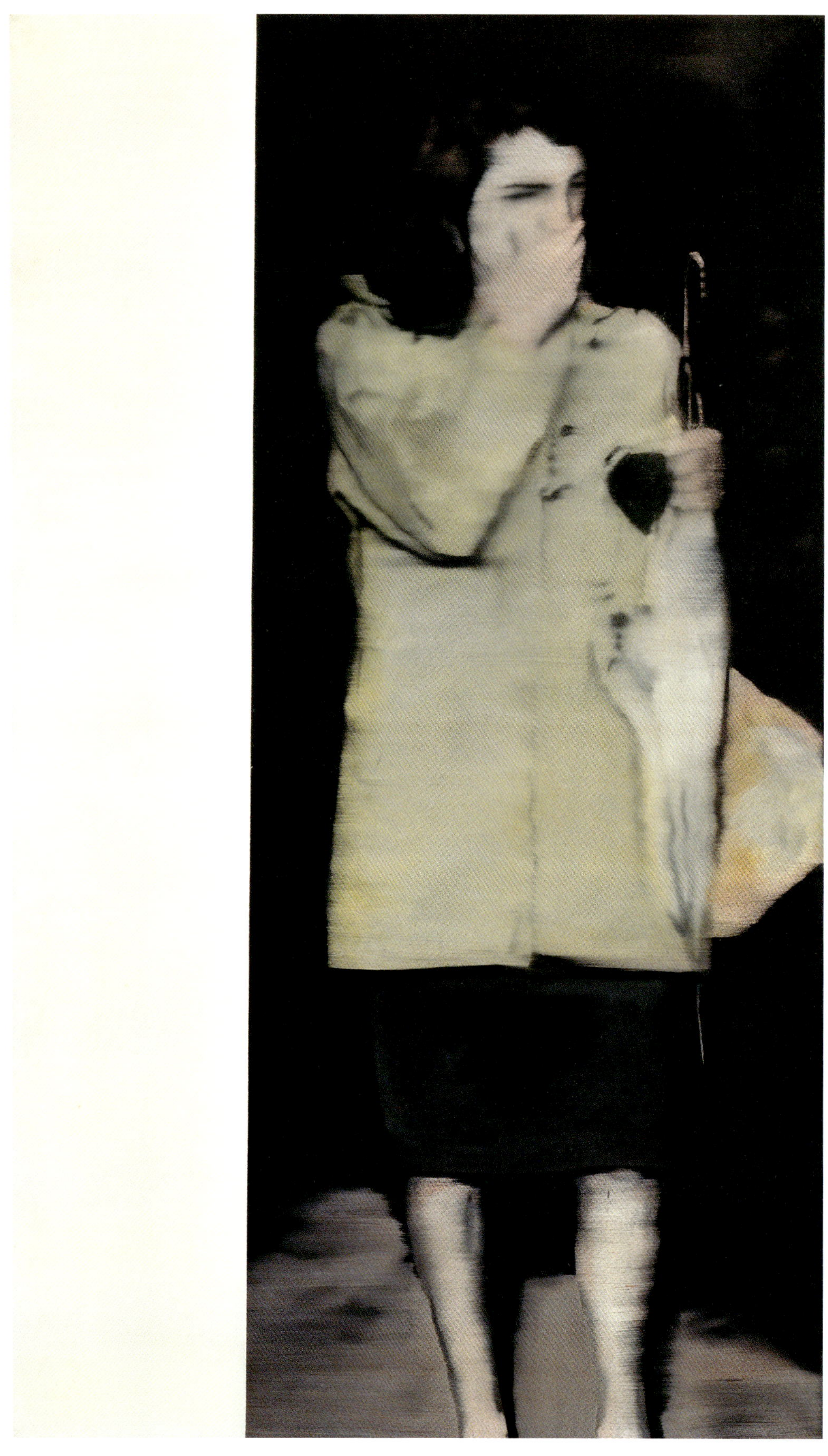

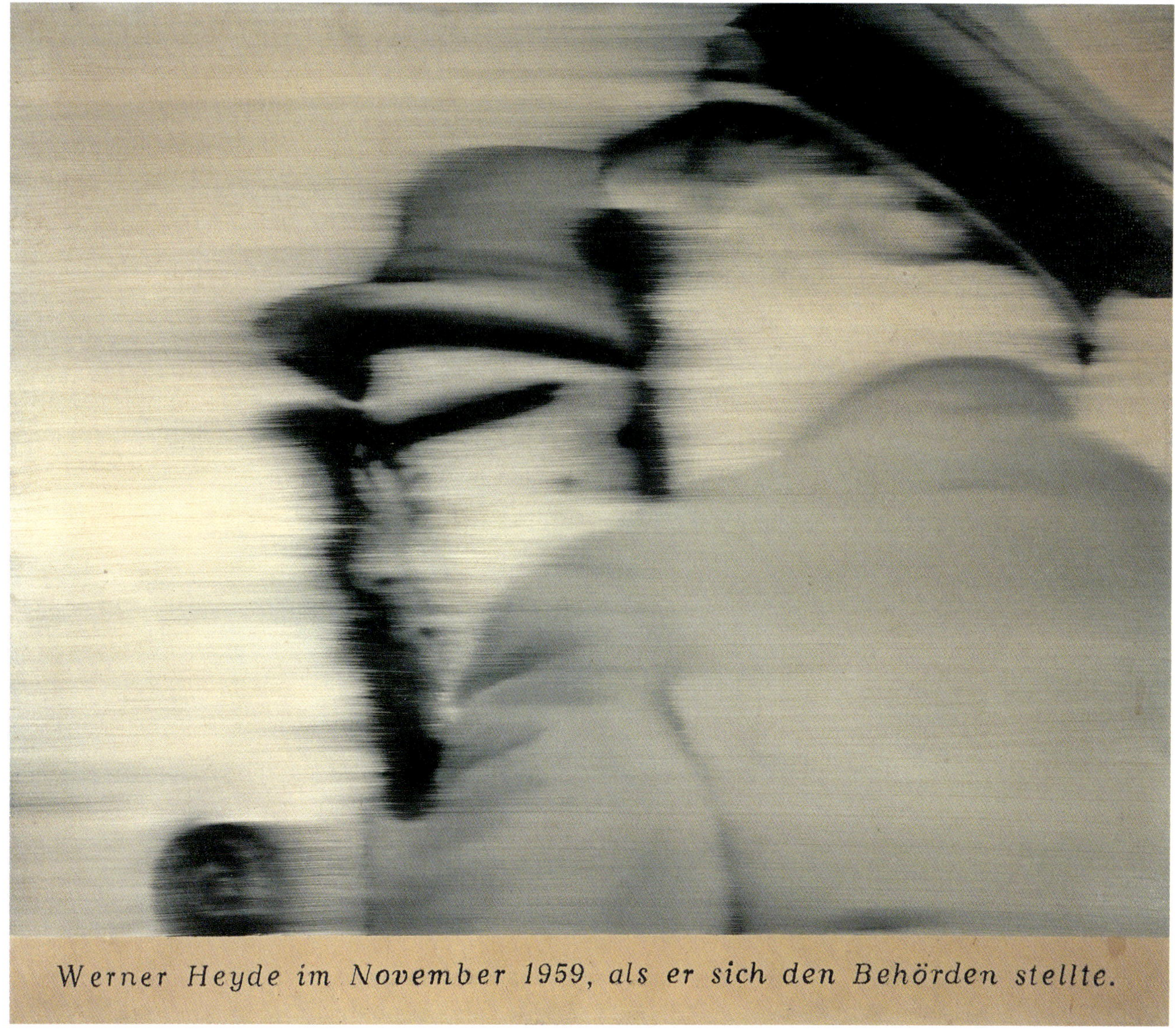

Mr. Heyde, 1965 (CR 100)
Oil on canvas, 55 x 65 cm (21¾ x 25⅝ in.)
Private collection

more precisely it portrays the other reality and, if you look at it like that, the photograph's only 'reality' is its own unreality—i.e., its quality of not being there."[17]

This insight into the apparent non-existence of the photographic image is one of the factors that encouraged Richter's decision to paint photographic images. The models for his photo paintings were taken from newspapers, magazines, calendars, and photo albums, and were all pictures devoid of any artistic ambition. Banal images. He also used some of his own photographs as models. Initially, the photographic parts share the picture with painterly passages. Fragments of words from the newspaper models penetrate the surface of paintings. The first picture in his catalogue raisonné, entitled *Table* (1962), reveals Richter's dilemma. A spontaneously daubed swirl of gray paint spreads out in the center of the picture, almost obliterating its subject, a table. Between paint swirl and photographic ground, a gaping spatial discrepancy in the visual impression opens.

Woman with Umbrella, 1964 (CR 29)
Oil on canvas, 160 x 95 cm (63 x 37½ in.)
Zurich, Daros Collection

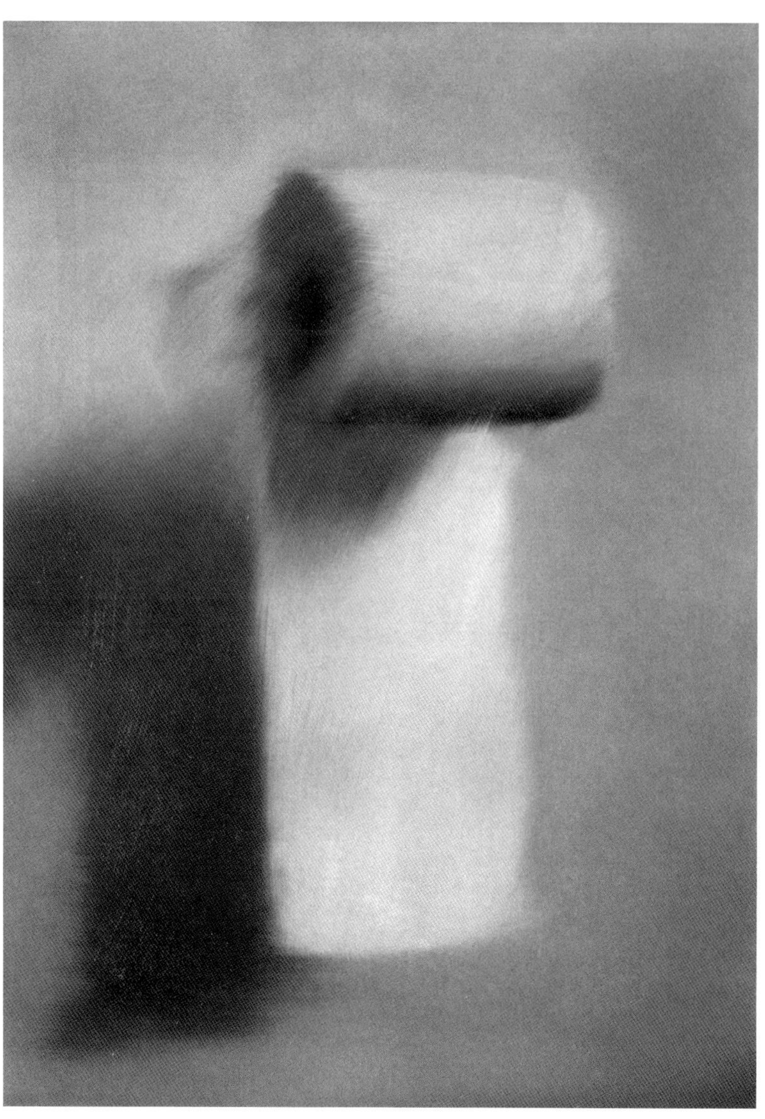

Toilet Paper, 1965 (CR 75-1)
Oil on canvas, 55 x 40 cm (21¾ x 15¾ in.)
New York, private collection

This beginning looks more like a full stop. Like *Coffin Bearers* (1962) and *Deer* (1963), this photo painting marks an unresolved conflict between painting and photography. Shortly afterwards, they merge seamlessly. Richter's motifs are banal but not unimportant. The artist points to Hannah Arendt's use of the term in the "banality of evil."

In the art sphere, these images were all the more provocative for being considered unimportant by virtue of their photographic origin and apparent triviality of their motifs. The selection of motifs seems random, but isn't. This is indicated by the fact that the artist consistently painted them in series: Airplanes and cars (1963/64), landscapes from travel brochures (1964), and vacation pictures like *Family at the Seaside* (1964), or utensils in everyday use such as *Kitchen Chair* and *Toilet Paper. Flemish Crown* (1965), a chandelier seen from below, bodes ill and is reminiscent of Alfred Hitchcock. Not all paintings are restricted to the familiar photo-graphic spectrum of black and white. Yellows and greens sneak in. The photographic images often hide longings and fears, the repressed and the despised. Non-political feelings, but

Flemish Crown, 1965 (CR 77)
Oil on canvas, 90 x 110 cm (35½ x 43⅜ in.)
Germany, private collection

absolutely political in total. Lacking the opportunity to be considered in the history books, they are significant reflections of collective repression.

Death is both openly and obliquely discernible in many of Richter's paintings: abruptly in the concealed corpse of *Dead* (1963), less directly and with a light undertone of irony and sarcasm in the *Coffin Bearers*, menacingly in *Stukas* and *Mustang Squadron*, with ambivalence in the soldier who is being trained to kill, somberly in the depiction of the widow of murdered US President John F. Kennedy in *Woman with Umbrella* (1964)—not to mention in *Mr. Heyde*, the Nazi doctor who commanded the Nazis' euthanasia program, as well as Richter's *Aunt Marianne*, a victim of this murderous policy, with him as a child (1965). Richter's experiential grasp of photography's essence is mirrored in both the images and subjects of these pictures.

Until the 1960s, photography was an artistically unencumbered medium that did not immediately maneuver itself back into the channels of painting's familiar forms. It provided the basis for a way of painting that was free of historically accumulated, formal ballast such as stylistic guidelines and rules

Helga Matura with her Fiancé, 1966 (CR 125)
Oil on canvas, 200 x 100 cm (78¾ x 39⅜ in.)
Düsseldorf, Museum Kunstpalast

PAGES 26/27
Eight Student Nurses, 1966 (CR 130)
Oil on canvas, 8 parts, each panel:
95 x 70 cm (37½ x 27⅝ in.)
Zurich, Crex Collection

of convention. Without the artist consciously emphasizing it, photography additionally gave his pictures the melancholy tone that underpins his entire artistic work. Feelings of loss, futility, grief, and failure shape them. However, photography also gave Richter the opportunity to hold on to painting in spite of everything. "Keep painting" became Richter's relentless motto in the face of the anti-form artists' protests that painting is an artistic form of expression that has historically resolved itself.

However, Richter's need for intellectual exchange compelled him to get close to them. Richter's contact with the leading artists in minimalist and conceptual art intensified when Konrad Lueg, under his real name Konrad Fischer, opened a towel-sized gallery in Düsseldorf that favored these fields. At the Ohme Jupp, Fischer's local café, where artists liked to meet, Richter was often seen in the company of Carl Andre and Sol LeWitt, Daniel Buren and Jan Dibbets, Robert Smithson, Lawrence Weiner, Bernd and Hilla Becher, and Hanne Darboven.

Administrative Building, 1964 (CR 39)
Oil on canvas, 98 x 150 cm (38⅝ x 59 in.)
San Francisco Museum of Modern Art
(on permanent loan from the Doris and
Donald Fisher Collection, San Francisco)

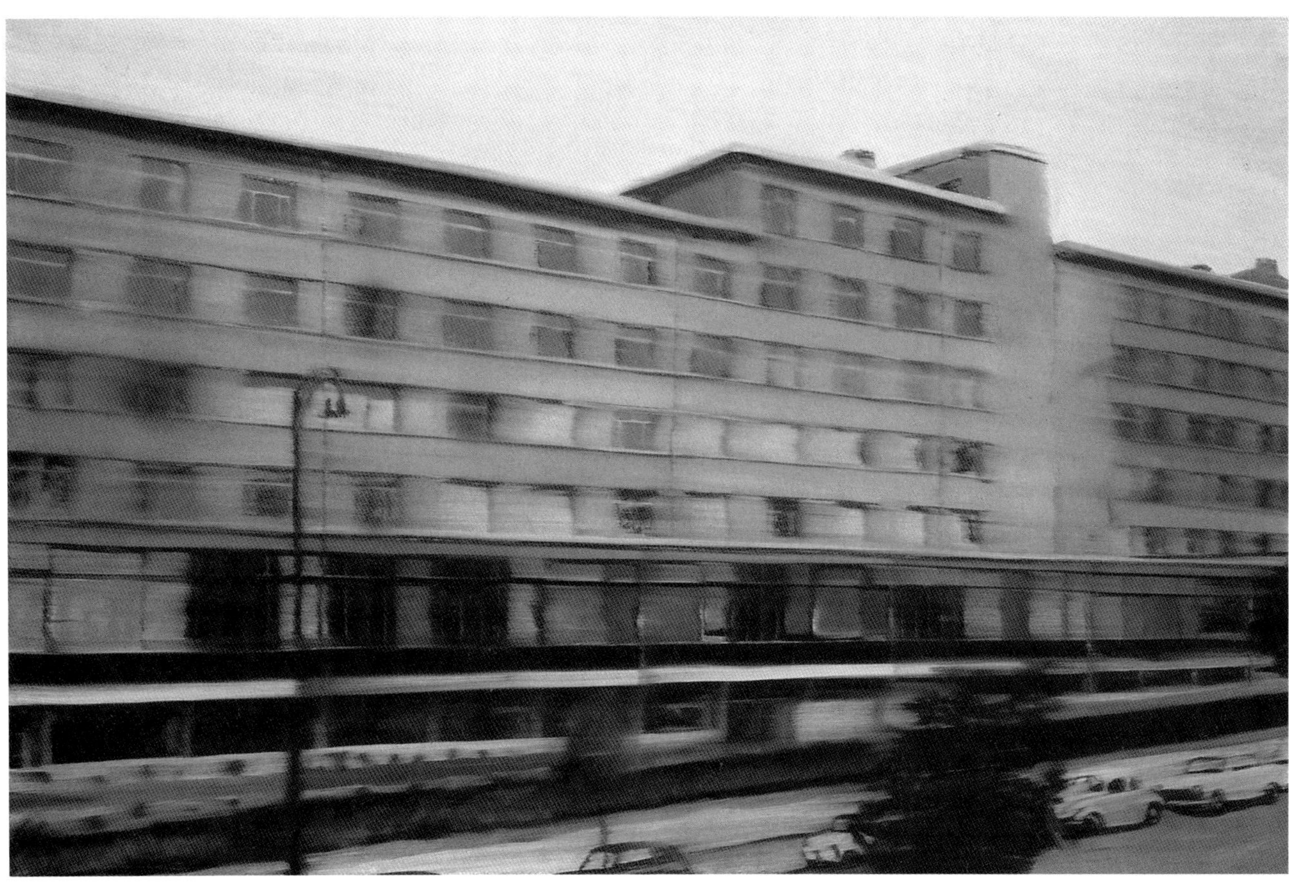

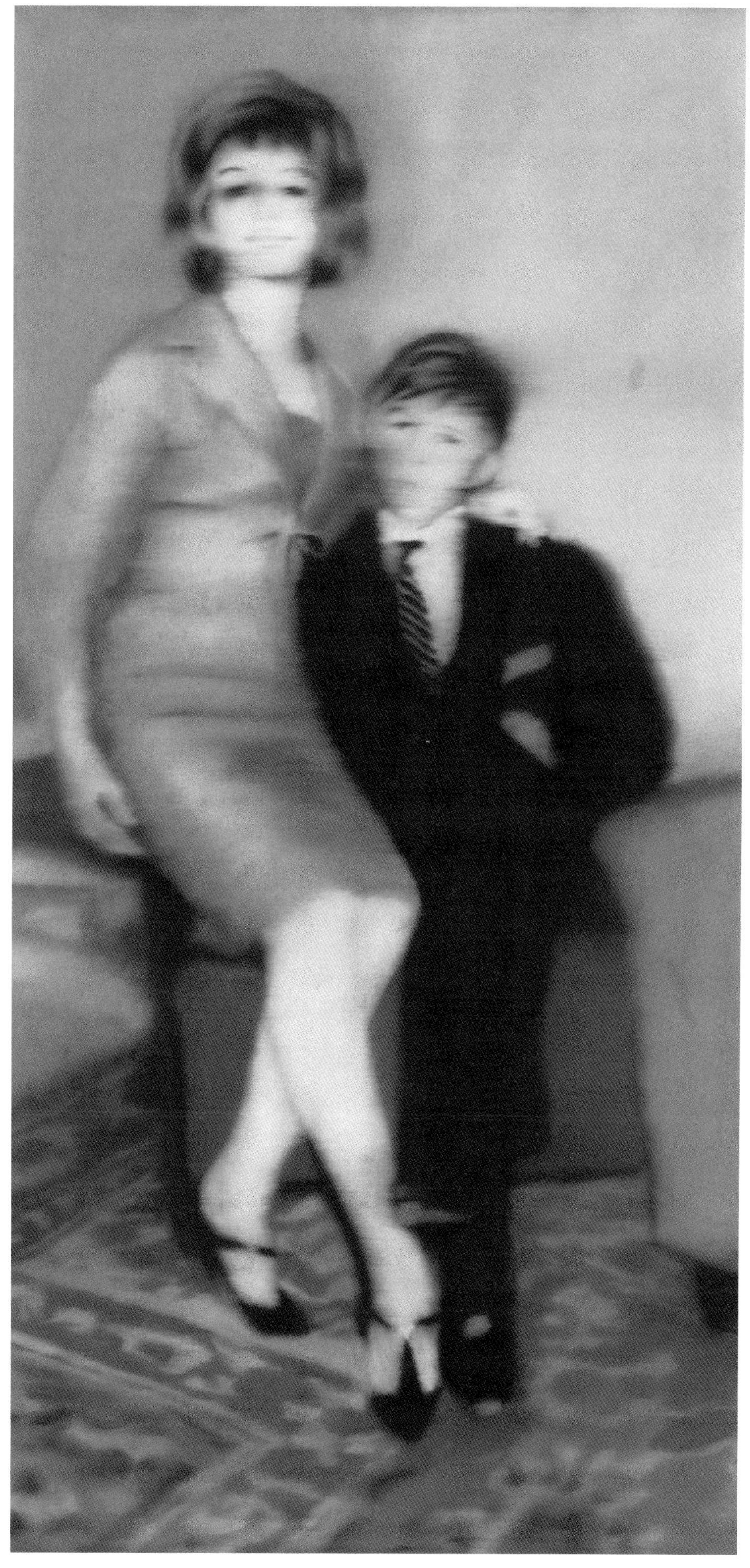

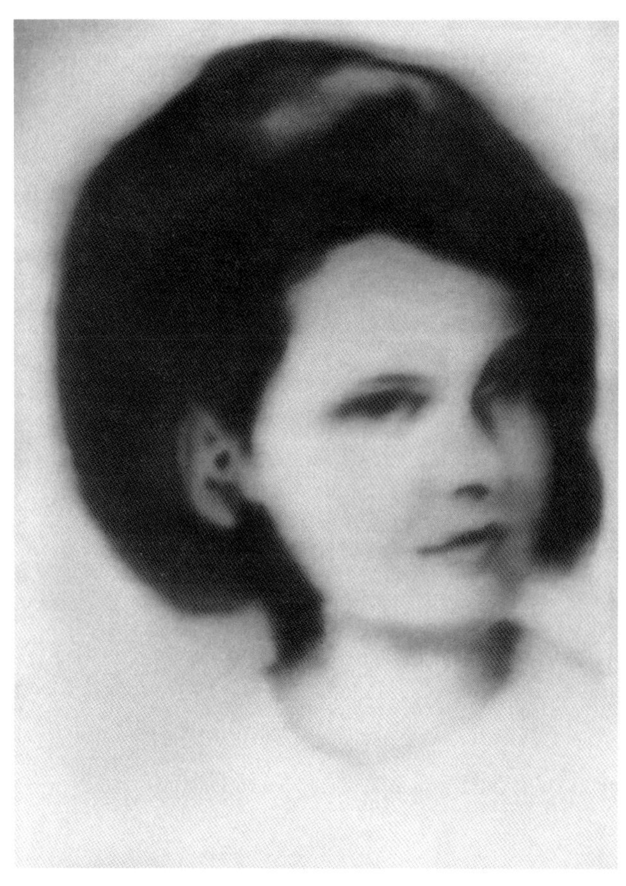
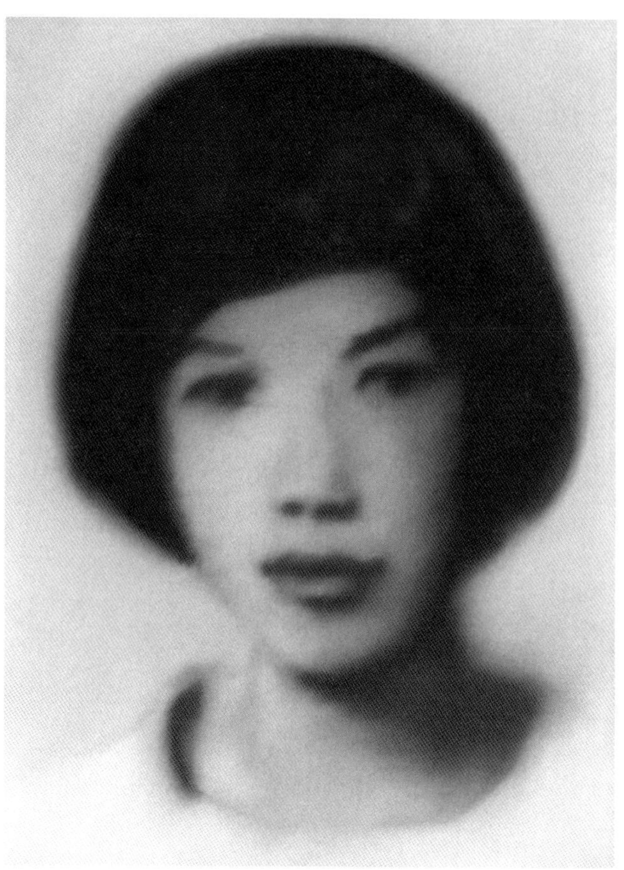
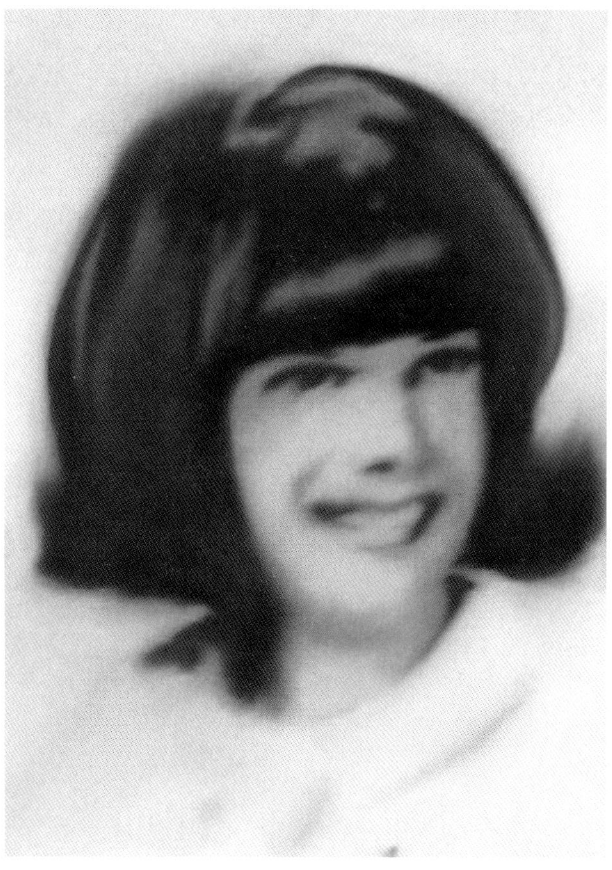
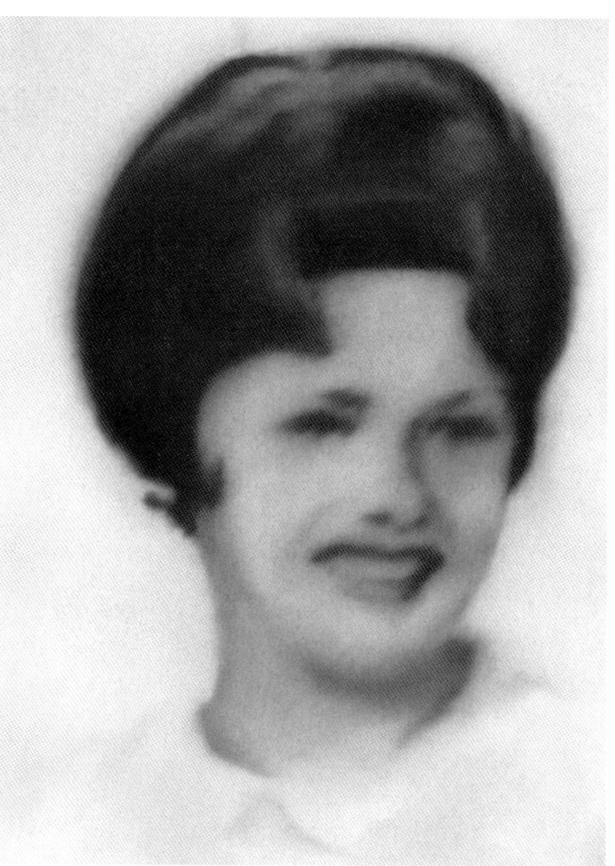

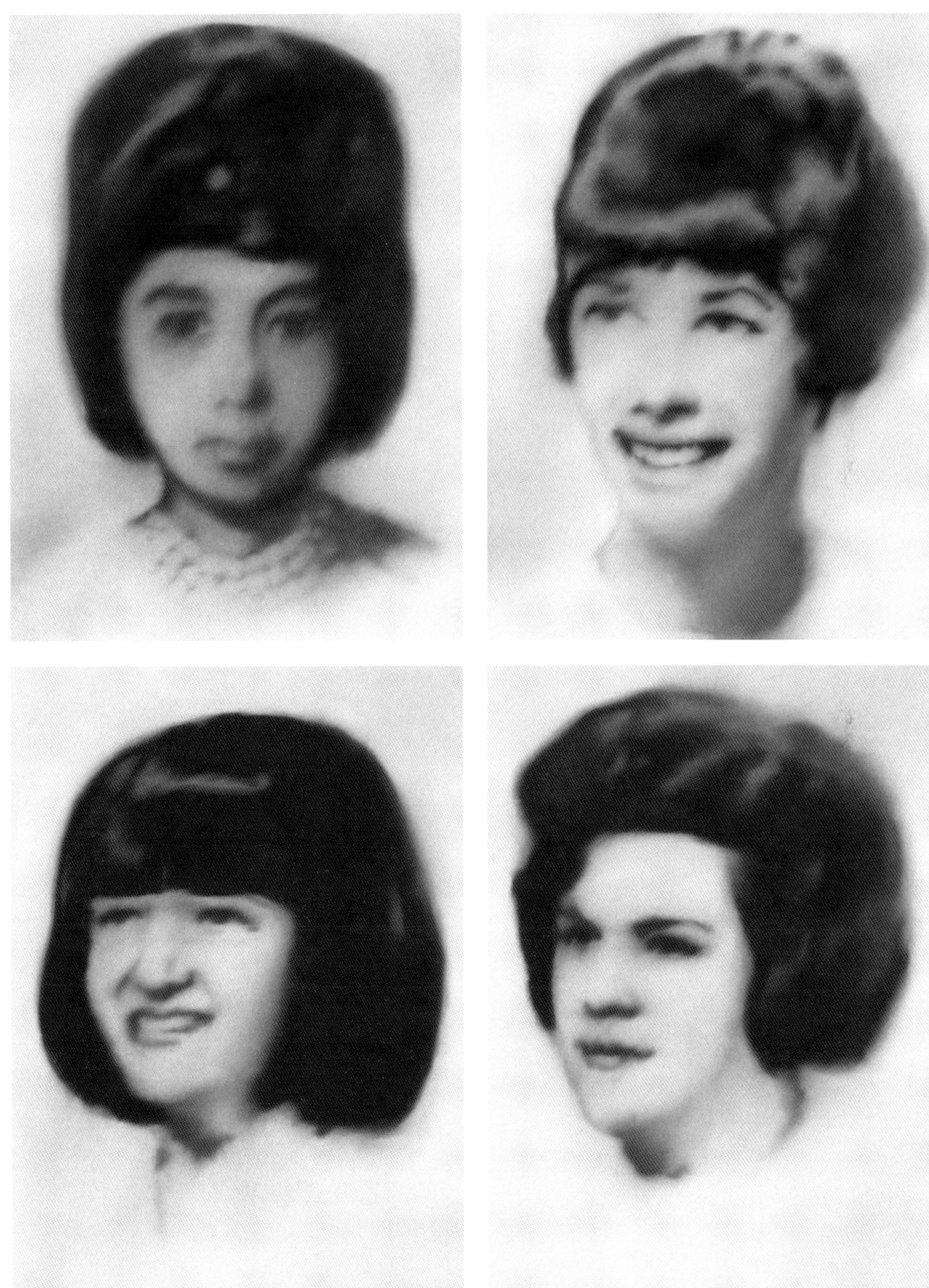

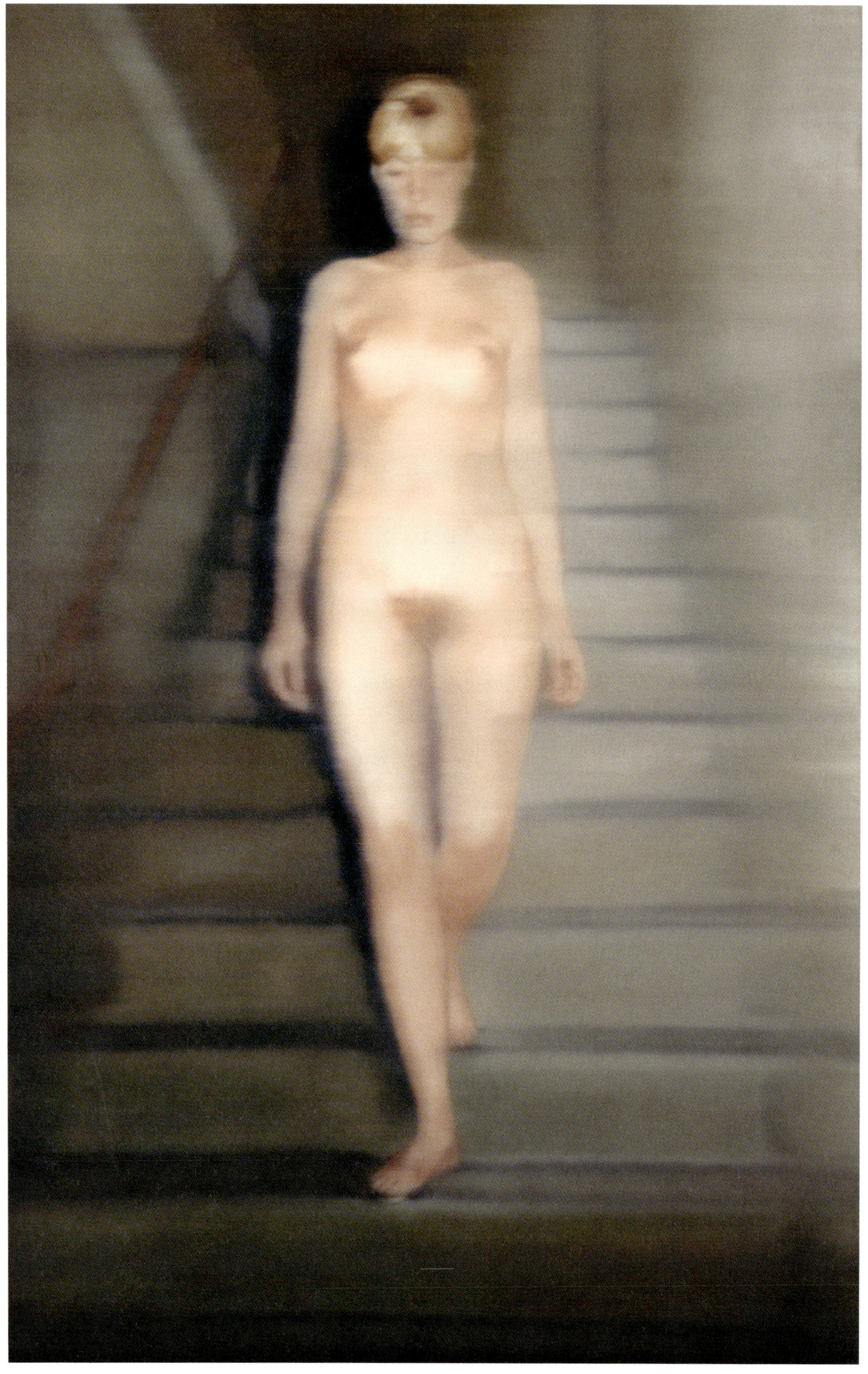

"That's how old-fashioned it was. Glass, metal, and Pop were fashionable."[18]

Richter has never denied that his painting *Ema* (*Nude on a Staircase*) (1966) alludes to Marcel Duchamp's famous futuristic painting *Nude Descending a Staircase, No. 2* (1912). "I knew Duchamp's work, and there certainly was an influence. It may have been an unconscious opposition."[19] Richter is not an artist who follows a specific idea or preconceived concept. In a conversation with his and Ema's daughter Babette, he emphasizes that not even the photographic original was made with a special intention, let alone the painting: "the fact that I photographed your mother on the stairs wasn't planned or intended as such, and neither was the painting that resulted from it."[20]

The similarities are striking nonetheless. Nudes descending staircases are rare in painting. (Richter had already painted another *Woman Descending the Staircase* (1965) based on a newspaper photograph—this one with an evening gown.) Perhaps the next sentence in this conversation sheds light on the unconscious processes of Richter's artistic thinking: "And so I barely dared to show it to anyone. That's how old-fashioned it was. Glass, metal, and Pop were fashionable."[21] Peter Ludwig added an ironic punchline two years after the painting was completed by purchasing it for his collection shortly after he acquired a taste for Pop Art.[22] At the time, Richter's photo paintings were considered a German version of Pop Art in the European art scene—this was partly a result of a sense of perplexity.

During the period in which Richter painted *Ema*, Duchamp had become the figurehead of the most influential branch of contemporary art. His anti-artistic readymades—objects of utility including a urinal, a bottle-drying rack, and a bicycle wheel—inspired the anti-form stance. This was especially so with their conceptual variants, which served as fetishes. They replaced the doing in art with thinking. Duchamp's Cubo-Futurist nude concluded his handmade artistic work.

When comparing the two paintings, the more recent is not only the more technically advanced, but also the more complex. Unlike the profile view of Duchamp's painting, Richter's nude faces the viewer. It also retains physical integrity. The descent is at a measured step, visually assisted by subtle blurring. By contrast, the French artist chopped the body into pieces, following the example set by Eadweard Muybridge and Étienne-Jules Marey's motion photographs, and offered a phased demonstration of the sequence

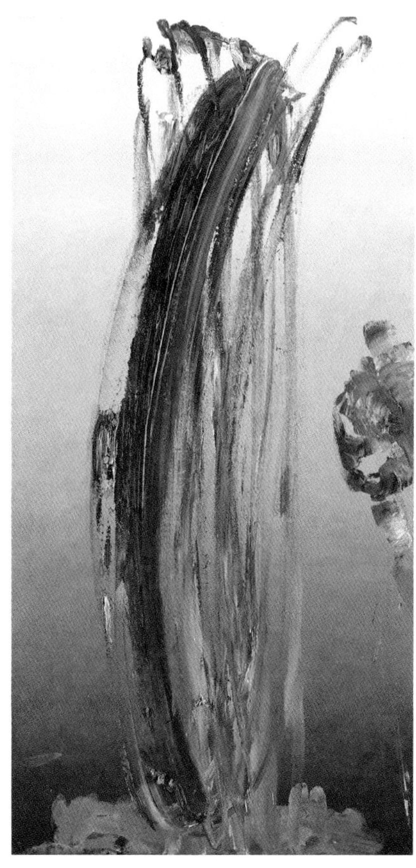

Untitled, 1968 (CR 194-9)
Oil on canvas, 80 x 40 cm (31½ x 15¾ in.)
Hamburger Kunsthalle
(loan from a private collection)

Ema (Nude on a Staircase), 1966 (CR 134)
Oil on canvas, 200 x 130 cm (78¾ x 51¼ in.)
Cologne, Museum Ludwig

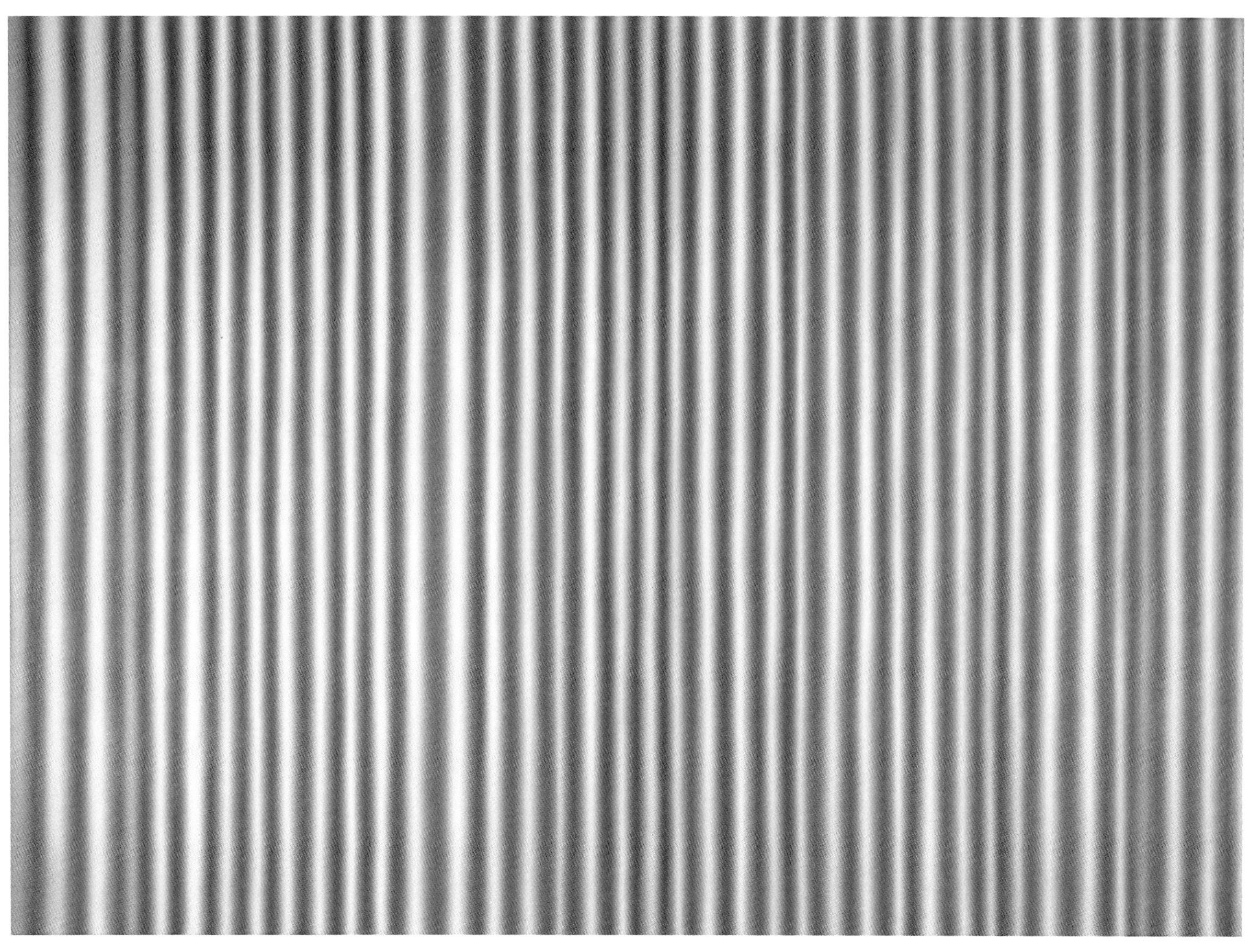

Large Curtain, 1967 (CR 163-1)
Oil on canvas, 200 x 280 cm (78¾ x 110¼ in.)
Frankfurt am Main, Städelsches Kunstinstitut und Städtische Galerie

of movement. Duchamp's color contrasts are more lurid, their application more blunt, the painting more violent, the nude more anonymous. The nude in *Ema* radiates an emotional distance. The longer you look, the more transient she becomes; both remote and close. The two-dimensional space throbs, its permanence dissolves, and the subtle tension between body and background transforms the body into an almost timeless manifestation. The painting does not deny its origin in photography.

This painting may not have been Richter's conscious declaration of war against modernist conceptual art, but we cannot dismiss the assumption that this was what he had in mind, albeit unconsciously. To be sure, the challenge was not aimed at Duchamp's ideas—Richter shared his views on the demystification of the artist—but on the rigid exclusion of the hand in the artistic process, the ideological component: "I could never accept that it had put paid, once and for all, to a certain kind of painting."[23]

Duchamp's painting is one of the countless images stored in his memory, even if not all are retrievable at all times. "The eye and the hand of the painter (rather than his memory) are full of pictures which form a sort of 'treasure' … brimming with the entire history of painting. This reservoir of ideas and forms accumulated by tradition," Richter confirmed.[24] "Half the history of art is in your head anyway."[25] His reservations about showing the

192 Colors, 1966 (CR 136)
Oil on canvas, 200 x 150 cm (78¾ x 59 in.)
Hamburger Kunsthalle
(loan from a private collection)

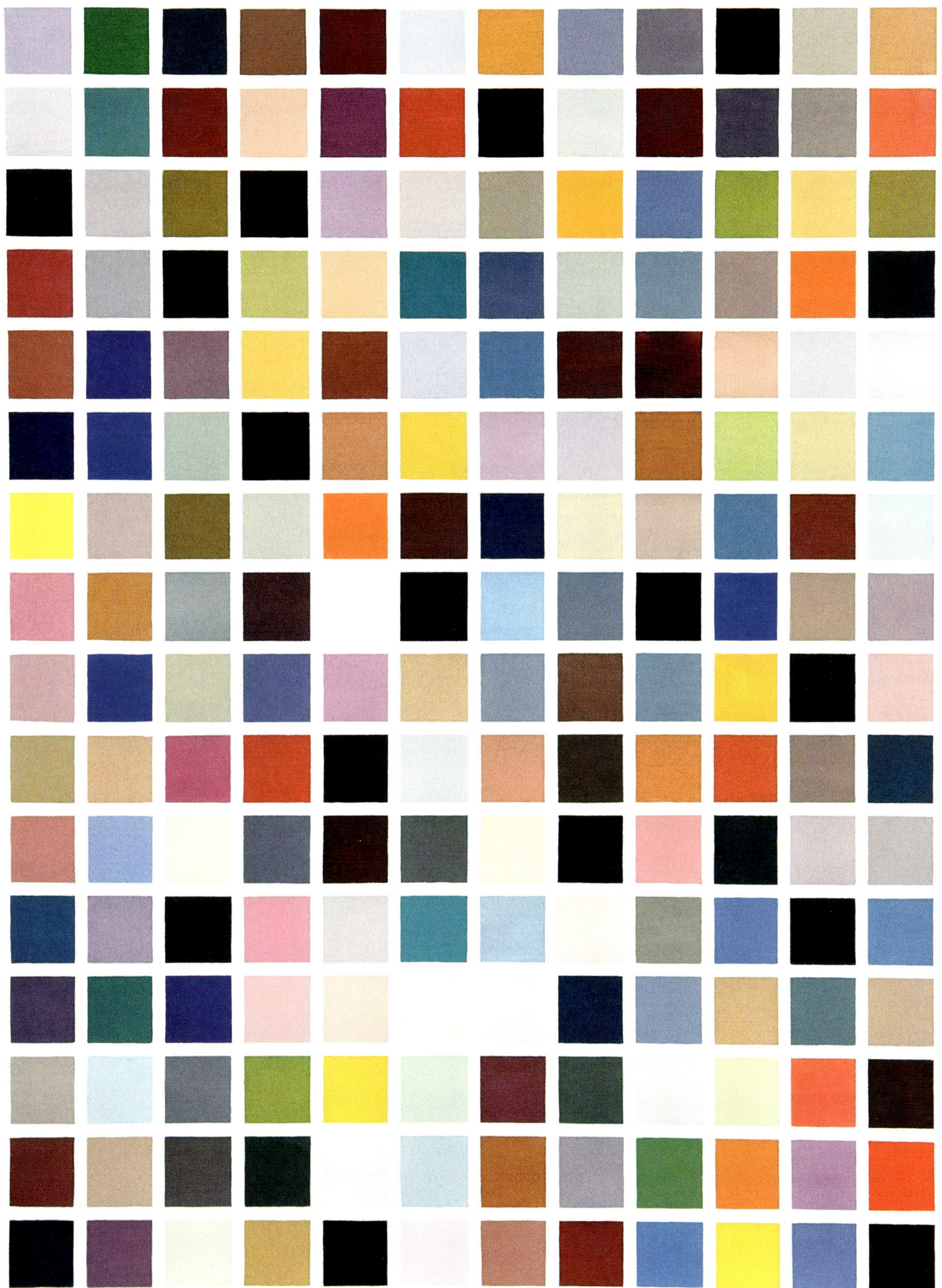

painting emphasize that Richter saw art's renunciation of all artistic traditions as a challenge.

Indeed, *Ema* steers the opposite course. The painting is smooth, the color nuances are delicate, and the presentation elegant. The relationship between space and figure is dynamic. Even half a century later, the painting has lost none of its power, unlike Duchamp's *Nude*, which now looks antiquated. *Ema* exemplifies Richter's particular notion of subversion that did not express itself as a political declaration. As Jürgen Harten writes, "by 'subversive' he actually meant his inner resistance to the crisis of art and the ideological tutelage that wanted to take offence at his painting."[26] The crisis of art is a crisis of representation, and it is the second since the dawn of the avant-garde in the second half of the 19th century.

This expressed itself in Richter's rapid shifts between forms of representation. In the mid-1960s, his insecurity increased as the anti-painting league gradually took hold of the exhibition industry. This development was backed by art criticism: "Ideas can be works of art," proclaimed Sol LeWitt in his *Paragraphs on Conceptual Art*.[27] They don't need to be executed materially. And Joseph Kosuth saw painting as merely an a priori concept of artistic possibilities.[28]

Keep painting? In spite of everything? One well-known note sums up Richter's way of thinking: "I pursue no objectives, no system, no tendency; I have no programme, no style, no direction … I steer clear of definitions. I don't know what I want. I am inconsistent, non-committal, passive; I like

Untitled (Gray), 1968 (CR 194-6)
Oil on canvas, 50 x 50 cm (19¾ x 19¾ in.)
Switzerland, private collection

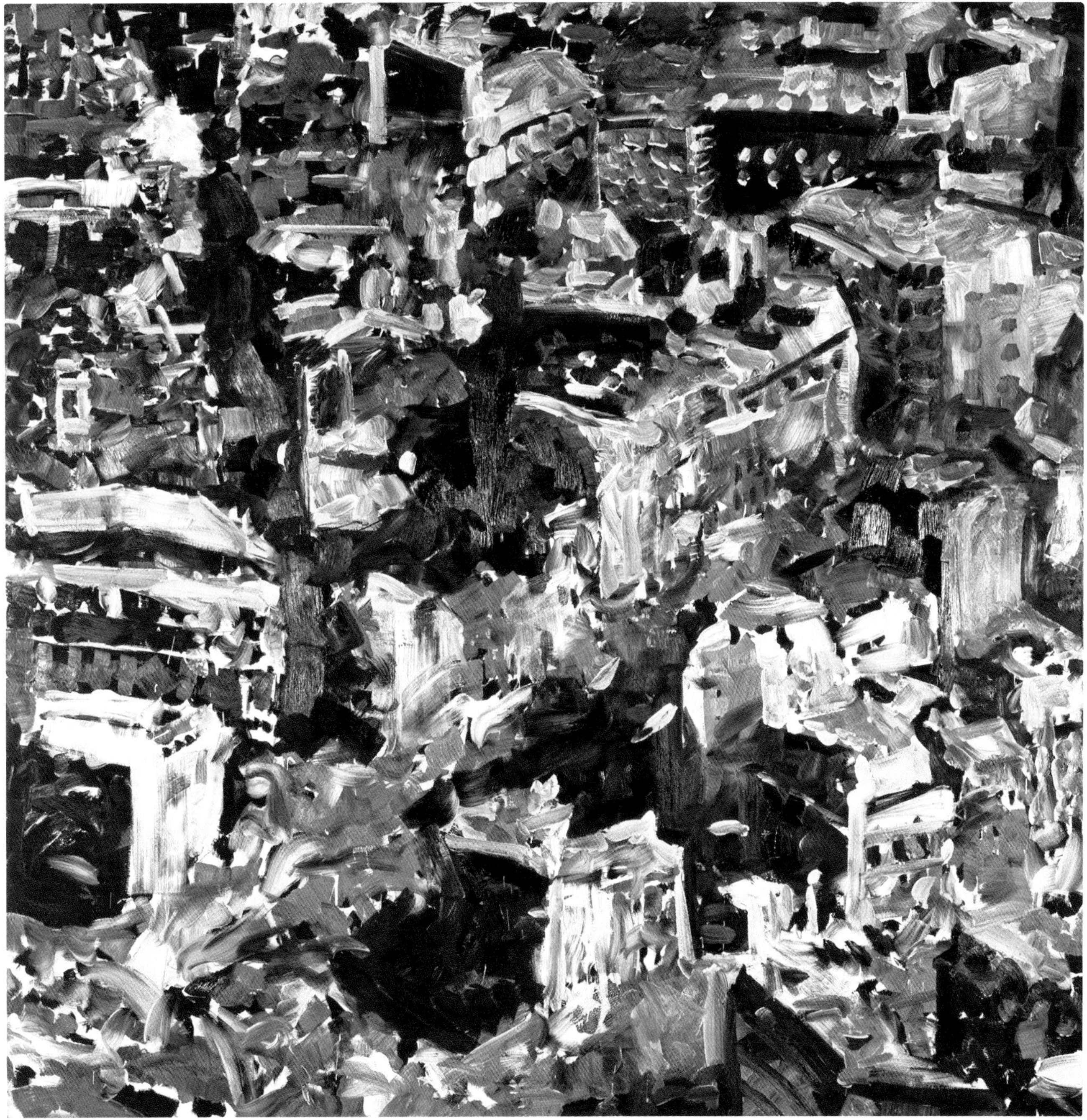

Townscape Paris, 1968 (CR 175)
Oil on canvas, 200 x 200 cm (78¾ x 78¾ in.)
Stuttgart, Froehlich Collection

the indefinite, the boundless; I like continual uncertainty."[29] Emphatic discontinuity characterized his artistic practice in the following years and his relationships to art, reality, and their specific associations were subject to enormous fluctuations.

Meanwhile, private galleries began to proliferate, heralding a time of aesthetic open-mindedness, risk-taking and commitment to unconventional artistic movements. Richter benefited: Rudolf Zwirner, first in Essen then Cologne; Heiner Friedrich in Munich; René Block in Berlin and his friend Konrad Fischer in Düsseldorf all opened galleries and regularly exhibited his

Gray (Bark), 1973 (CR 348-7)
Oil on canvas, 90 x 65 cm (35½ x 25⅝ in.)
Cologne, private collection

work. Sales were not uncommon. Alfred Schmela in Düsseldorf arranged his first solo show in 1964. As their reputations grew, the galleries established successful relationships with other European countries and the US.

By then New York had replaced Paris as a hub of contemporary art. The world's first art market, Kunstmarkt Köln '67, was held in 1967 in the Gürzenich, Cologne's old festival hall, and the Verein progressiver deutscher Kunsthändler (Association of Progressive German Art Dealers) was formed especially for this purpose. Abstract Art—whose unique selling point in the postwar period had been as a liberated art, beholden only to itself—was in retreat, and the artists' gaze was once more turning to the outside world.

Richter responded with a wealth of seemingly aimless artistic explorations that included experiments with pivoting panes of glass (1967). Duchamp's

Gray, 1970 (CR 247-1)
Oil on nettle, 200 x 150 cm (78¾ x 59 in.)
Bremen, private collection

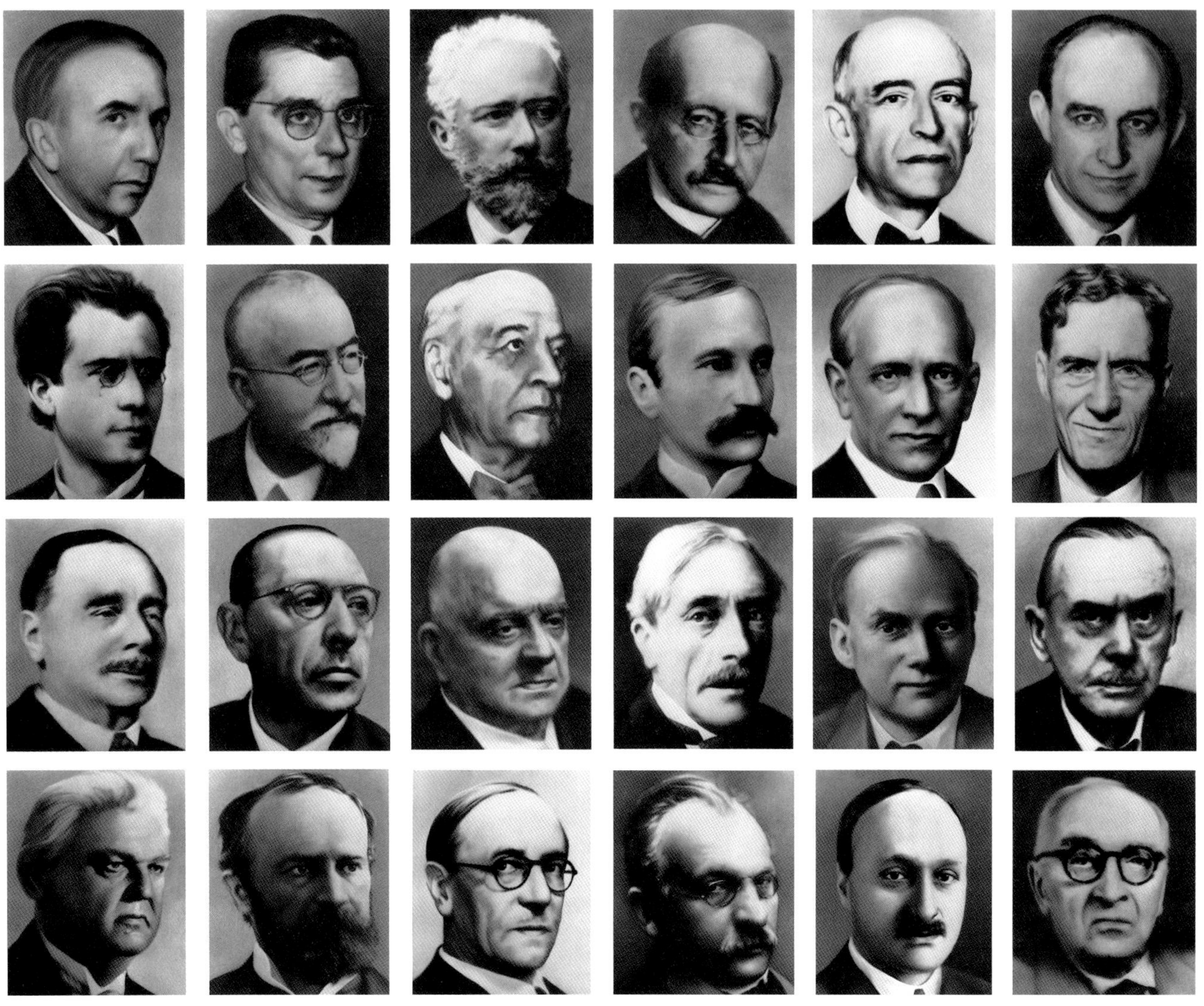

The Large Glass (1915–23) was inspiring but his esoteric theorizing that accompanied the work troubled Richter. "I think something in Duchamp didn't suit me—all that mystery-mongering—and that's why I painted those simple glass panes and showed the whole windowpane problem in a completely different light."[30]

During that time, Richter also broadened the thematic and methodological range of "photorealistic" images, as they were then called, from the supposedly banal subjects of everyday life to the poignant portrait series depicting *Eight Student Nurses* (1966), who were murdered in the United States.

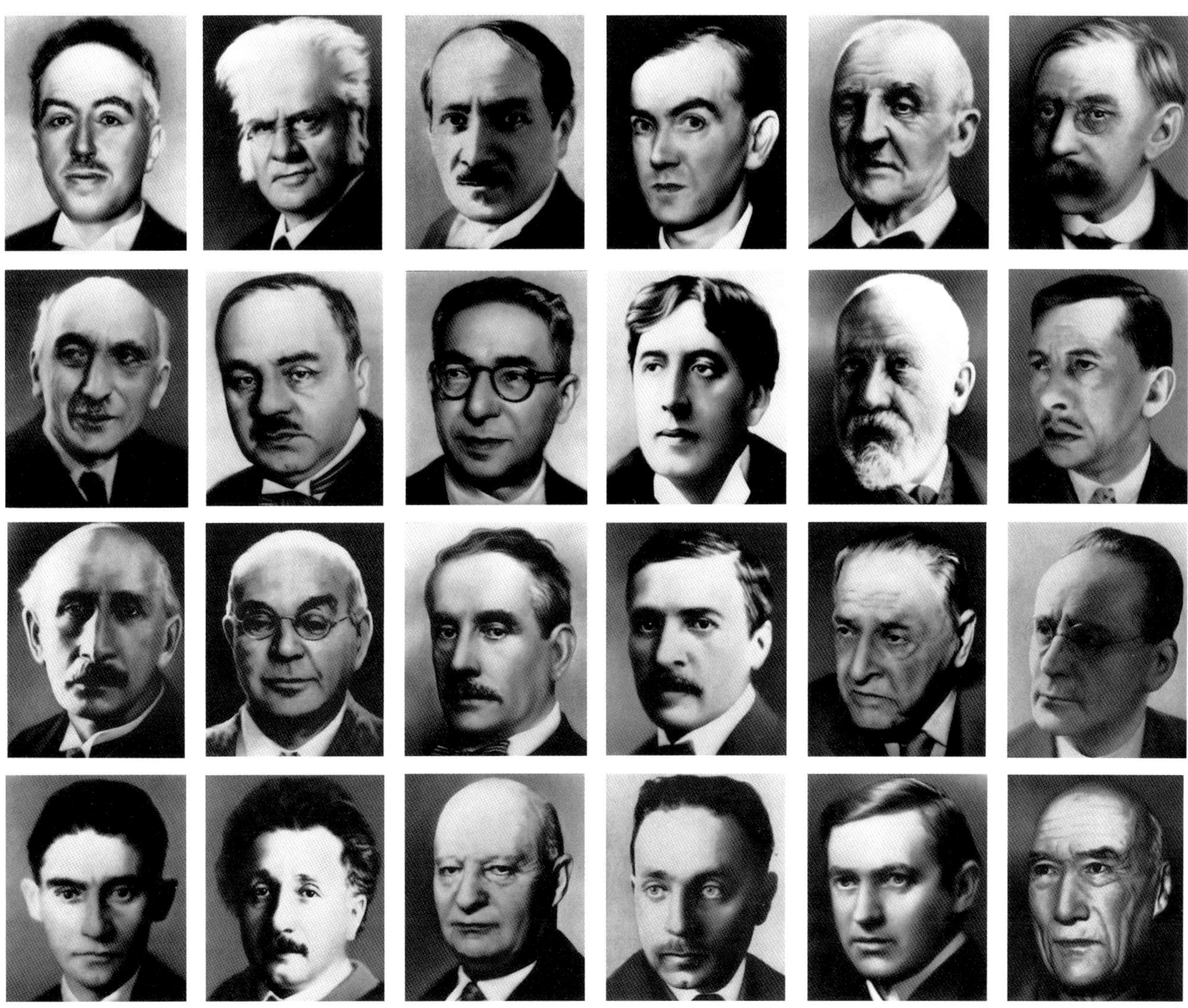

Stylistically, his spectrum ranged from photo-based paintings to Tachist images such as *Untitled* (1968); from constructed, non-photo-based "photographic" images (1966) to geometric pictures based on color charts (1966); from bird's-eye-view, black-and-white townscapes (1968) and thickly painted mountain landscapes (1968) to large, monochrome gray paintings (1970).

Richter also made a film for his exhibition at Galerie Schmela, named after a member of Düsseldorf's art scene who hoped to make his mark as an artist: *Volker Bradke* (1966). The film see-saws between homage and irony, deliberately amateurish and, naturally, blurred. This was Richter's only excursion

48 Portraits, 1971/72 (CR 324-1 to 48)
Oil on canvas, 48 parts, each panel:
70 x 55 cm (27⅝ x 21¾ in.)
Cologne, Museum Ludwig

Corsica (House), 1969 (CR 211)
Oil on canvas, 115 x 130 cm (45⅜ x 51¼ in.)
Seattle Art Museum

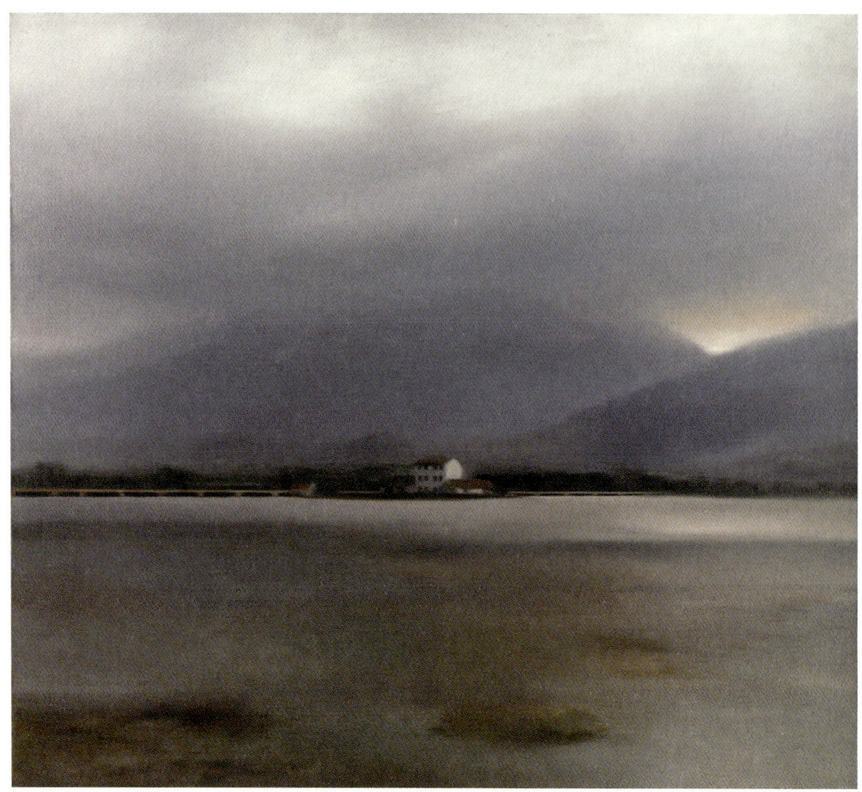

into the world of film. What seems haphazard to the impartial eye unfolds its own logic in the artist's mind. In fact, this was an extremely fruitful period with few wrong turns. With the exception of the film, Richter affirmed all the modalities of visual "communication" as well as those he was yet to systematically explore or modify. He was gradually testing painting's potential. As he grew bored by gentle smudging, he switched from the flowing application of paint to rough impasto brush strokes.

The delicacy of Richter's "blurring" turned the portraits of the eight murdered student nurses into a touching epitaph. The young women's posed smiles are frozen through a transparent blur; unspeakable pain becomes suddenly manifest. The uniformly photographic gray of their hairstyles transforms them into ominous, black helmets that seem almost to crush the girls' pale faces. Additive in their effect, these portraits extend Richter's death series and anticipate the *October 18, 1977* (1988) cycle, connected across time by grief at the senseless death of young people.

By contrast, the black-and-white townscapes that appear expressive close up but, paradoxically, exhibit impressionistic, showy effects from a distance have no clear successors in the artist's oeuvre. Beneath the surface, however, they are forerunners of his abstracts. By making blow-ups of aerial photographs of Paris, Madrid, and other major cities Richter transformed them into massive paintings that are hard to "read." It is as if some cities are saturated with creeping destruction. Sometimes from a distance, sometimes from up close, a multitude of personal styles is illustrated in the seas of buildings, which nonetheless deny any hint of subjective investment. In this regard, the variously sized color panels modeled on commercial color charts are only counterparts on a formal level. In fact, they substantiated Richter's artistic unintentionality and indifference: He often arbitrarily changed the combination of colors or let friends decide. His conclusion is that "each color adapts marvelously to whichever other color is used."[31]

With mirrors and panes of glass, Richter withdrew completely from practical implementations and, like his conceptual artist friends, confined himself to design. In the pivoting panes of glass and mirrors, the visible reality that Richter never lost sight of is produced as a dynamic, uncontrollable space of experience rather than merely as a static image plane. Visual counterparts, they correspond to images of imaginary windows and doors that are not based on any photographic originals. Richter painted them like photographs; windows reflect the shadows of their frames, doors lead to nowhere, and curtains billow in a steady rhythm of light and dark shades of gray.

Detail (Brown), 1970 (CR 271)
Oil on canvas, 135 x 150 cm (53¼ x 59 in.)
Essen, Museum Folkwang

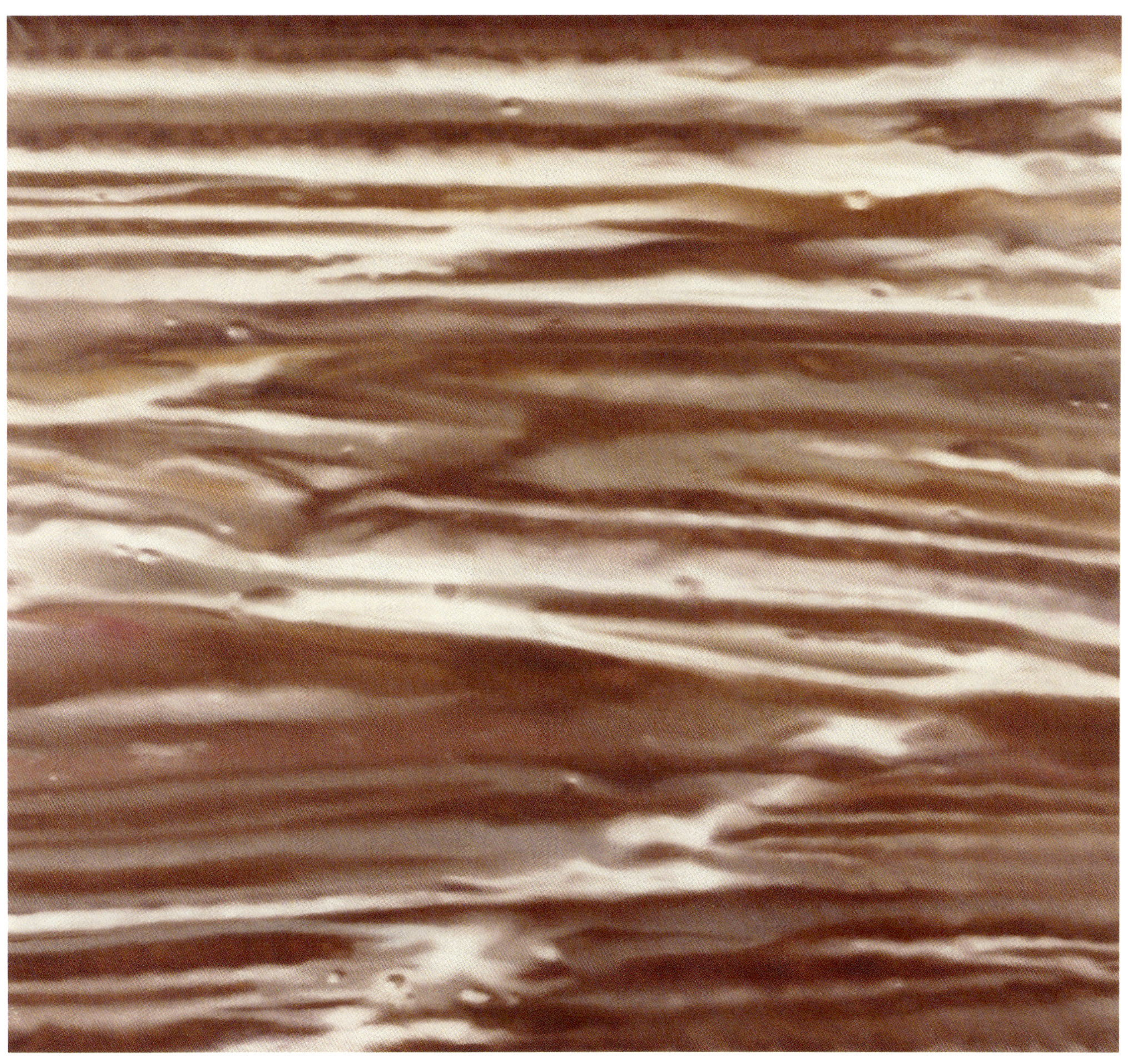

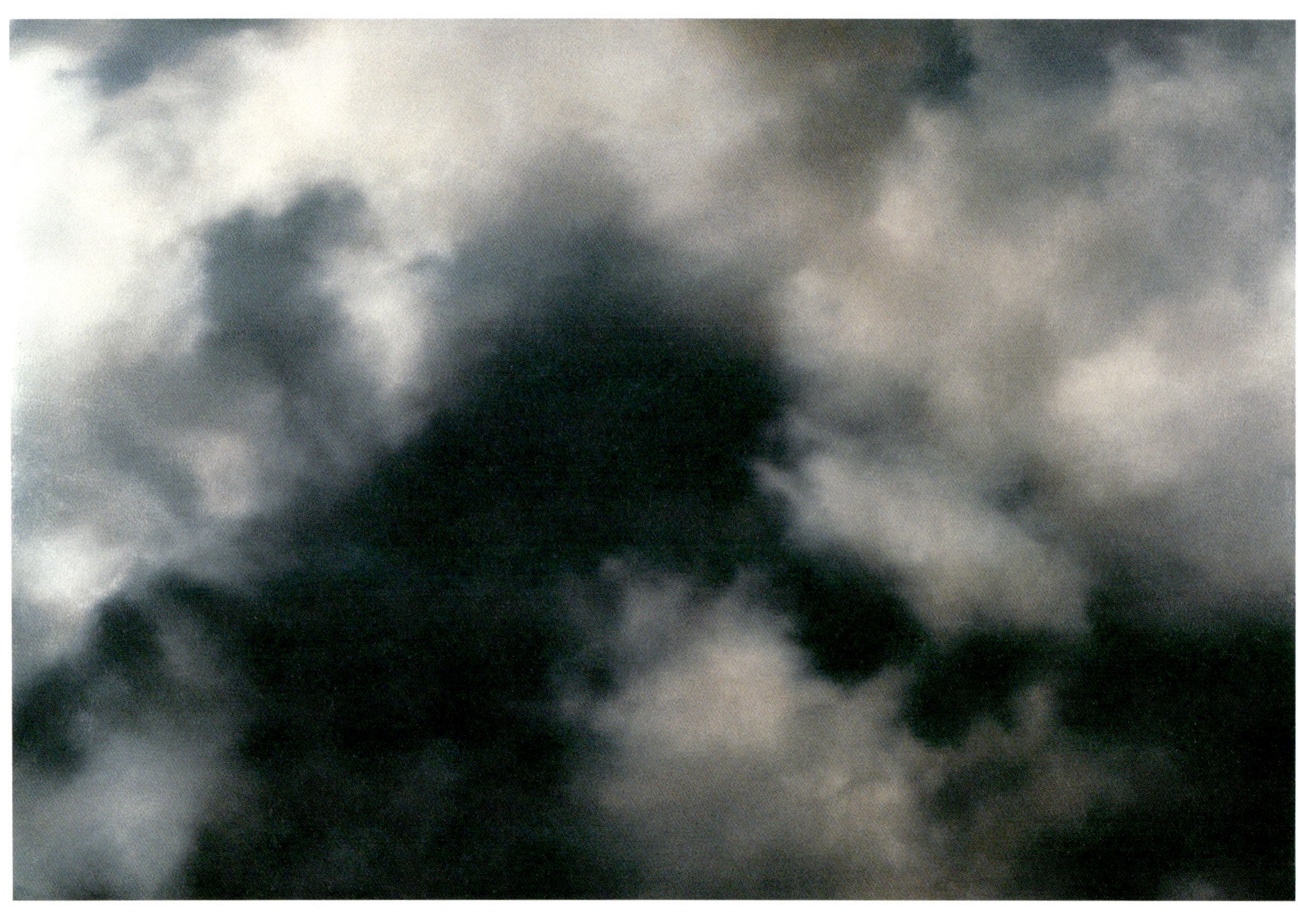

Clouds, 1970 (CR 265)
Oil on canvas, 200 x 300 cm (78¾ x 118⅛ in.)
Essen, Museum Folkwang

The artist was nevertheless stuck in an artistic quandary, as is shown by his overpainted pictures and gray paintings with and without visible brushstrokes. The grays of the photo paintings are independent as a "visibly proportioned color surface" (Richter) or as a flat monochrome. Undoubtedly, the paintings display a tangible aporia. As do the curtains against which the gaze rebounds, and the doors and windows which deny their function. In a letter to Edy de Wilde (February 23, 1975), Richter concedes: "When I first painted a number of canvases gray all over … I did so because I did not know what to paint."[32] Eight years later, by which time the gray paintings had acquired an intrinsic aesthetic value, he added: "To me, gray is the welcome and only possible equivalent for indifference, noncommitment, absence of opinion, absence of shape."[33]

Seascape (Contre-jour), 1969 (CR 233)
Oil on canvas, 200 x 200 cm (78¾ x 78¾ in.)
California, private collection

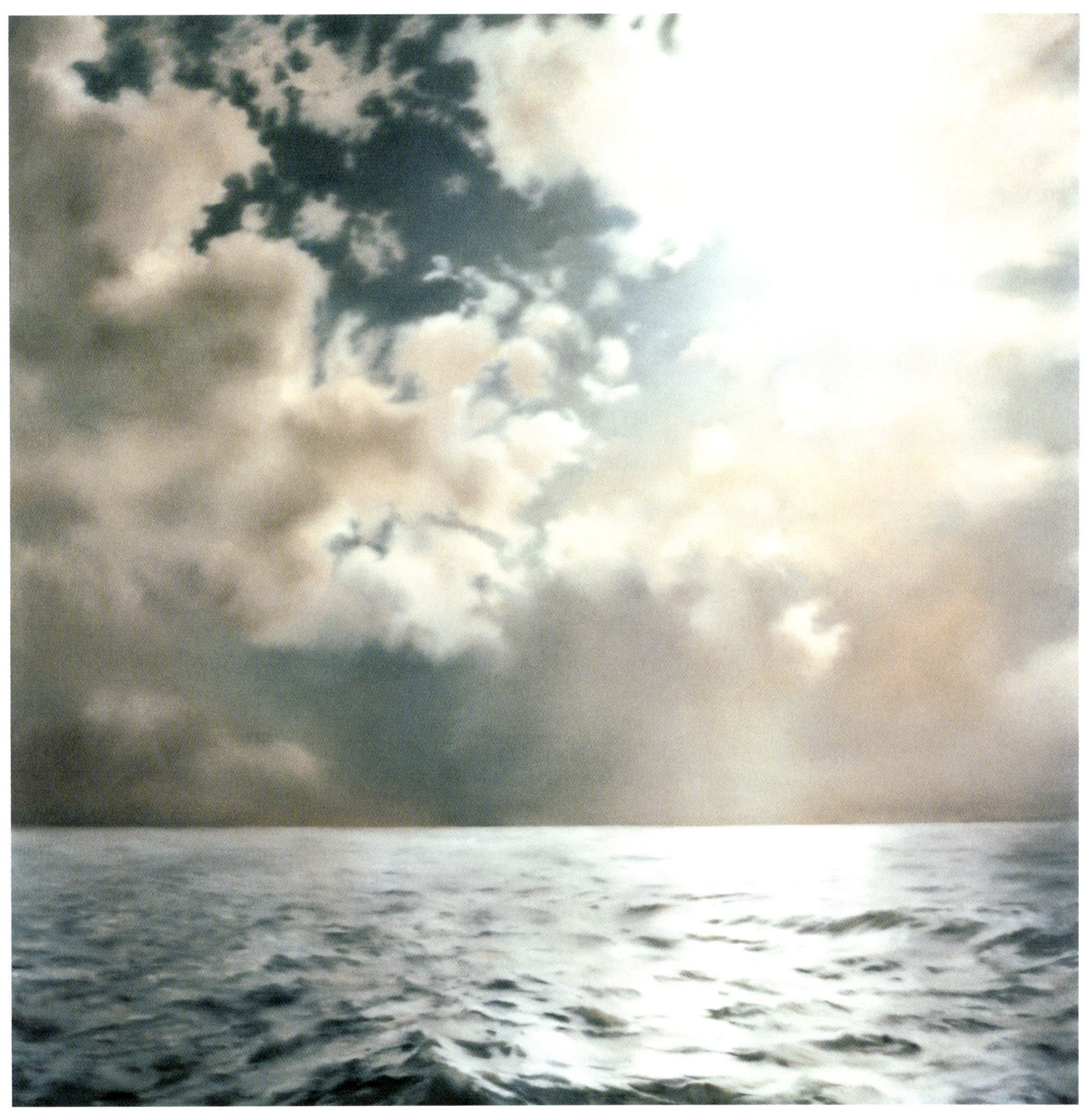

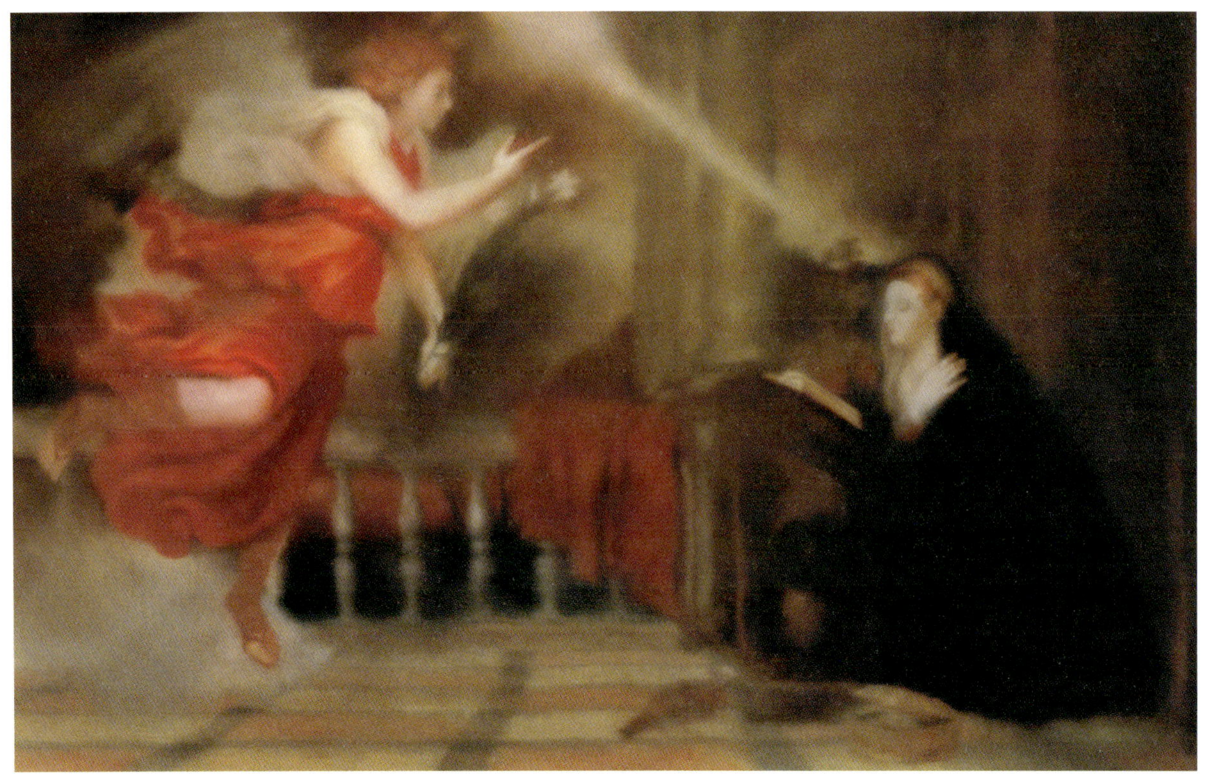

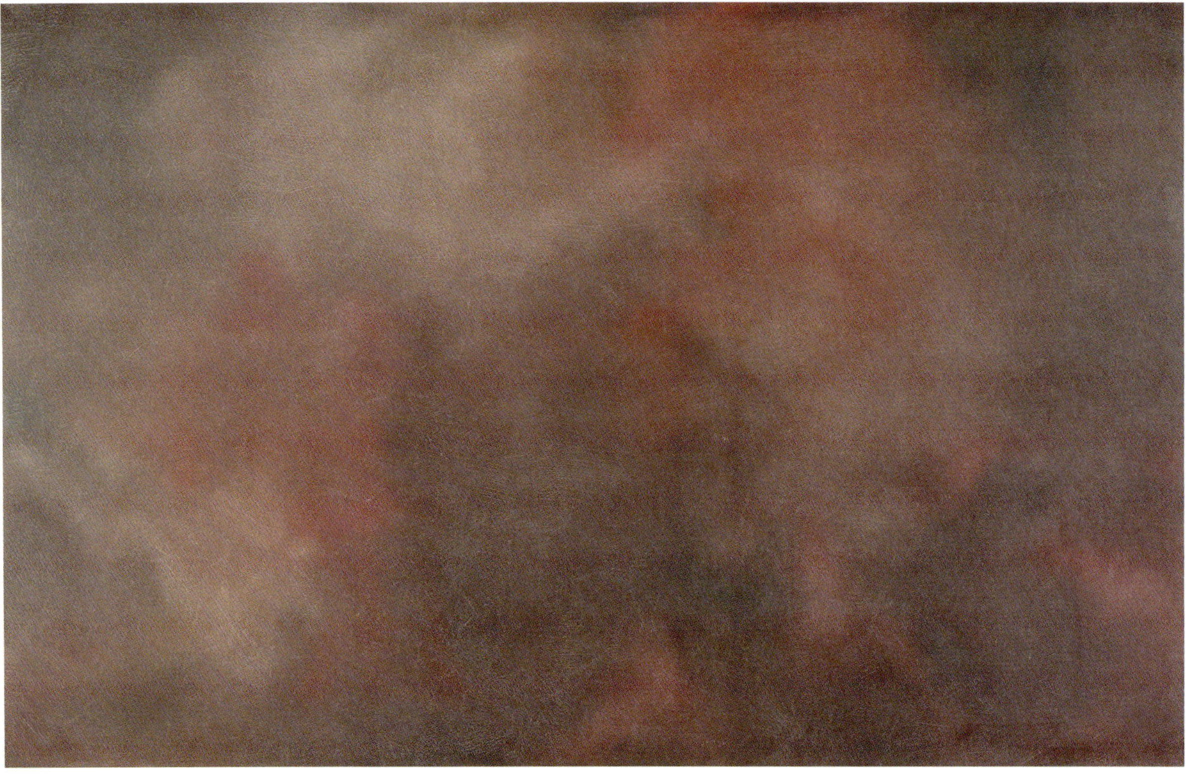

ABOVE
Annunciation after Titian, 1973 (CR 343-1)
Oil on canvas, 125 x 200 cm (49¼ x 78¾ in.)
Washington, D.C., Hirshhorn Museum

BELOW
Annunciation after Titian, 1973 (CR 343-2)
Oil on canvas, 125 x 200 cm (49¼ x 78¾ in.)
Kunstmuseum Basel

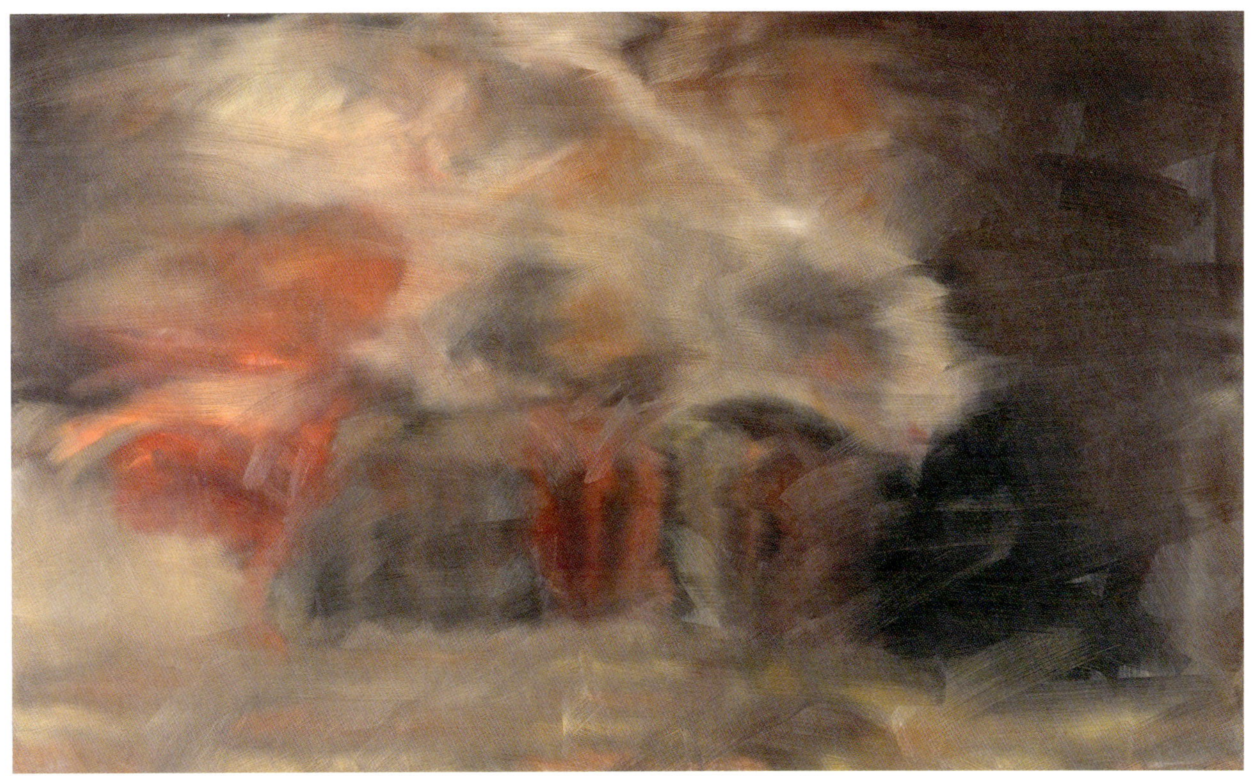

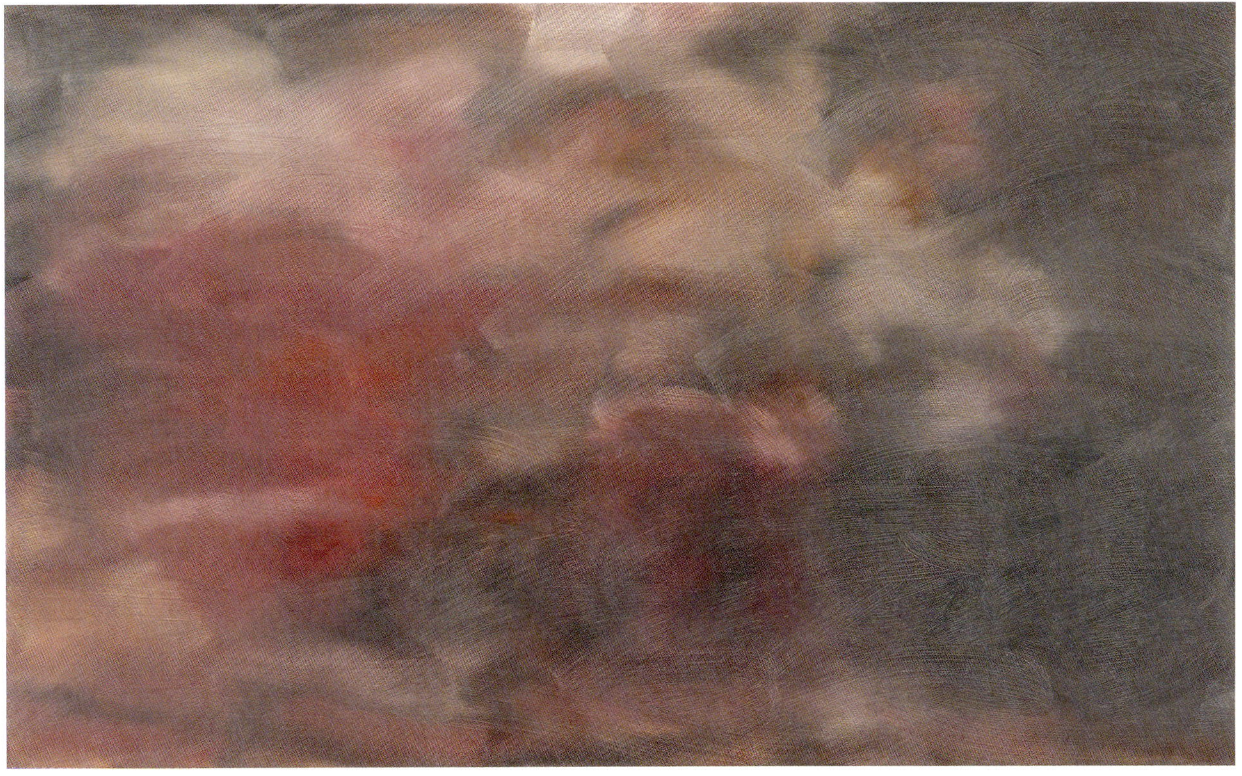

ABOVE
Annunciation after Titian, 1973 (CR 344-1)
Oil on canvas, 150 x 250 cm (59 x 98½ in.)
Kunstmuseum Basel

BELOW
Annunciation after Titian, 1973 (CR 344-3)
Oil on canvas, 150 x 250 cm (59 x 98½ in.)
Kuntsmuseum Basel

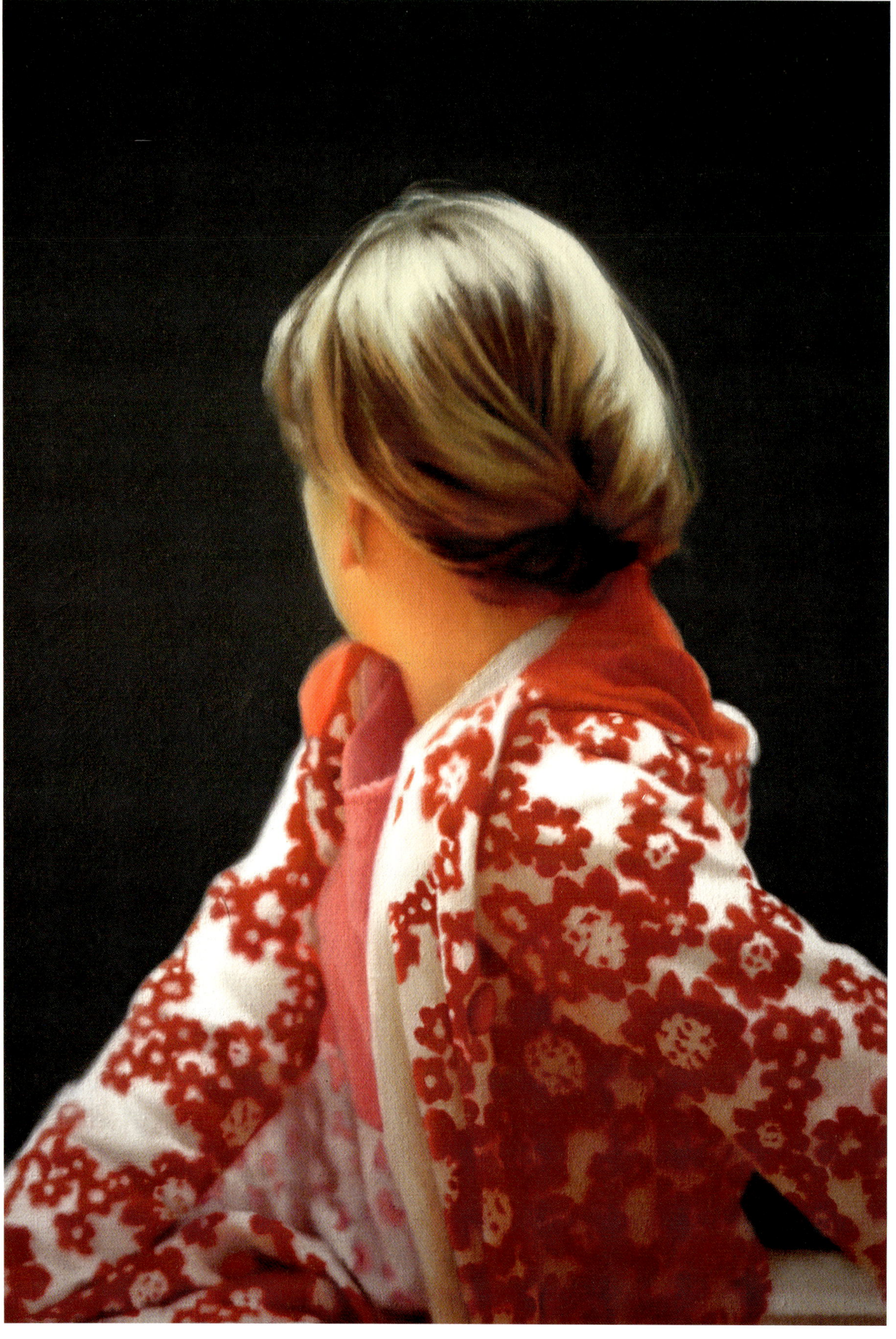

"To try out what can be done with painting."[34]

In 1973, an unusual cycle of themed paintings emerged from among the gray paintings: canvases of intertwined, colored brushstrokes and color panels modeled on color charts. The postcard that the cycle is based on is not of an everyday occurrence but a scene from the world of mythology painted by Titian in 1540: the Archangel telling the Virgin Mary that she will conceive and become the mother of the Son of God. A ray of light emitted by a dove at the top of the picture symbolizes the event.

What prompted Richter to refer to art history again after *Ema* (and a group portrait of Dutch origin) and to select, of all things, a painting by an artist of such high repute, was probably his own aspiration. Encountering Titian's painting in Venice was the impetus. An extensive conversation with Gislind Nabakowski about the cycle fails to provide adequate clarification.[35] During the interview, Richter concedes that the aspect of Titian's *Annunciation* that attracted him was something that holds true for all works of art of a similarly high standing—i.e., that they are "good" (if they are good) regardless of their impact at the time, why they were made, or the story behind them.[36] Although a vague attribute, "good" testifies to the artist's undiminished quest for guidance. He denies that his objective was to lock horns with Titian, while slyly adding, "perhaps we should ask a psychiatrist. Maybe he could tell me why I wanted to do the painting."[37]

It is noteworthy that Richter treats the term "art" as absolute. Tracing the mystery of "good art" to the past, capturing it and saving it for the present would be a plausible reason. "But … I don't accept the principal difference between 'pure' pictures that only represent themselves and others that just illustrate something."[38] However, Richter resolutely rejects art for art's sake; This would contradict his suggestion that art is and shall remain a medium of "communication." Instead, he sets his sights on a form of art that is self-referential while at the same time containing a kind of numinous, invisible moment that transcends self-reference. He mentions the paintings of Robert Ryman, Brice Marden, and Palermo as examples: "in a way their paintings are also illusionistic, and you can only just identify the actual paint or the material if you have the eyes of a paint salesman."[39]

With his paraphrasing of Titian, the artist unintentionally but nonrandomly touches upon the subliminal overlap between art and religion. Art

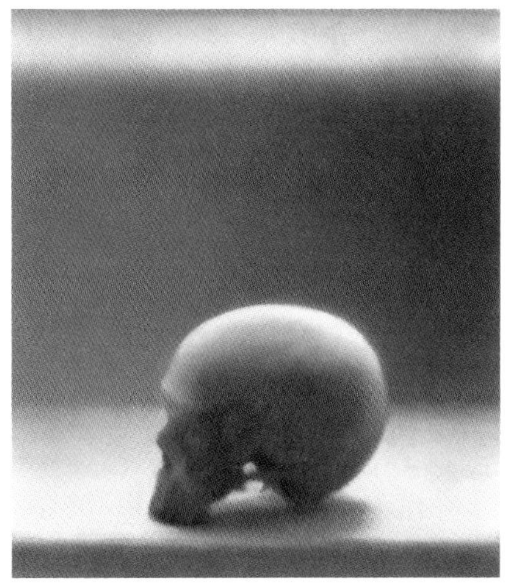

Skull, 1983 (CR 545-3)
Oil on canvas, 55 x 50 cm (21¾ x 19¾ in.)
Switzerland, private collection

Betty, 1988 (CR 663-5)
Oil on canvas, 102 x 72 cm (40¼ x 28⅜ in.)
Saint Louis Art Museum

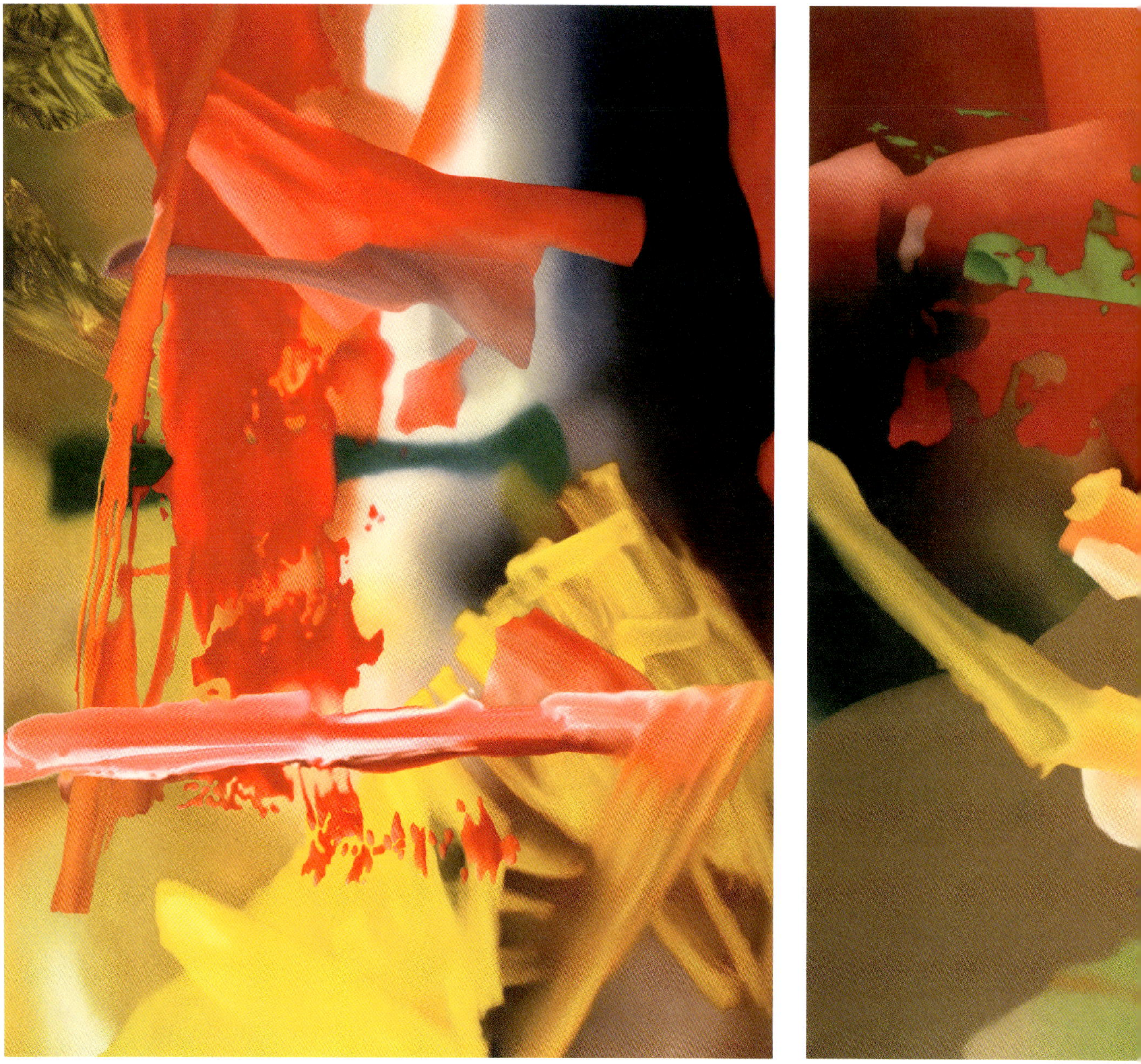

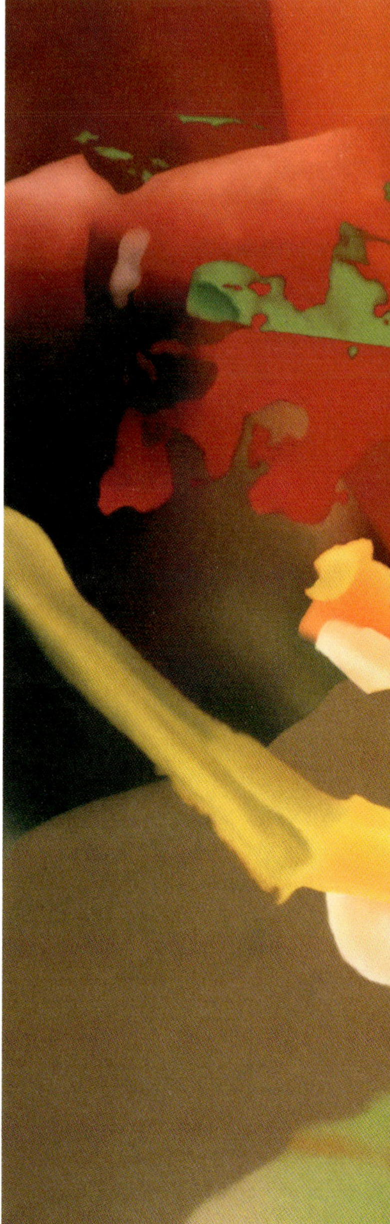

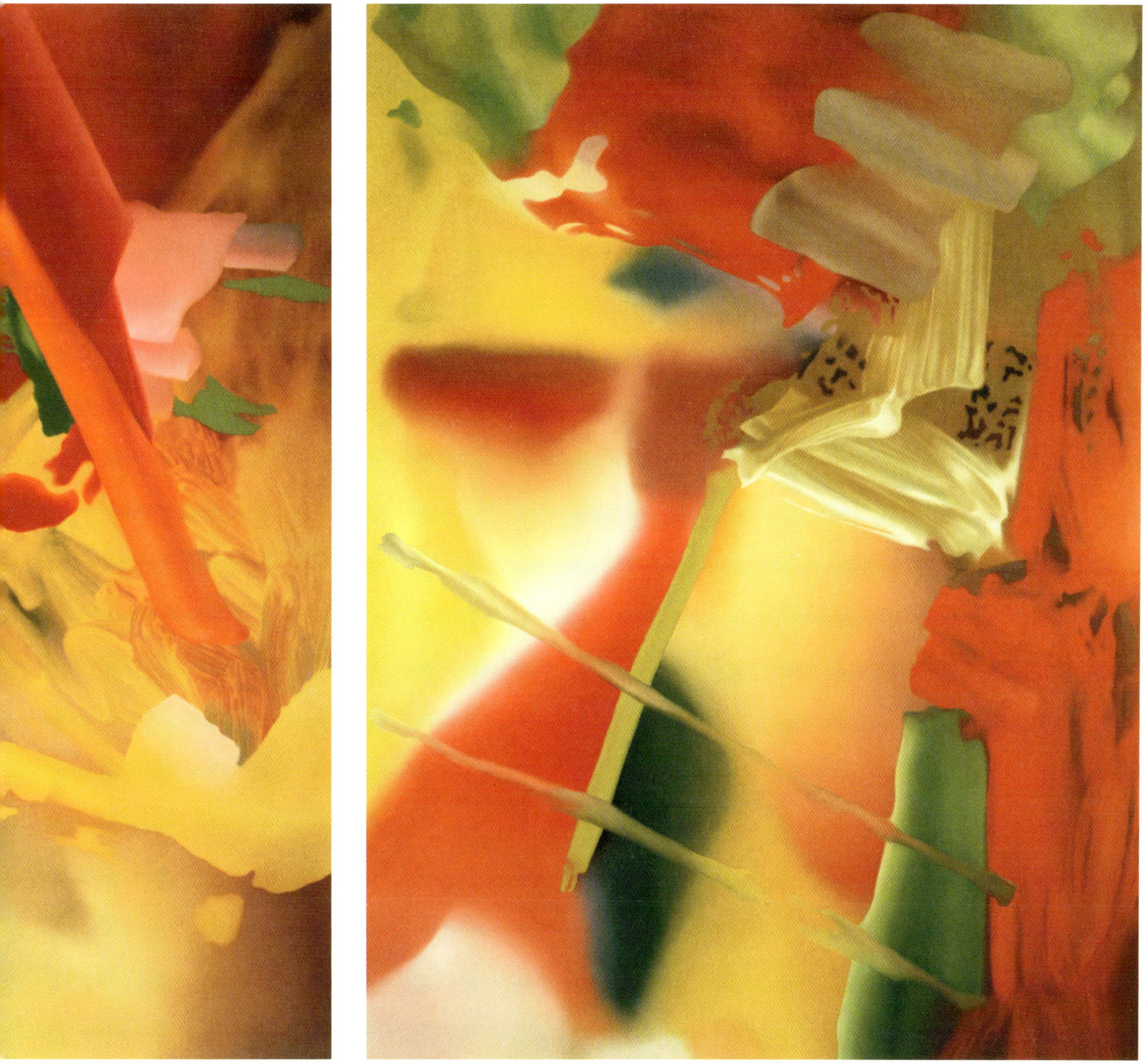

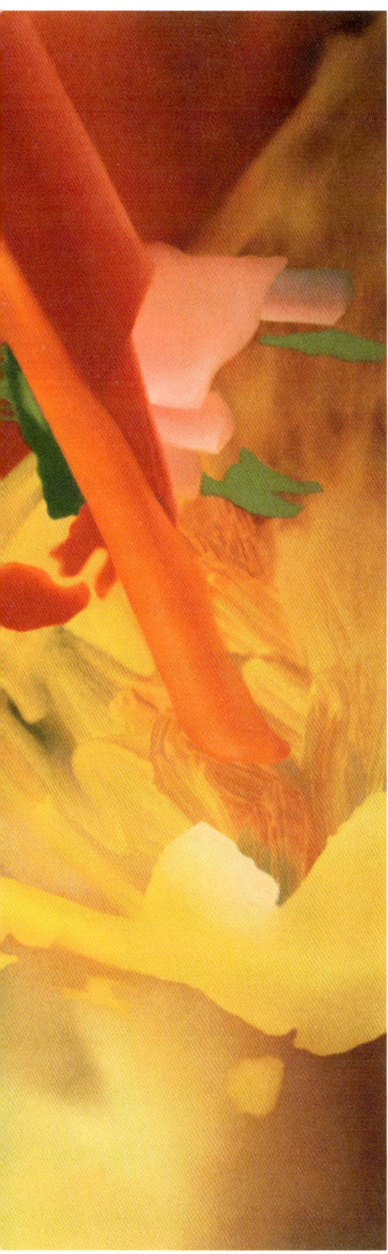

Faust, 1980 (CR 460)
Oil on canvas, triptych, each:
295 x 225 cm (116¼ x 88⅝ in.)
Frankfurt am Main, Deutsche Bank Collection

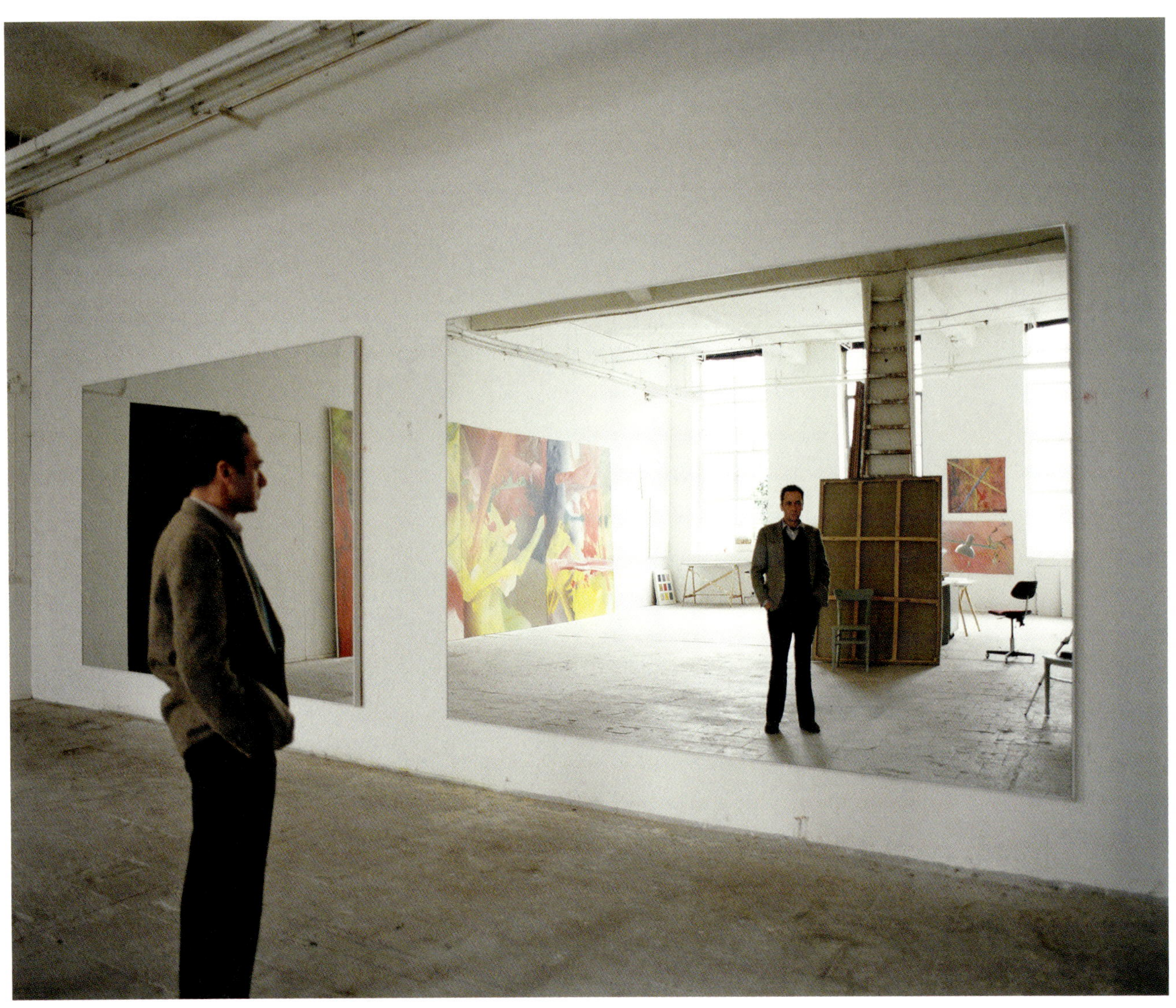

Mirror, 1981 (CR 470/1–2)
Crystal mirror glass, each:
225 x 318 cm (88⅝ x 125¼ in.)
Kunsthalle Düsseldorf

Abstract Painting, 1979 (CR 444)
Oil on canvas, 300 x 250 cm (118⅛ x 98½ in.)
Paris, Musée National d'Art Moderne,
Centre Georges Pompidou

and religion share a necessary condition. Both require a collectively credible narrative for social presence and power. Richter occasionally addresses this in his early notes, revealing a hidden inclination to allow art a quasi-religious function. Agnostic modernism offers no realistic outlook for metaphysical art beyond the esoteric. Certainly not for undiluted Christian art. Unlike the mode of their staging, the traditional characters have had their day. Our understanding of the Angel and the Virgin Mary is evaporating, and most people think of Madonna as merely a showbiz superstar.

Nevertheless, Titian's *Annunciation* posed a problem for Richter: How to distill an appropriately artistic and aesthetic communication without resorting to the staged message of the Immaculate Conception? Doesn't his undertaking in fact represent an artistic test of strength—albeit not explicitly deliberate—that excludes the competitive ambition to prove who is the "better" painter? The artist solved this problem with his tried and tested set of tools. He blurred the contours of the Angel and the Madonna and moved them towards the horizon of disappearance.

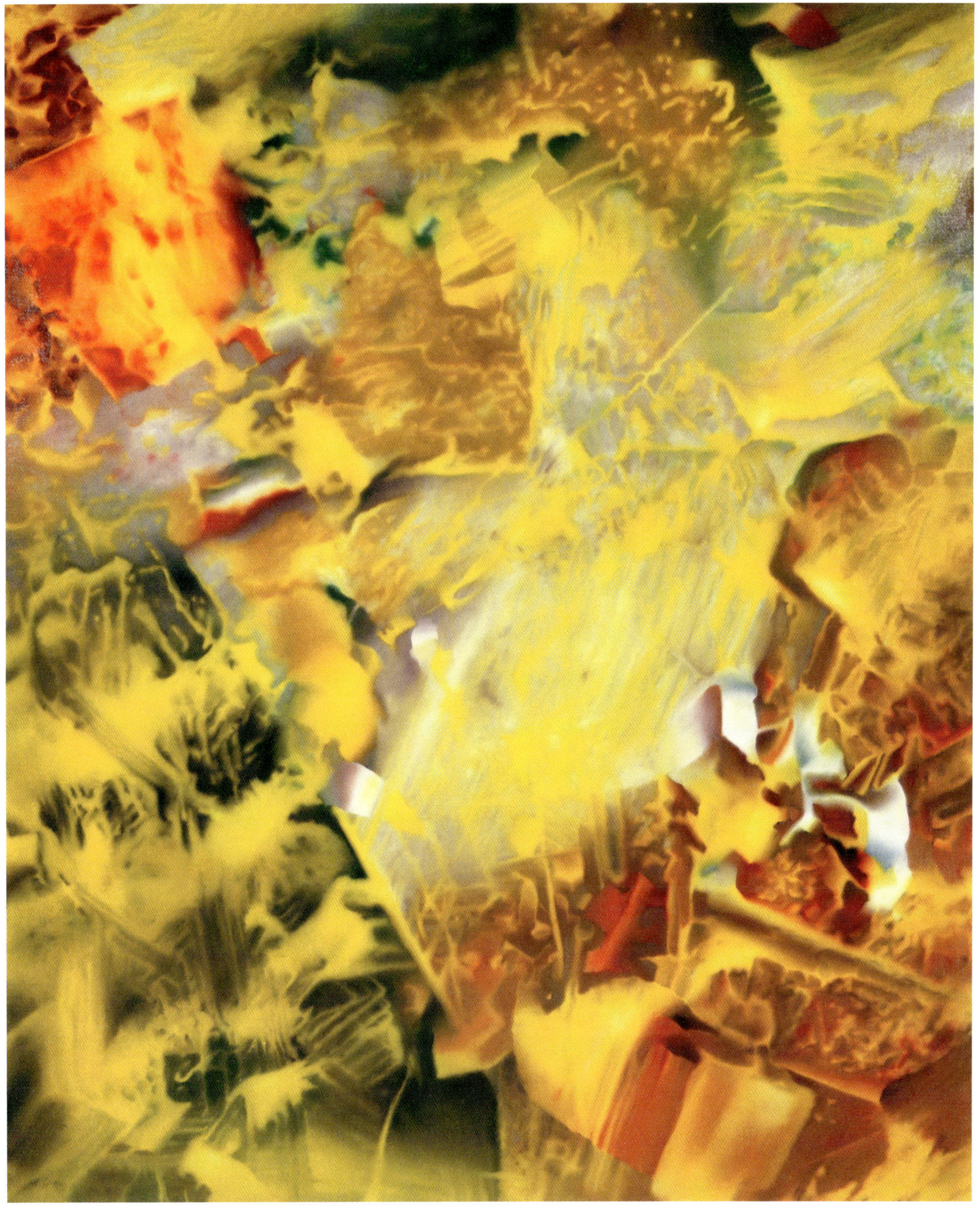

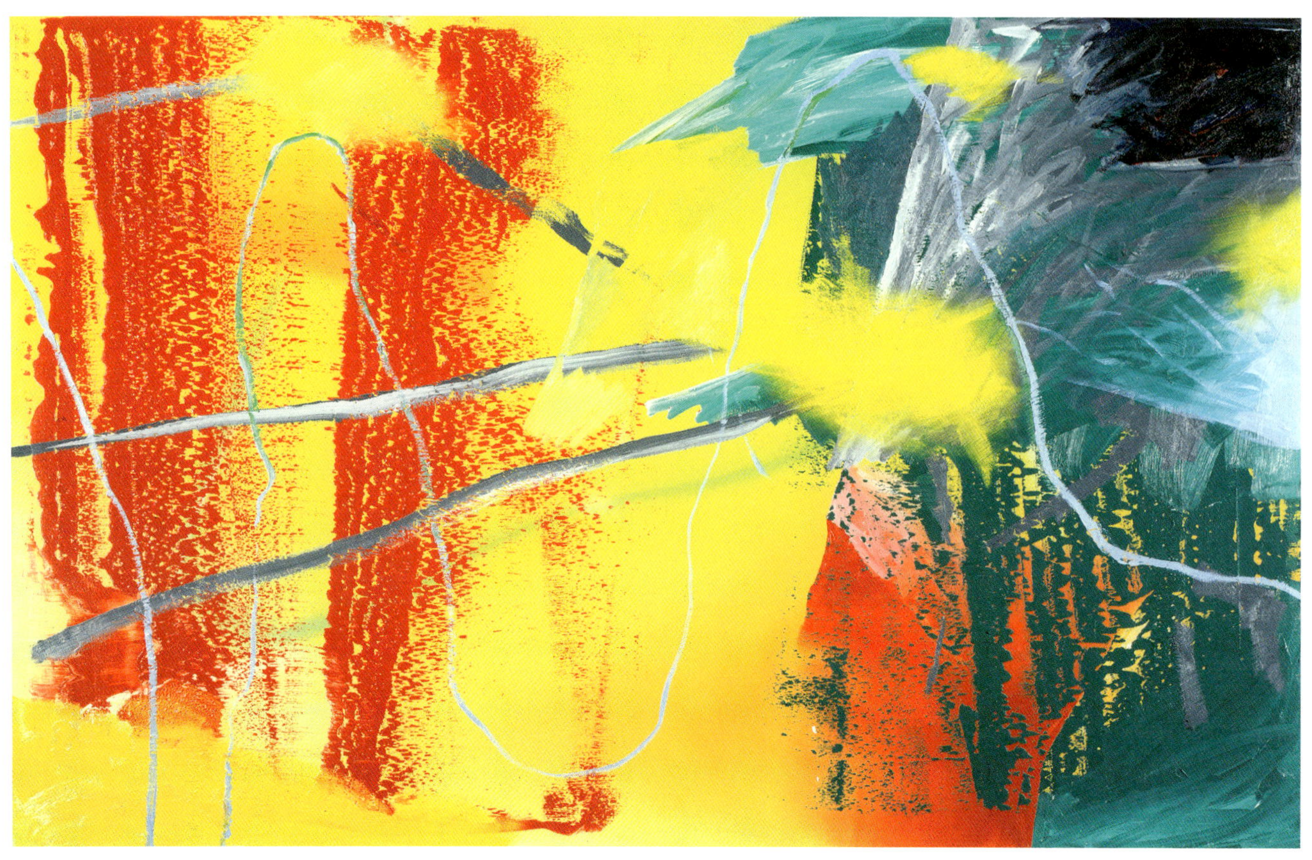

War, 1981 (CR 484)
Oil on canvas, 200 x 320 cm (78¾ x 126 in.)
Cologne, Museum Ludwig

The blurring intensifies the painting's dynamic effect, while the Angel "rushes" towards Mary, whose inertia provides gentle and formal resistance. Form and content still correspond but in a parodic way: the ray of light directed at Mary dissolves in smoke and the dove turns into a blotch.

All the figures and objects in subsequent versions of the painting dissolve, becoming cloudy, floating, colored shapes. All that remains in the series' fifth and final picture is a dark area of vibrant, extraordinarily differentiated brown with diffuse, lighter areas and a red undertone. It is the red of the robe worn by Titian's Angel—a tonal bracket for all five paintings—and a delicate echo of the model.

The purpose of the blurring technique in these paintings is not to arouse visual perception, as in the case of the photographic images. Instead, the aim is to obliterate the painting's subject. Here, unlike Richter's early *Table* photo painting, annihilation is achieved by means of subtly refined, space-creating color. It is the result of a sophisticated technique that endows the paint with an indefinable yet evident effect in order to lift the supposedly invisible into visibility, and the depicted beyond the purely empirical. In Richter's hands, paint becomes a fleeting, liquid substance: physical, yet transcending material boundaries.

Long after its completion, the group of paintings based on Titian's *Annunciation* was considered a failure. Dietmar Elger's biography of the artist refers to it just twice and then only in the margins.[40] Richter dismissed the works when he stated in summary that the continued attachment to Renaissance painting no longer worked, "even as a copy."[41]

With the passage of time, the paintings are viewed quite differently. The failure of this endeavor turned out to be the only "realistic" and, ultimately, plausible prospect for daring the impossible—and for prevailing in the end. A prerequisite for mastering an artistic challenge is the ability to reflect its factual impossibility in the specific form of its implementation. The objective is an irrevocable sense of loss at the purported failure, which is the actual impossibility of transferring the past's "good art" into the present without rupture, loss, or change. Only an artist who has the mastery to reflect visual language vividly and at the highest artistic level can truly succeed in doing so.

The indication of loss is a feature of a way of painting that clearly rejects the conceivability of a return to historical positions. Contemporary art may only be able to materialize the metaphysical, which enriches experience and stimulates things outside the visible and palpable by failing, by an apparent lack of success. Richter's failure is the heroic failure of painting in defiance of everything. At the time, references to the art history preceding the emergence of the avant-garde remained exceptions in Richter's work.

Five years after Richter completed *Annunciation after Titian*, he photographed his daughter Babette, who turned away abruptly when she saw the

Table, 1982 (CR 508)
Oil on canvas, 225 x 294 cm (88⅝ x 115¾ in.)
Germany, private collection

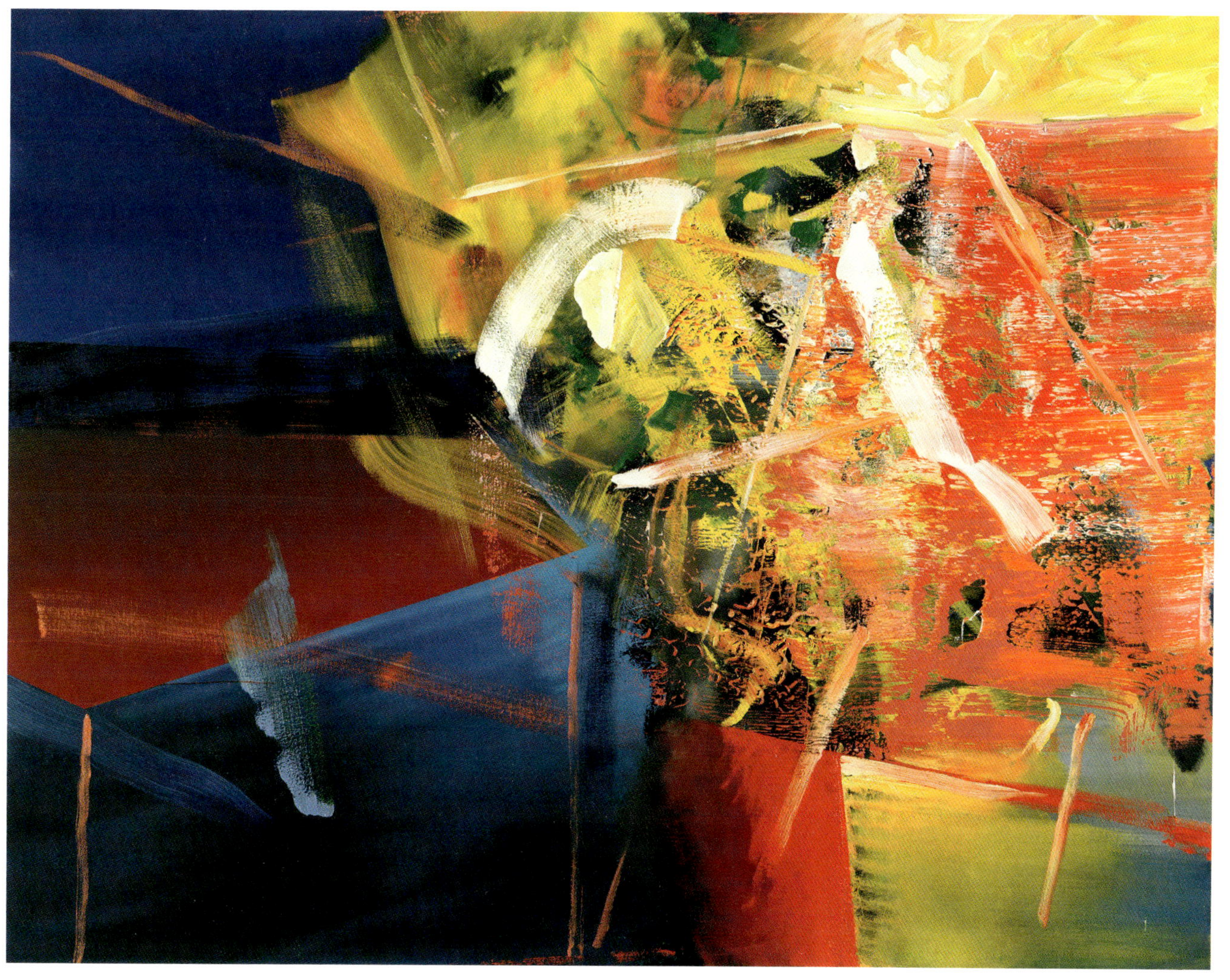

camera. In the *Atlas*, the photograph is an isolated snapshot amidst many still lifes. In 1988 Richter produced the photograph for *Betty* (1988), one of his most beautiful paintings. It's an artistic bow to Johannes Vermeer's compelling images of women and an exemplary modernist portrait: reflected beauty.

Photography continued to provide a way of escaping perplexity and insecurity, although it did not completely eliminate it. Richter photographed extensively in color during this period. Landscapes, seascapes, the sky, clouds, and portraits provided templates for painted images. He also indulged in a few experiments with photographic blurring as well as random cut-outs. Chronologically, the color photographs he collected in the *Atlas* begin with pictures of small fires. At that point, color was not yet the norm in photography. While working on the paintings he based on paint charts, Richter started by subjecting the colors to extensive tests before testing them in his photographic paintings, and then combining them in a wide variety of compositions. He also made numerous precise architectural drawings of special rooms to test the effect and radiance of the color charts.

Another incentive for focusing more on color was that the reputation of his photographic black-and-white images had changed. Over the years, the trivial objects they depicted had begun to bask in the glow of a nostalgic aesthetic. They had become familiar and were no longer provocative. Richter's emerging unease that the black-and-white photographic images seemed to be instituting some kind of style may have been a third motive for focusing on color: "If black and white turns into color, I may as well use the right colors."[42] He temporarily abandoned his excursions into abstract painting, which had also initially been based on color photographs. The source material was provided by detailed shots of horizontal brushstrokes in the paintings, which the artist blew up and then copied. Irregular wavy and blurred horizontal stripes stretched across the canvas, hiding their photographic origins. This type of painting would initiate the most momentous change in the painter's entire work. Did his landscapes build a passable bridge?

Richter's first pure landscape was still black and white: *Corsica I* (1968). The model was a montage of landscape and seascape. The sea in the foreground, a narrow dark strip of vegetation above, and mountains enfolded by clouds in the background. He was reluctant to exhibit the picture as he didn't think it would be possible to show it. The artist gave an offset print of the subject to the Gegenverkehr—Zentrum für aktuelle Kunst contemporary art center in Aachen. The Gegenverkehr had been established six months earlier, and is where I organized his first solo exhibition in a public institution,[43] which opened on March 26, 1969. "This exhibition was important for Richter," wrote Dietmar Elger, "because in addition to providing an overview of his work so far, he was also able to produce a catalog whose 122 small-format illustrations reflected its diversity. Thus, Gerhard Richter rectified the public's identification of his work with the gray photo paintings and gave his current images an equal position."[44]

Corsica I (1968) and the canvases that share its subject, title, and consecutive numbering play an essential part in Richter's work. They introduced an engagement with landscape painting, albeit subject to constant interruption. The genre offered a suitable territory for the use of color.

The way in which Richter handled them almost casually set the mood of loss conveyed in the distinctive colors of the *Annunciation after Titian* cycle. It would become a dominant leitmotif in his future work; the other, more

Candle, 1982 (CR 511-2)
Oil on canvas, 70 x 70 cm (27⅝ x 27⅝ in.)
San Francisco Museum of Modern Art

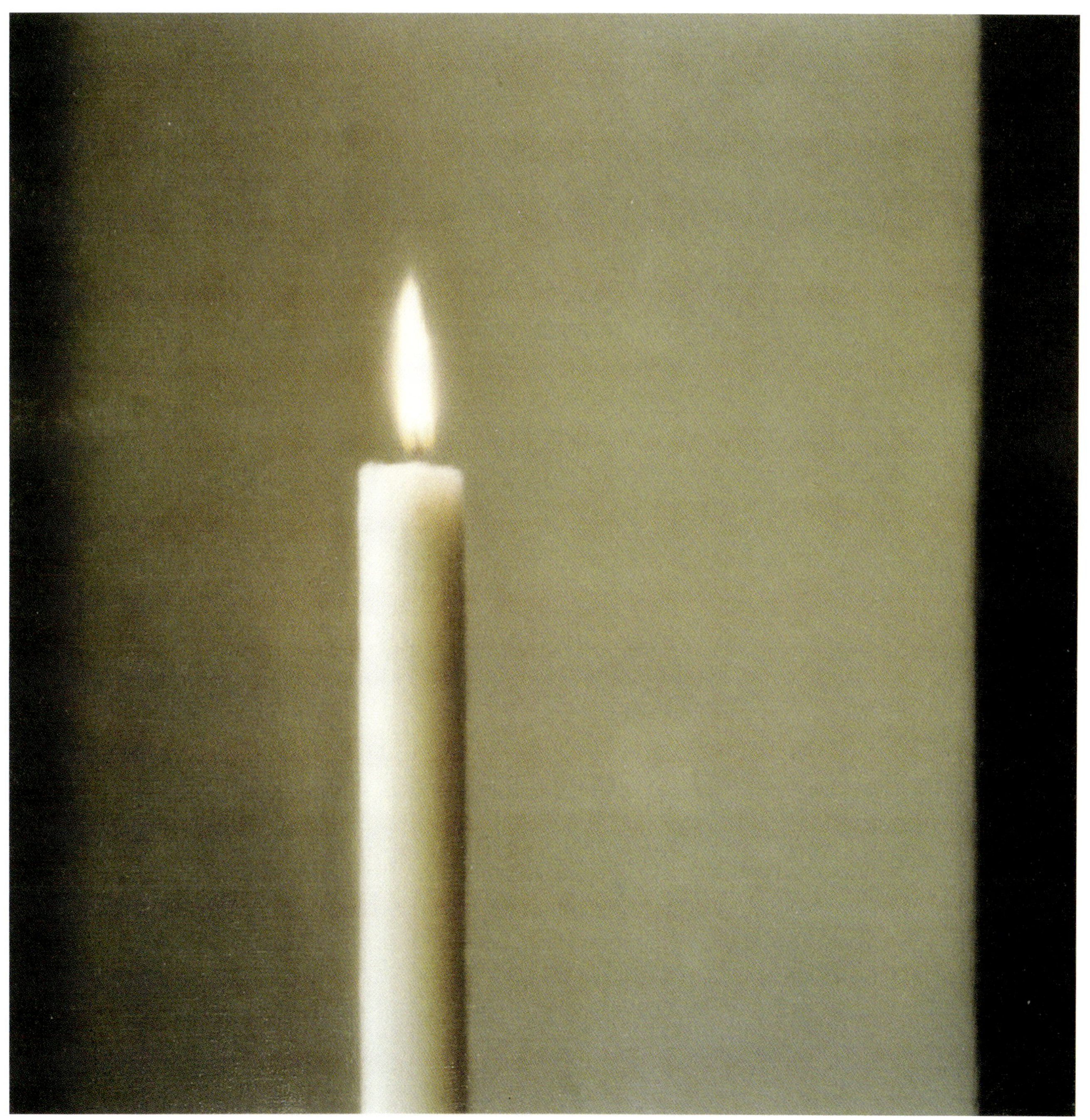

Abstract Painting, 1984 (CR 551-7)
Oil on canvas, 50 x 70 cm (19¾ x 27⅝ in.)
Private collection

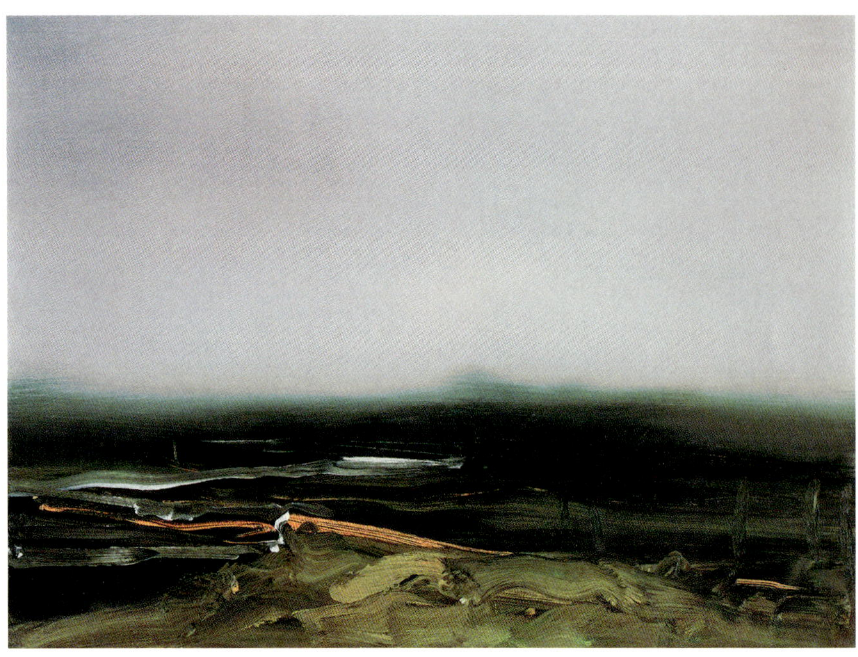

confident variant, would be his intention to create the unexpected, the unseen, the disconcerting.

Richter's first appearance in the spotlight of the international art scene was in 1972 at the Venice Biennale, where his contribution was extraordinarily haunting. Dieter Honisch had invited him as the only artist to exhibit in the German Pavilion. This was unusual as several artists typically share the space. For the building's central rotunda, Richter produced 48 70 x 55 cm black-and-white portraits of male luminaries from science and culture based on photographs taken from encyclopedias: "Using an episcope, I project the small photograph from the encyclopedia onto the larger canvas. I draw the facial contours directly from the photo projection. The rest I transfer to the canvas without mechanical assistance."[45] Hung side by side at equal distances, the portrait series captured the Pavilion's pompous atmosphere and provided a caustic backlight by virtue of the aesthetic sparseness of the encyclopedia's uniform photographic images that had "no artistic style of their own."[46] Richter's profound understanding of the interplay between painting and architecture allowed him to stage a visual and emotional game of ping-pong. Ever since then, the Pavilion, which was altered by the Nazis in 1938, has been controversial. Square columns replaced Ionic columns, and the former parquet was traded for a marble floor. Calls for its demolition are repeated before every Biennale.

Exhibitions in renowned German and foreign museums followed, as well as in leading international galleries, which now included the German galleries that first exhibited Richter's pictures. The Palais des Beaux-Arts in Brussels granted Richter his first retrospective in 1976. He has regularly exhibited at the *documenta* in Kassel since 1972. In New York, Konrad Fischer and Gian Enzo Sperone, Italy's most famous avant-garde dealer, opened a gallery with Angela Westwater, where they introduced his pictures to the American public. Recognition followed across the board and was much appreciated by Richter.

Not everything went to plan. Despite *documenta 5* (1972), the Biennale, and low prices, the commercial success of Richter's work was disappointing. In 1966, life became financially difficult when he decided not to renew the exclusive contract with Galerie Friedrich that guaranteed him a monthly income. Richter felt artistically restricted and wanted to avoid working for the market at all cost.[47] A state professorship promised security with less dependency so in 1971 the artist accepted the offer at Düsseldorf's Art Academy. Additionally, New York's art scene was perturbed by his photo paintings, and sales were unspectacular. The Americans took particular exception to Richter's ceaseless visual style changes, which contradicted their idea of artistic identity and seriousness. Years later, his abstract paintings were much more successful among American art critics and collectors. His private life, however, was tinged with sadness. The relationship with his wife Ema became strained and the marriage officially ended in the spring of 1979. Earlier, his close friend Blinky Palermo had unexpectedly died on February 17, 1977, while on holiday in the Maldives. During this time, the art market started flying high, reflecting the growing popularity and social prestige of "progressive" contemporary art, backed by art critics and an increasing number of museum exhibitions. Prices began to rise. Even the German museums relaxed their reticence towards contemporary art and offered up

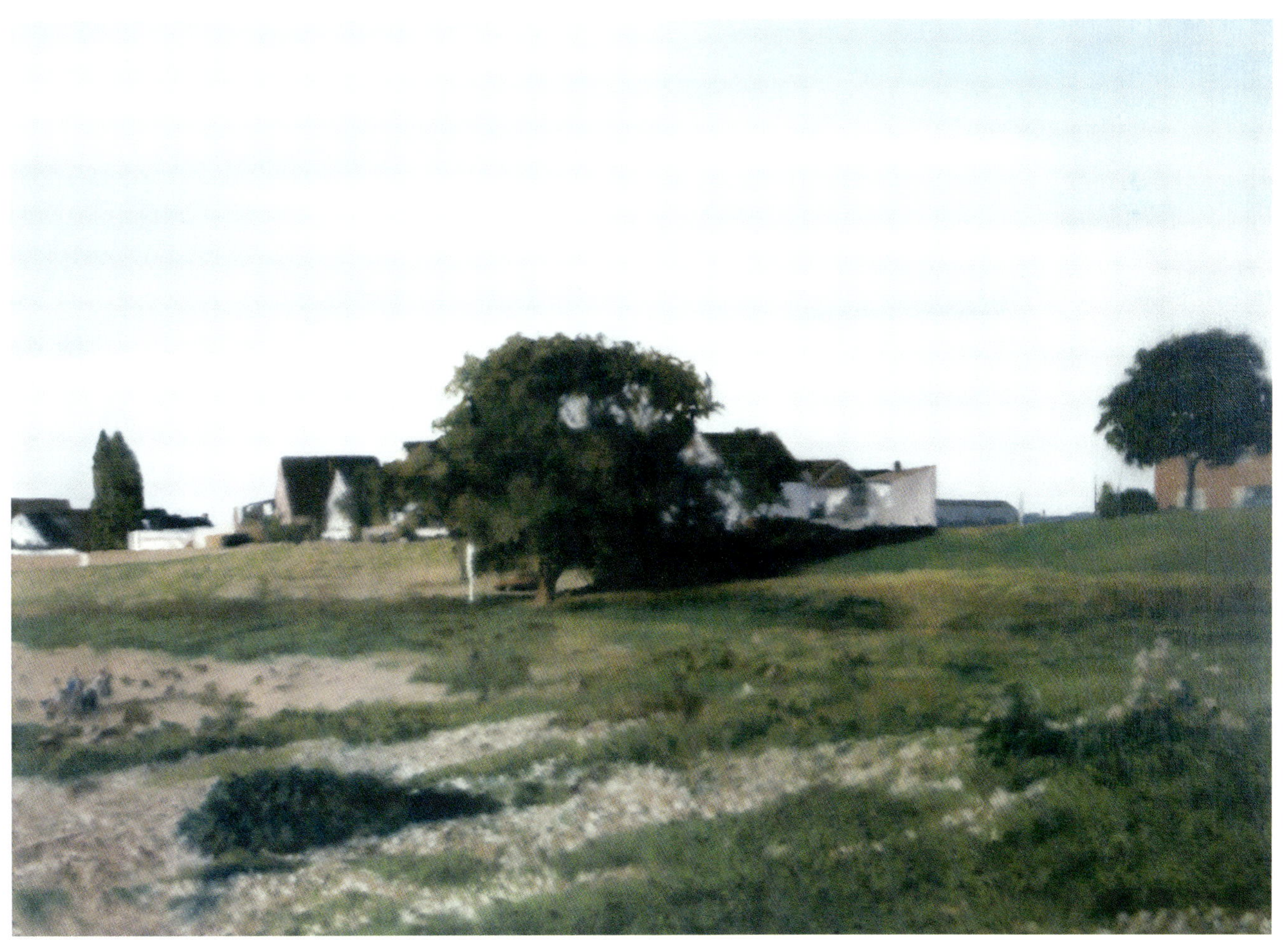

Rhinescape, 1984 (CR 550-3)
Oil on canvas, 100 x 140 cm (39⅜ x 55⅛ in.)
Private collection

Abstract Painting, 1984 (CR 568-2)
Oil on canvas, 200 x 180 cm (78¾ x 70⅞ in.)
Private collection

rooms for changing exhibitions, emulating American and Dutch museums. Western art criticism was in bloom.

The political and economic situation helped. Closer economic ties within Western Europe intensified international trade and the boom in the exports of (West) German goods provided the middle classes of the World War II losers with hitherto unfamiliar prosperity.

It may not have ended the political divergences between East and West, but the global policy of détente created the political prerequisites for economic success. Rising government revenues improved public sector support for cultural purchases, exhibitions, and contemporary art museums. Apart from a few exceptions, the younger generation's recent protests became institutionalized.

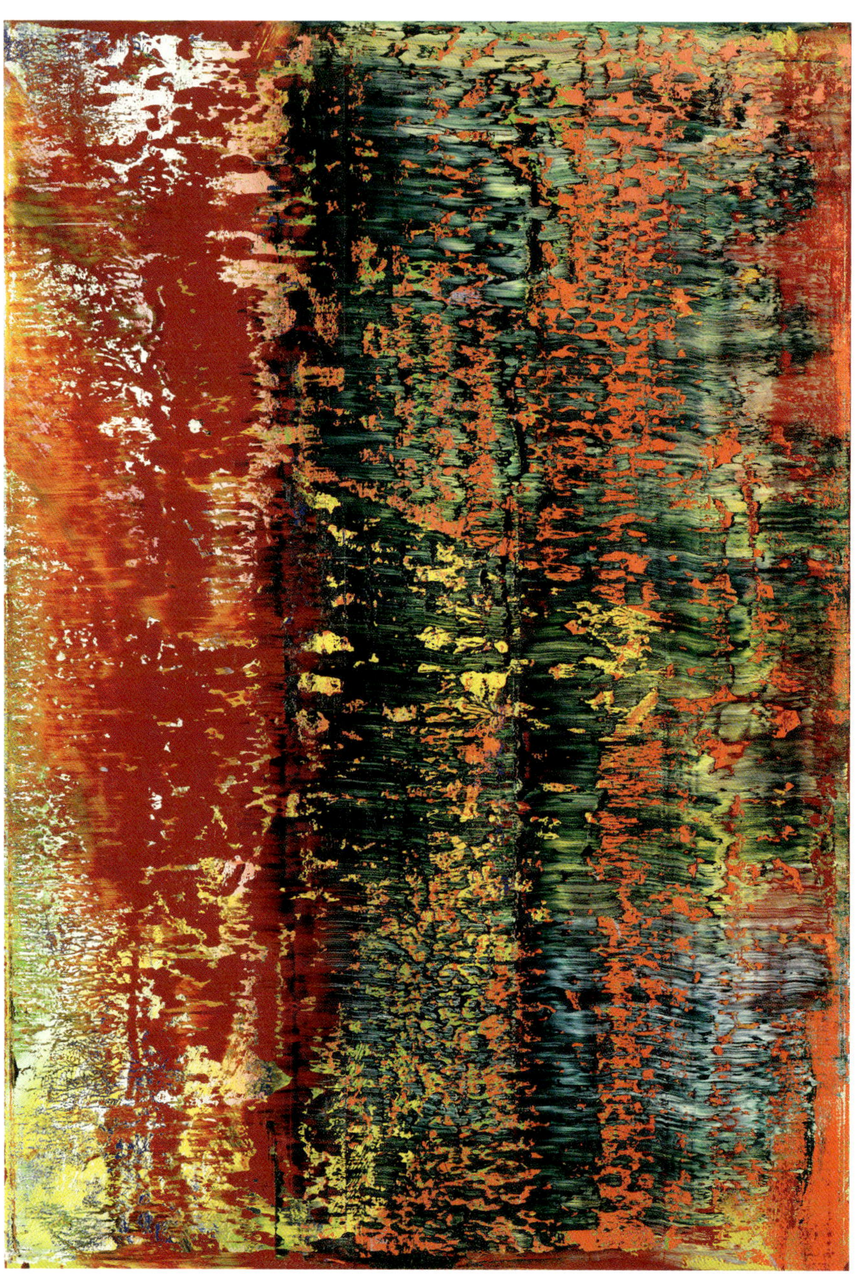

A B, Brick Tower, 1987 (CR 643-1)
Oil on canvas, 200 x 140 cm (78¾ x 55⅛ in.)
Private collection

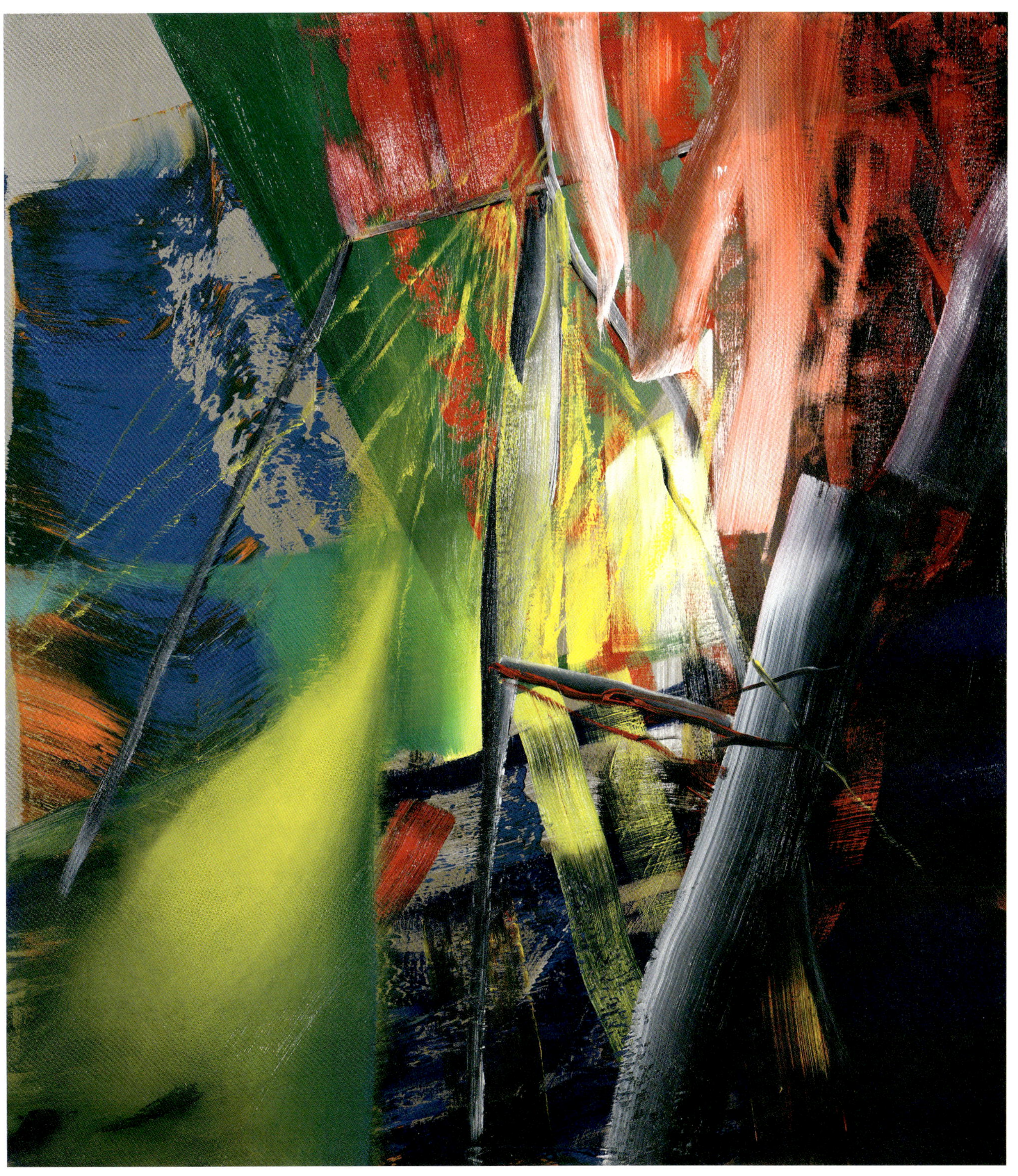

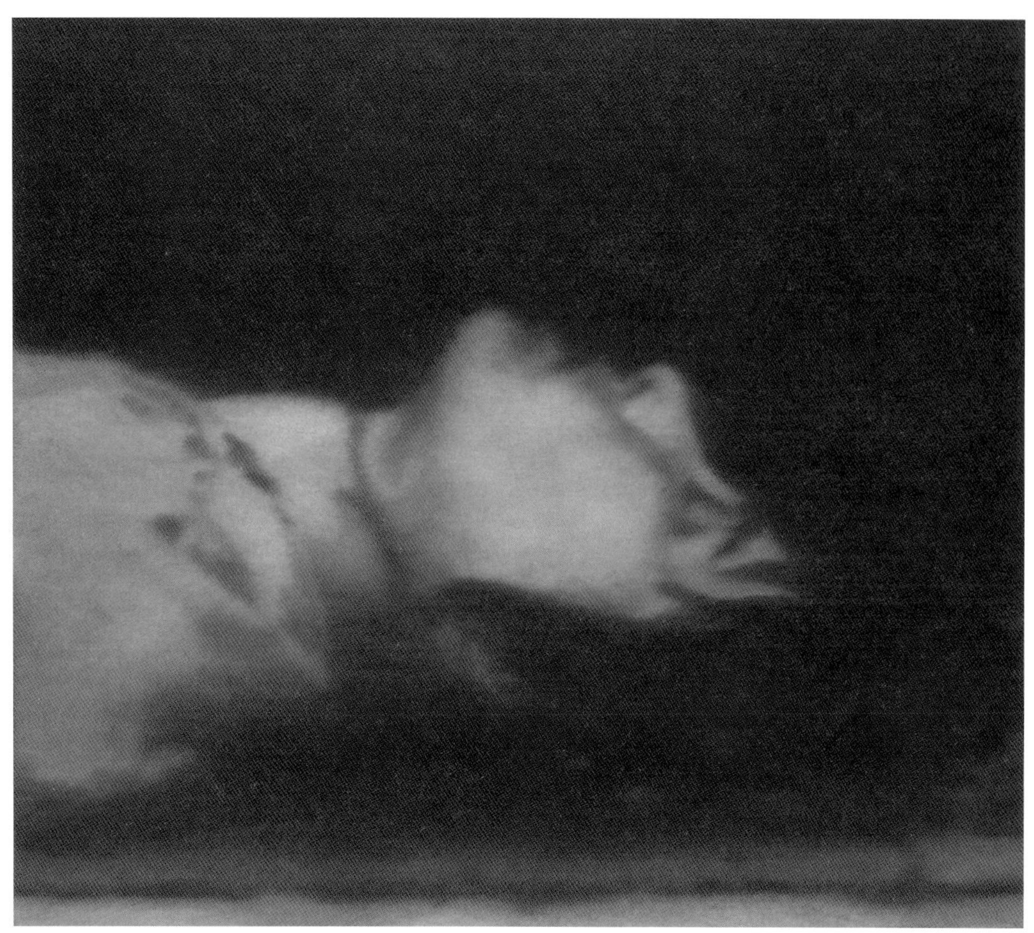

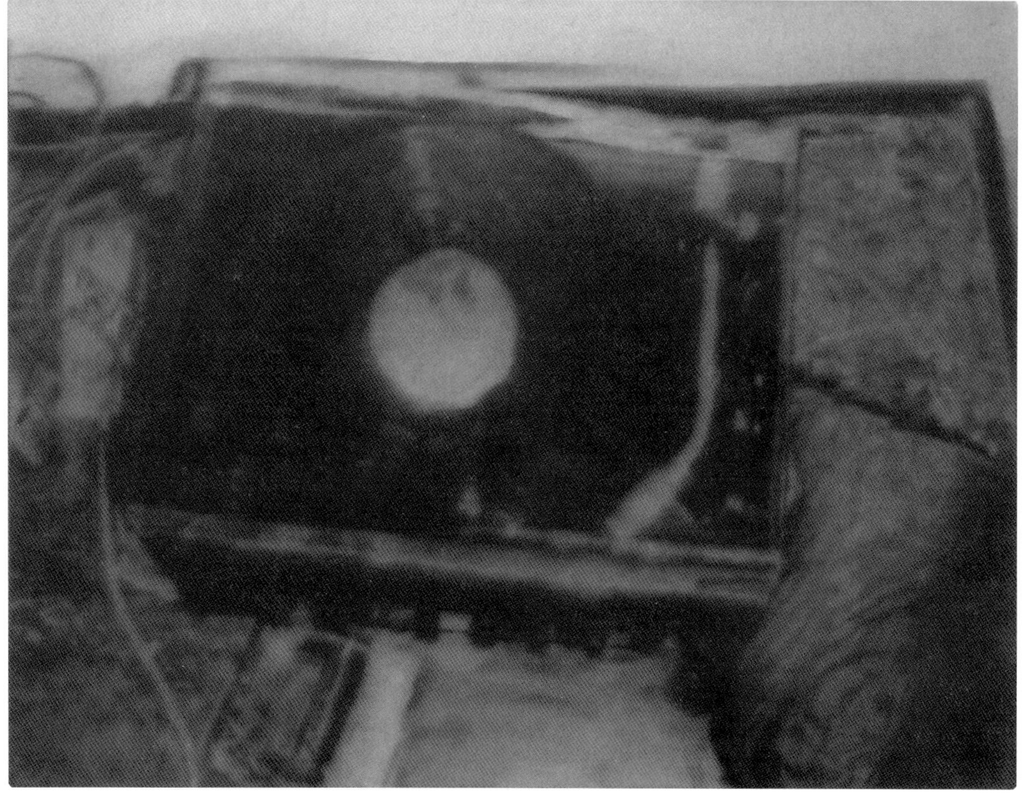

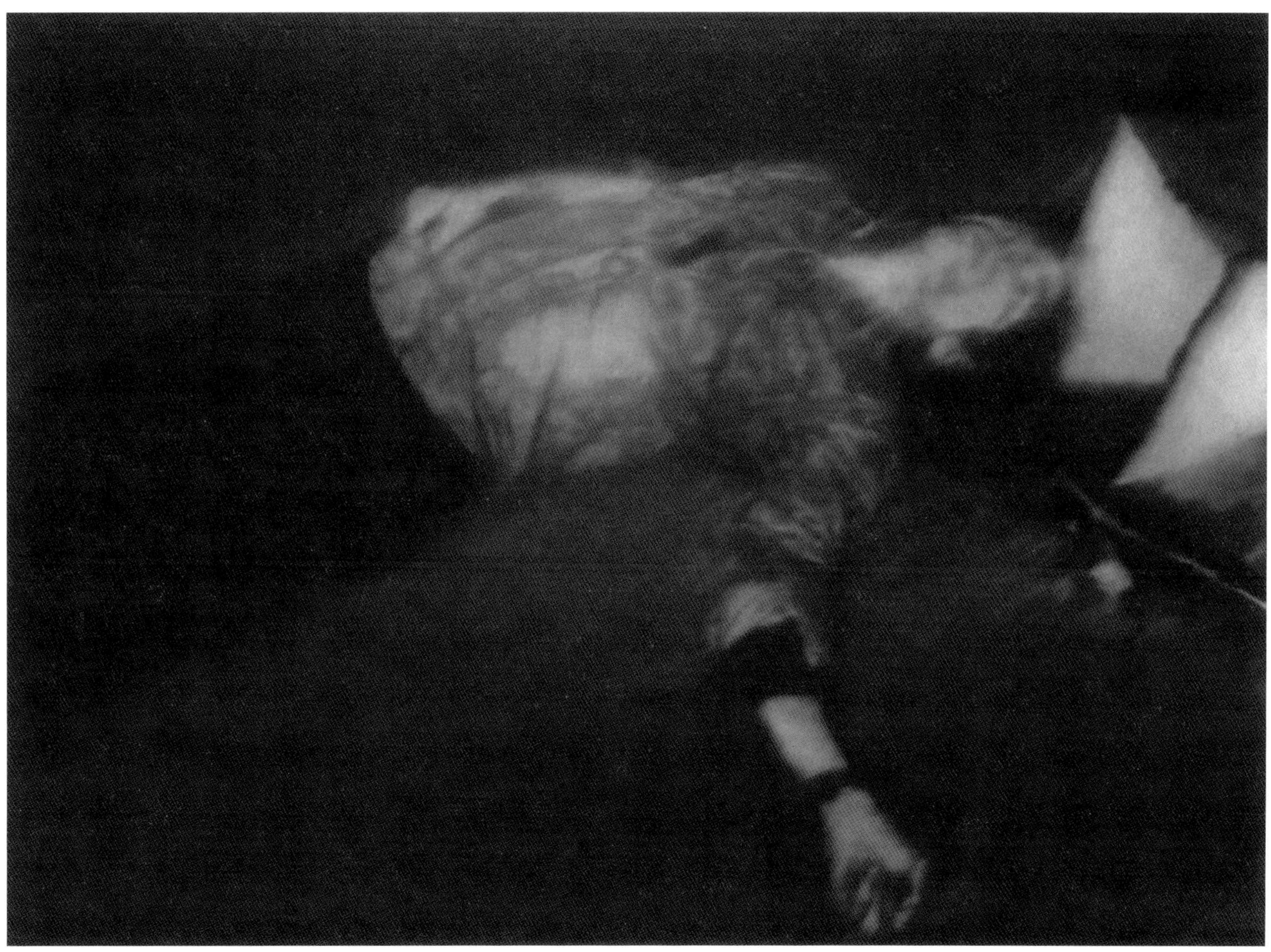

Man Shot Down 1, 1988 (CR 669-1)
Oil on canvas, 100 x 140 cm (39⅜ x 55⅛ in.)
New York, The Museum of Modern Art

In the 1980s, landscapes, depictions of candles—alone or combined— as well as brightly colored, large-format abstract pictures made up Richter's artistic practice. Earlier sea and cloud pictures developed into colored landscapes from the area around Düsseldorf. Some displayed a touch of the romantic, but the majority were rougher. The green vegetation of jagged meadows took over the canvas up to and beyond the horizon line. The landscapes do not deny their photographic origins, whether accessible or not. The photographic element has the ability to either ramp up romantic sentiment to a state of kitsch or to add cool sobriety. Richter's masterly control of color ensures a fine balance between image area and space, relativizing the photographic portion. He illustrated the weight of modern landscape painting's losses of nuanced sentiment when compared to romantic conceptions. The most obvious feature of his landscapes is an emotional and objectifying emptiness. The paintings do not offer a refuge for sensitive souls. When asked how he felt about romanticism, he stated that he lacked the spiritual foundation on which romantic painting was based. "We have lost the feeling of 'God's omnipresence in nature.' For us, everything is empty."[48]

The burning candles—some accompanied by a skull, set against flat, neutral backgrounds, painted with extraordinary mastery in muted colors—act as

PAGE 58 ABOVE
Dead, 1988 (CR 667-1)
Oil on canvas, 62 x 67 cm (24½ x 26½ in.)
New York, The Museum of Modern Art

PAGE 58 BELOW
Record Player, 1988 (CR 672-2)
Oil on canvas, 62 x 83 cm (24½ x 32¾ in.)
New York, The Museum of Modern Art

exhortations to contemplation that underline the memento mori in Richter's art. By contrast, the magisterial abstract images in splendid red, yellow, blue, and green and their high-contrast image narrative seem to embody contrary artistic positions. The broad spectrum of his work reminds us of the ebb and flow of nature's rhythms: between awakening and demise, birth and death.

On the other hand, the abstract pictures also signal the start of a significant incision in his artistic work. Richter's personal life took a turn for the better, which might have encouraged him to systematically explore the unfamiliar artistic terrain of abstraction. In 1982 Richter married the artist Isa Genzken, whom he had first met in the early 1970s when she was his student and with whom he reconnected after his separation from Ema. The artist bid Düsseldorf adieu and moved to neighboring Cologne. The new annual art fair, numerous new art galleries, far-sighted local cultural policies, and the relocation from Aachen of most of the Ludwig Collection, which quickly became Germany's most important contemporary art collection, focusing on Pop Art, temporarily turned Cologne into the European counterpart of New York as a center of contemporary art.

Richter's shift from photographic to abstract images also had pragmatic reasons. He was running out of subjects and the time was not yet ripe for new ones. It would take ten years before he could decide to process the Baader-Meinhof terrorists' suicide artistically by making a series of black-and-white

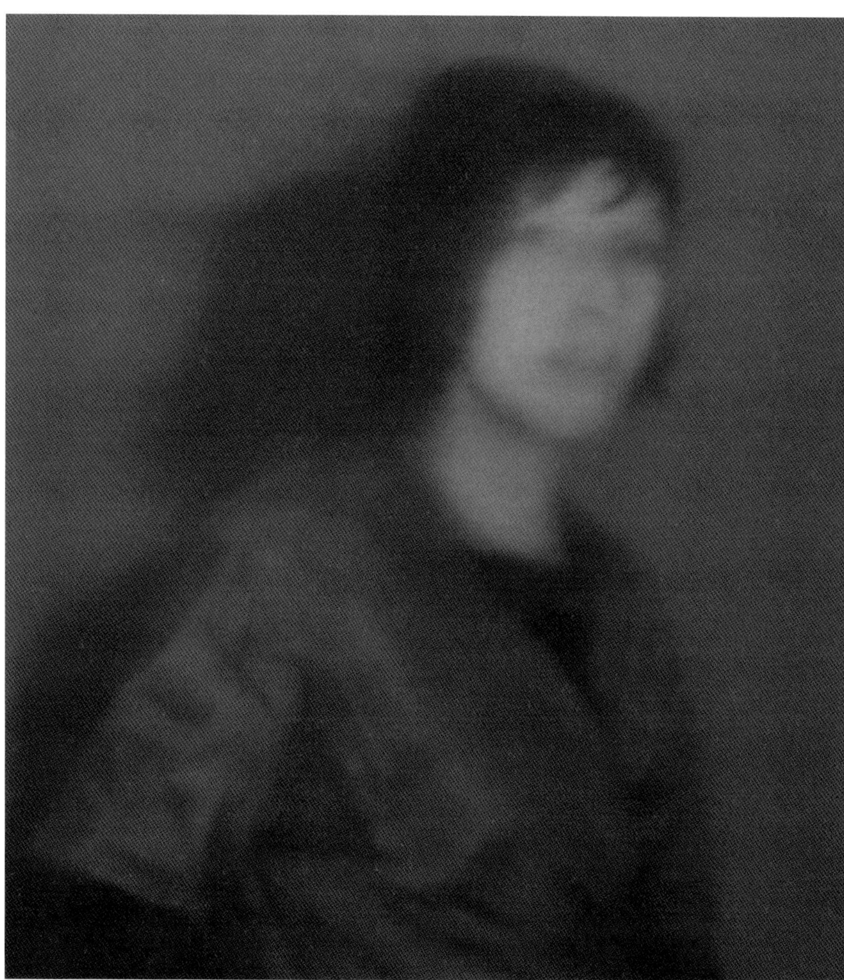

Confrontation 1, 1988 (CR 671-1)
Oil on canvas, 112 x 102 cm (44 x 40¼ in.)
New York, The Museum of Modern Art

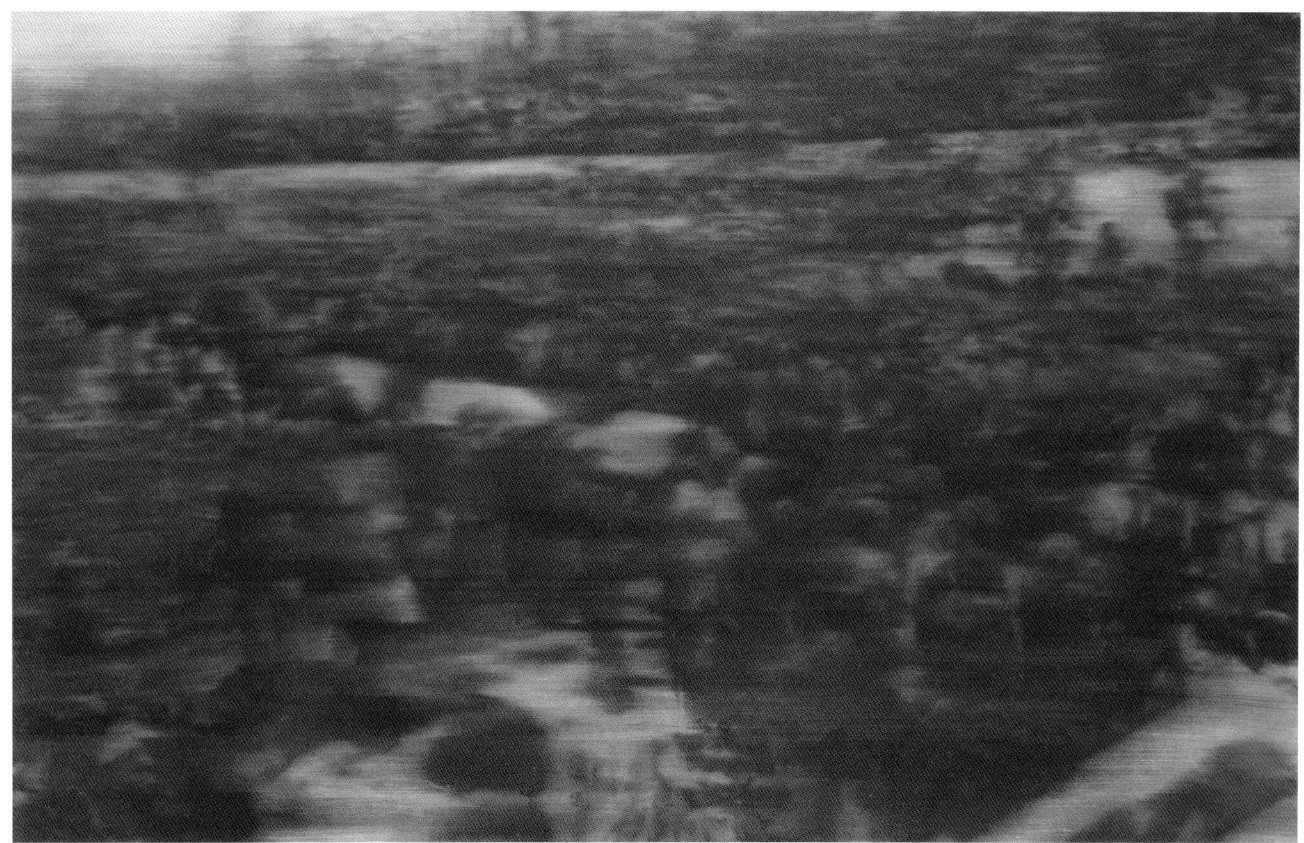

Funeral, 1988 (CR 673)
Oil on canvas, 200 x 320 cm (78¾ x 126 in.)
New York, The Museum of Modern Art

photo paintings entitled *October 18, 1977*. Both randomly and purposefully, he had collected pictures of this event. Perhaps using them for paintings had always lingered at the back of his mind. His response when asked which images from his stock he decided to use: "The ones that weren't paintable were the ones I did paint. The dead."[49] Richter was originally considering doing something large and comprehensive, "but then it all evolved quite differently, in the direction of death. And that's not really all that unpaintable. Far from it, in fact. Death and suffering have always been an artistic theme. Basically it's *the* theme. We've eventually managed to wean ourselves away from it, with our nice, tidy lifestyle."[50]

But back in 1988 this project stirred up a hornet's nest. The Red Army Faction had left a bloody trail and traumatized West Germany with abductions, armed raids, assassinations, and murders. Its members considered themselves revolutionaries, while most Germans thought them criminals. They represented a branch of the earlier youthful political and social protest which sought to achieve change by violent political subversion. Mostly, the others set off on the "the long march through the institutions" and eventually became functionaries of the state.

Richter was not a sympathizer of the Baader-Meinhof group, which was officially designated a gang. But for understandable reasons, their fates touched him, despite the disgust he felt at their ideological delusions and resulting violence. "There is sorrow," he said, explaining his decision to work on paintings that revolved around the deaths of the group's leaders, "but I hope one can see that it is sorrow for the people who died so young and so crazy, for nothing."[51]

Gray Mirror, 1992 (CR 765-6)
Color-coated glass, 53 x 63 cm (20⅞ x 24⅞ in.)
Switzerland, private collection

The *October 18, 1977* cycle has been classified as a contemporary variation of the now-faded genre of history painting. Not unreasonably. Nevertheless, all the paintings reflect the factual impossibility of reviving history painting in an age when technology offers far better means. Thus the task Richter set himself was similar to the *Annunciation after Titian* series, but the result is more complex. Regular smudging makes the faces of the young people anonymous; death overshadows them and makes them almost uniform. The finely weighted blurring reflects the conflicts in our memory of the dead, whose figural identity sinks into the imaginary depths of the image space. It is painting alone that gives a lasting impression as well as sadness. The paintings' colorless coloring places Richter among the phalanx of the great masters of "black," from Frans Hals to Francisco de Goya and Édouard Manet.

Mirror, Gray, 1991 (CR 735-1)
Color-coated glass, 280 x 165 cm (110¼ x 65 in.)
Musée des Arts de Nantes

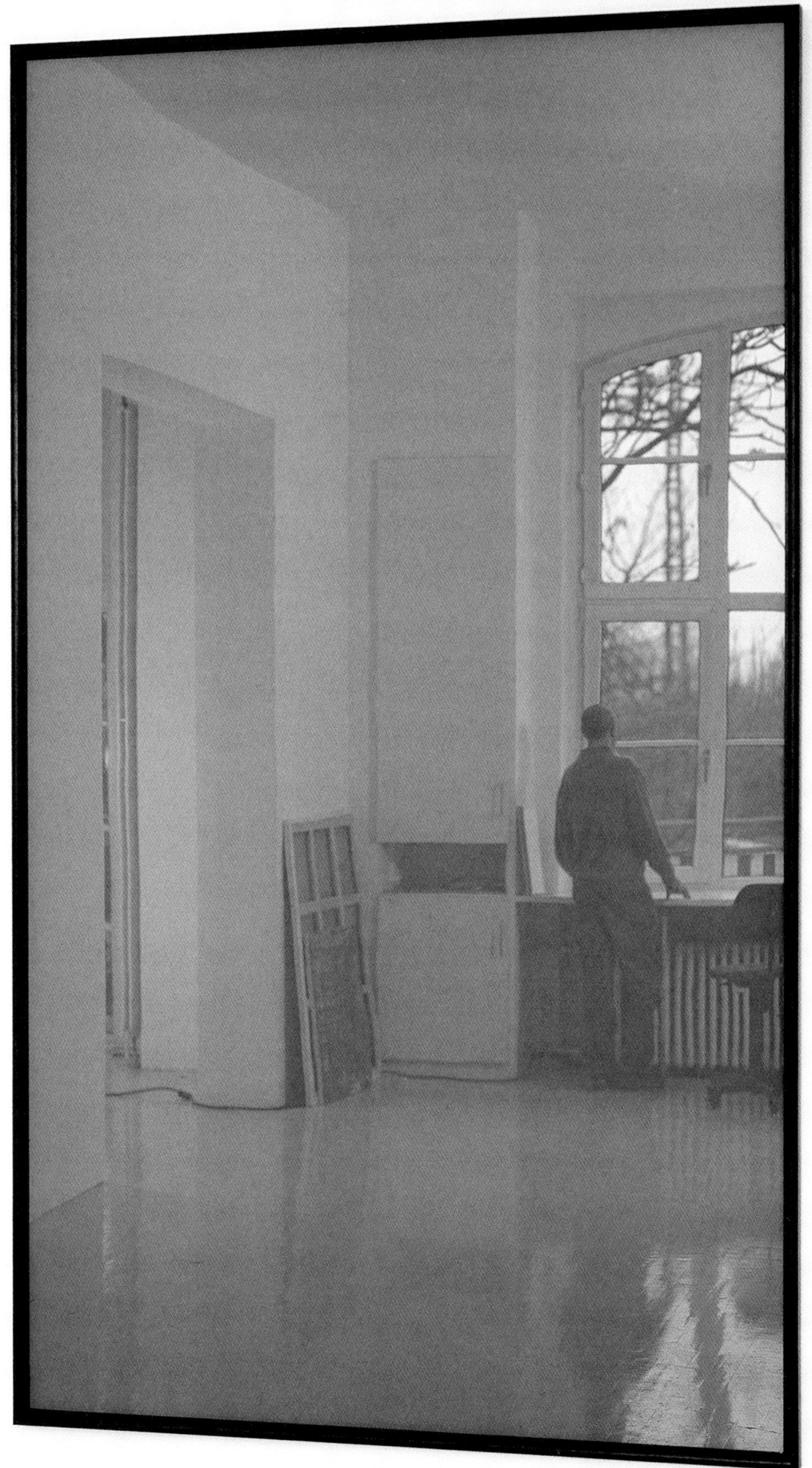

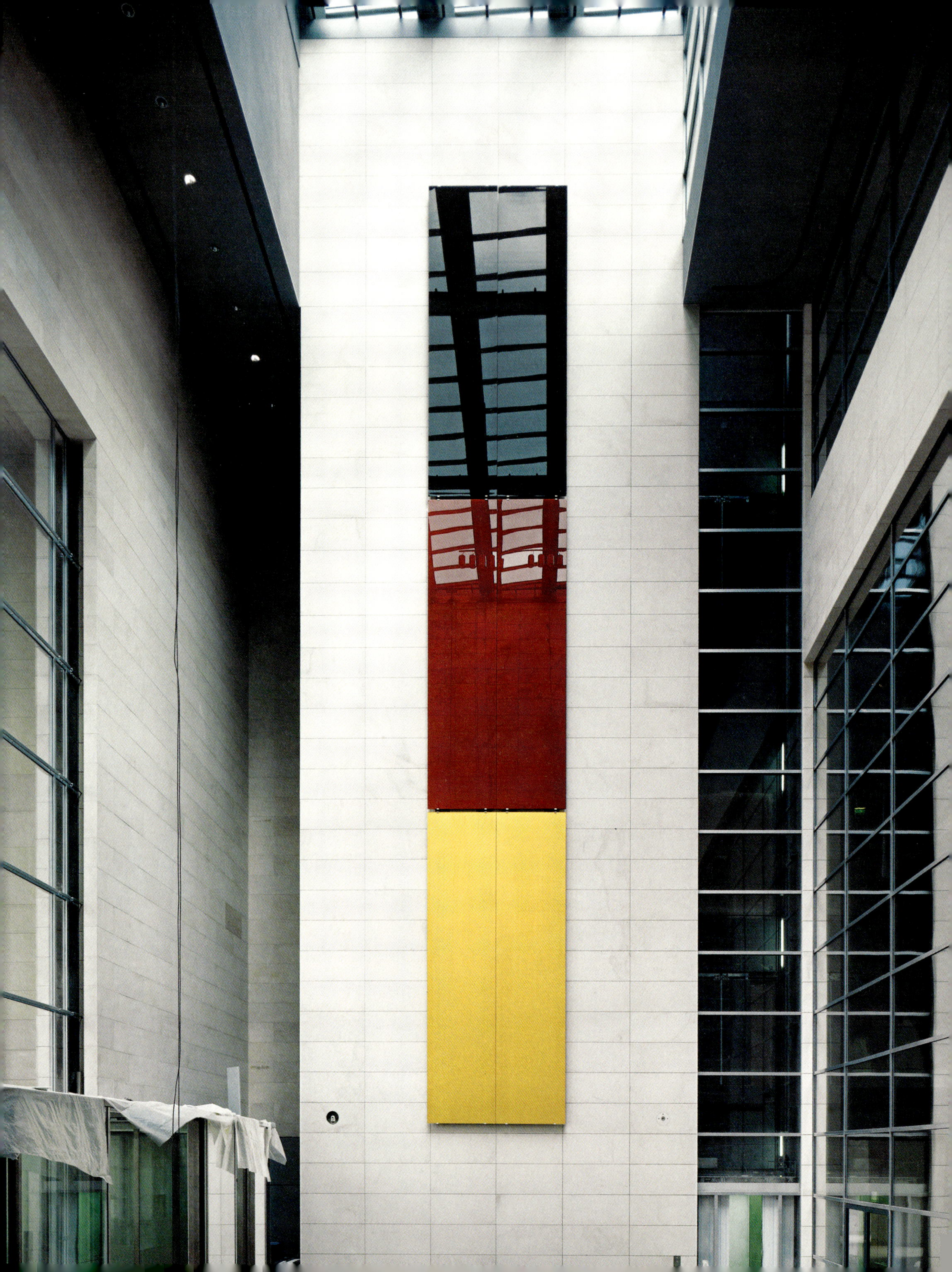

“What I decide to do grows within my mind and body.”[52]

Black, Red, Gold: the colors of the German flag—and the title of a commanding painting by Gerhard Richter. Created shortly before the millennium, the picture reflects the title’s promise. Three colors in equal proportions form the subject. Who would think to question its identity? Is it a picture or a flag? This question inspired aesthetic discourse in view of Jasper Johns’s *Flag* (1955), a depiction of the Stars and Stripes. Richter’s painting, a 20-meter-tall (2,043 x 296 cm / 3,218 ½ x 116 ½ in.) vertical format, consists of three equal rectangular panels made of enameled glass plates with applications of black, red, and gold on the reverse. Neither material nor format are evocative of flags.

On the other hand, the painting’s location is not random. It is a permanent fixture of the Reichstag building in Berlin, where the Bundestag, Germany’s lower house of parliament, is located. Although only its colors offer a visual association with the German flag, its location fills it with political meaning. In France or the United States, the painting would be no more than an unusual Color Field painting. Johns’s *Flag*, on the other hand, raises more questions in the context of art.

As is often the case with Richter’s work, there are factors beyond the sphere of art that give his paintings a dimension extending beyond their autonomy. Mostly it is the locale, as in the *October 18, 1977* cycle, whose acquisition by the Museum of Modern Art in New York broke the spell of German collective memory over them; or the German Biennale Pavilion in Venice, which turned the parade of scientists’ and artists’ portraits into a panopticon; or *Black, Red, Gold*, which invokes the tradition of democracy for the Reichstag. These were declared national colors by the first freely elected German parliament in 1919. Unlike most of his other work, Richter made it intentionally: “I wanted to present the three colors in the best possible way—or, rather, manufacture them for this space, for this purpose. It had to have a strong visible presence and be more or less tangible, like a thin pane floating in front of the wall—big and simultaneously fragile, and with a smooth, reflective surface, of course.”[53]

When he adds in a wry undertone that “It would be nice if it were cleaned occasionally,”[54] it becomes clear that the self-reference of this modern work of art in a historical location amounts to more than a formal gesture. Above all, it is a declaration of political independence against any attempt to exploit it.

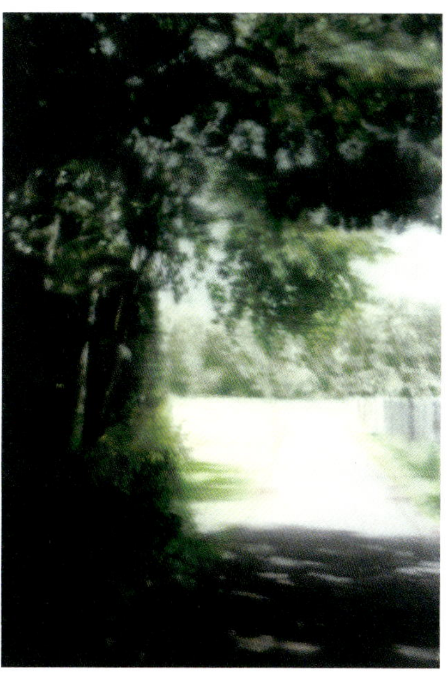

Summer Day, 1999 (CR 859-1)
Oil on canvas, 117 x 82 cm (46 x 32⅜ in.)
Vienna, Albertina (permanent loan from a private collection)

Black, Red, Gold, 1999 (CR 856)
Glass covered with colored enamel, 2043 x 296 cm (804⅜ x 116⅝ in.)
Berlin, Deutscher Bundestag

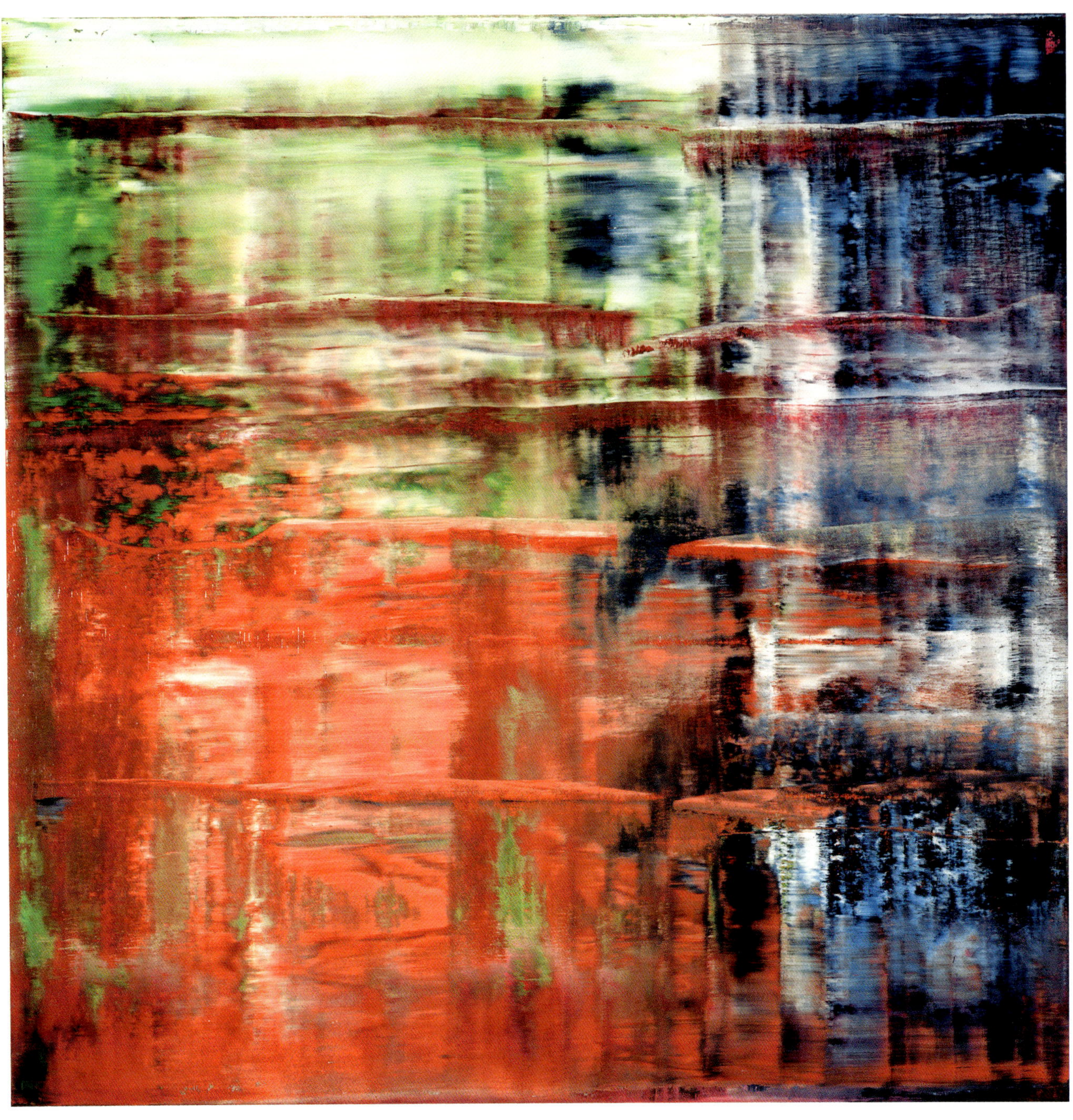

Bach (1), 1992 (CR 785)
Oil on canvas, 300 x 300 cm (118⅛ x 118⅛ in.)
Stockholm, Moderna Museet

Nowhere would such a "proclamation" be more appropriate than in the German Reichstag, with its eventful history. Here, *Black, Red, Gold* has to assert itself daily against the superficial acceptance of voters, non-voters, and the elected. The heated discussion sparked by the image is part of his "message." A pronouncement, not least thanks to its reflectivity, which creates a dialogue between the image and each viewer. But there is always an underlying risk that the picture may be dirtied.

Richter reached the peak of his artistic career in the late 20th century: he is world-famous and his work achieves astronomical prices. Meanwhile,

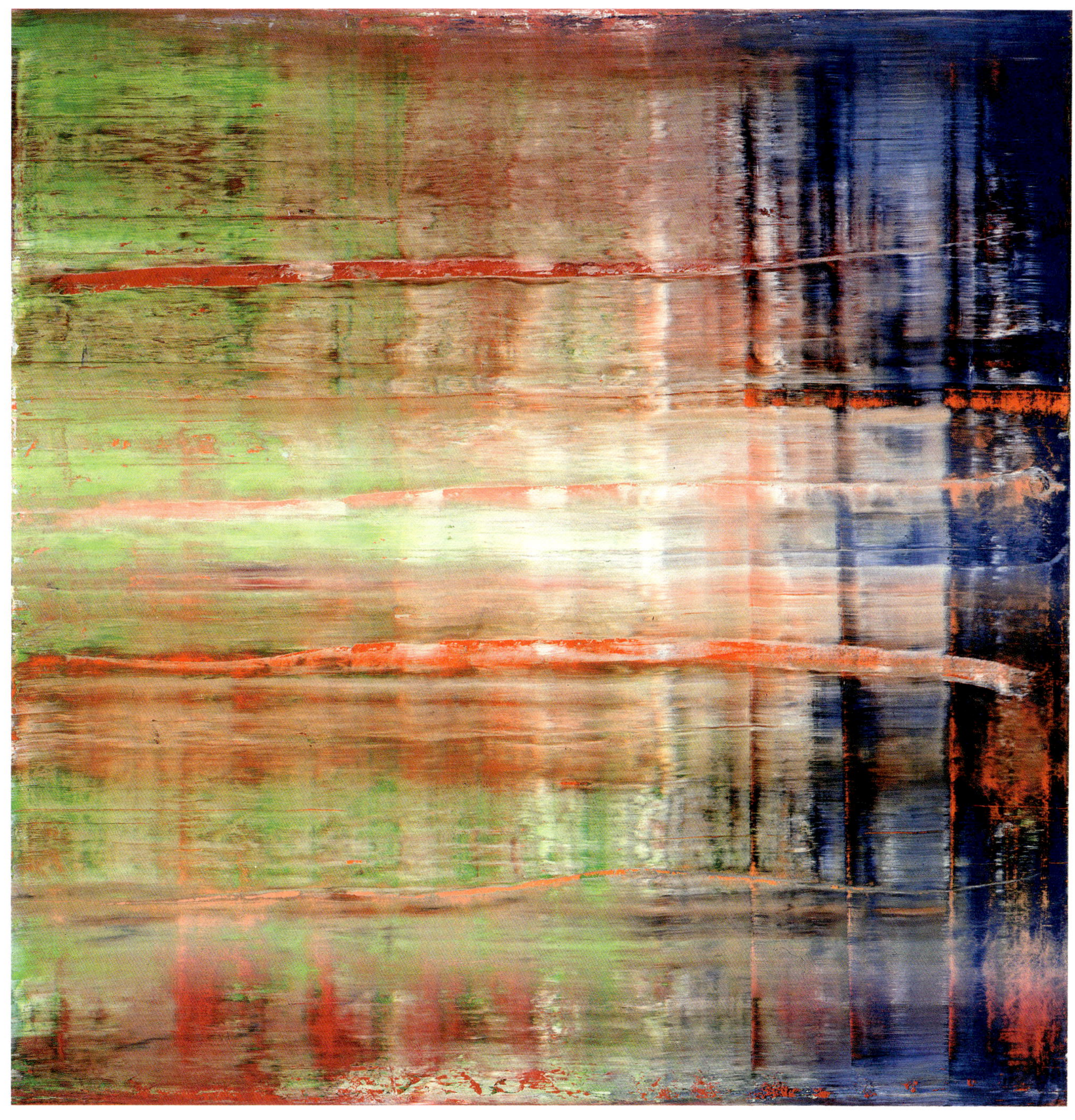

Bach (2), 1992 (CR 786)
Oil on canvas, 300 x 300 cm (118⅛ x 118⅛ in.)
Stockholm, Moderna Museet

the auction industry, responsible for accelerating the commercial trajectory of contemporary art, pushed up prices even more than the dealers. Since the 1980s Richter's commercial interests in New York and London, the centers of the art trade, have been represented by the influential Marian Goodman and Anthony d'Offay galleries, which regularly exhibited and stimulated interest in his work. German artists, with Richter at the forefront, enjoyed unprecedented international renown, and reputable museums organized major exhibitions and bought their works for their collections.

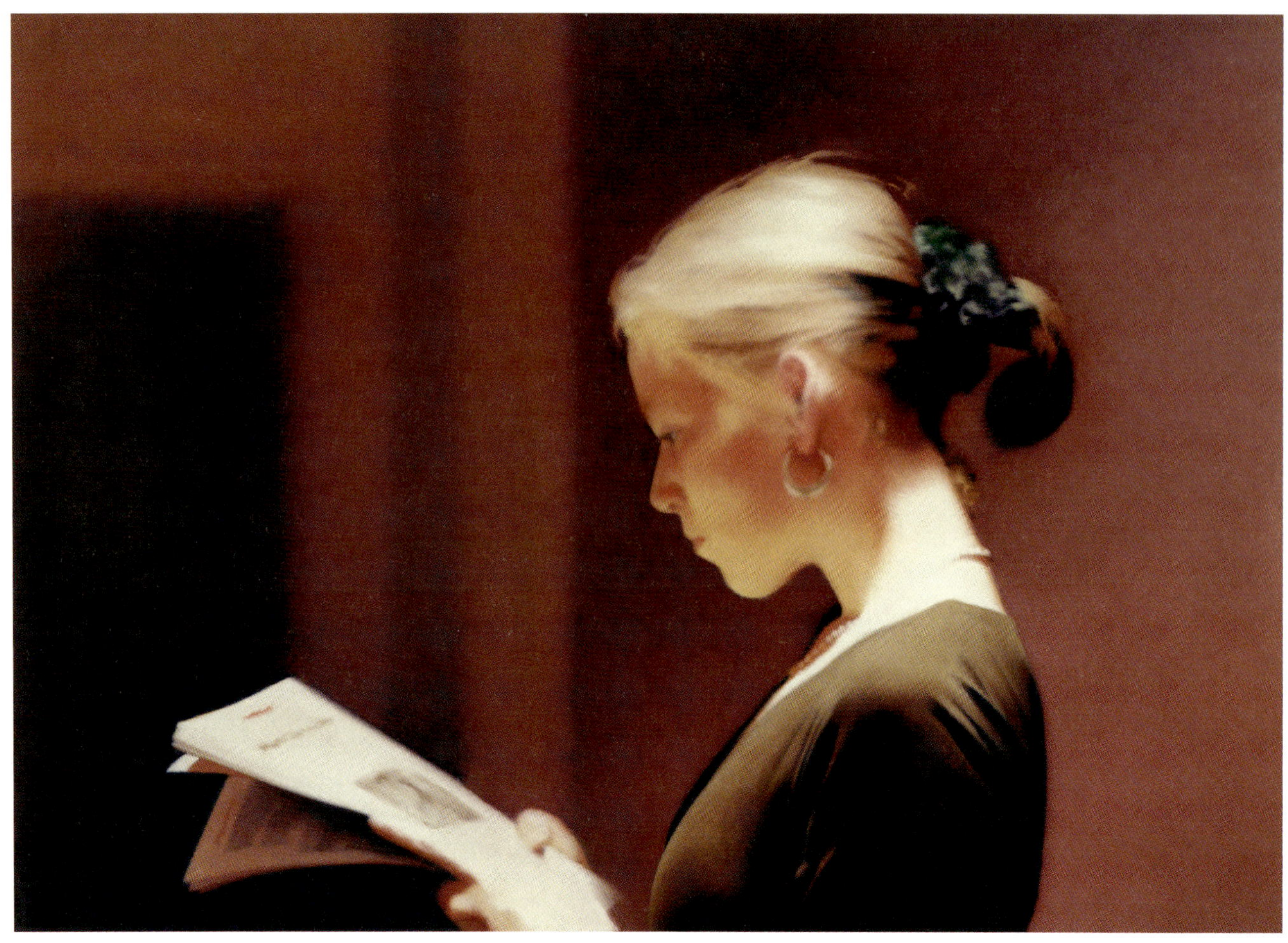

Reader, 1994 (CR 804)
Oil on canvas, 72 x 102 cm (28⅜ x 40¼ in.)
San Francisco Museum of Modern Art

Since conceptual currents had temporarily lost their way, neo-figurative and neo-expressive tendencies fueled turnover, and helped to bring about an unexpected revival in painting. At the same time, the art scene was increasingly keen to submit to the dictates of showbiz and fashion. The changing attitude of contemporary art's clientele created a tailwind that replaced traditional bourgeois values, such as education and connoisseurship, with money and prestige.

Richter noted with revulsion the upheavals in the art world that found expression in high regard for art's commercial aspects at the expense of aesthetic value.[55] He regretted the absence of artistic substance in neo-figurative and neo-expressive painting: "I only became an intellectual painter because I was always the opposite of fashionable, and fashion was all that silly, funny, spontaneous, ugly stuff that could be produced on the fly."[56]

His own artistic activity focused on painting abstract images. Occasionally, Richter returned to using mirror and glass, combining them with color: sublime gray or rich red; green and red; brown and blue; or black, red, and gold. In 1989, Richter made a stained-glass window containing 625 colors for Haus Otto in Berlin-Zehlendorf, using his color chart paintings as a guide for this commission.

Seascape, 1998 (CR 852-1)
Oil on canvas, 290 x 290 cm (114¼ x 114¼ in.)
San Francisco Museum of Modern Art
(long-term loan from The Doris and
Donald Fisher Collection, San Francisco)

Although the artist refers to his non-representational pictures as abstract in the common sense, they by no means fit smoothly into the tradition of

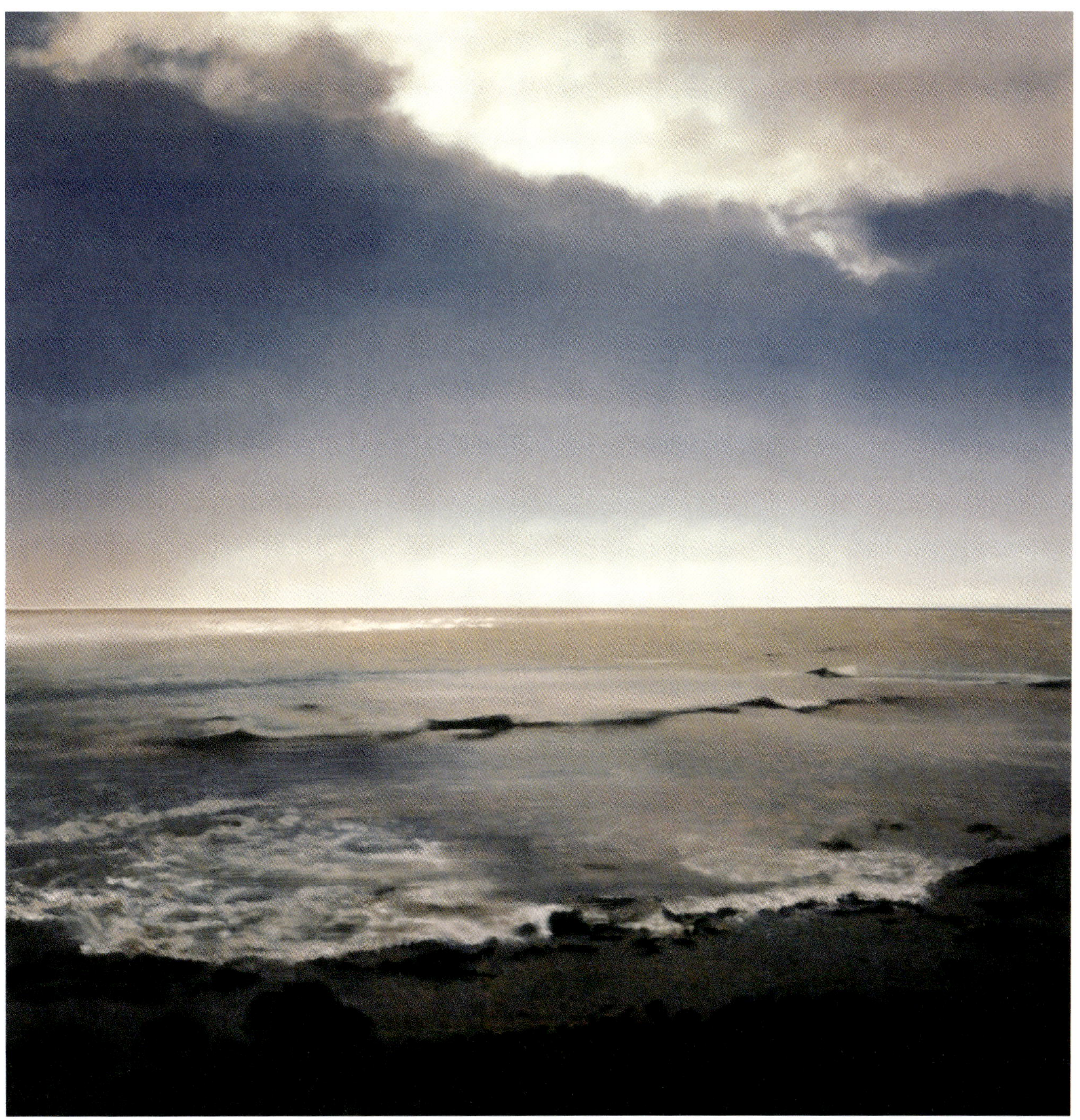

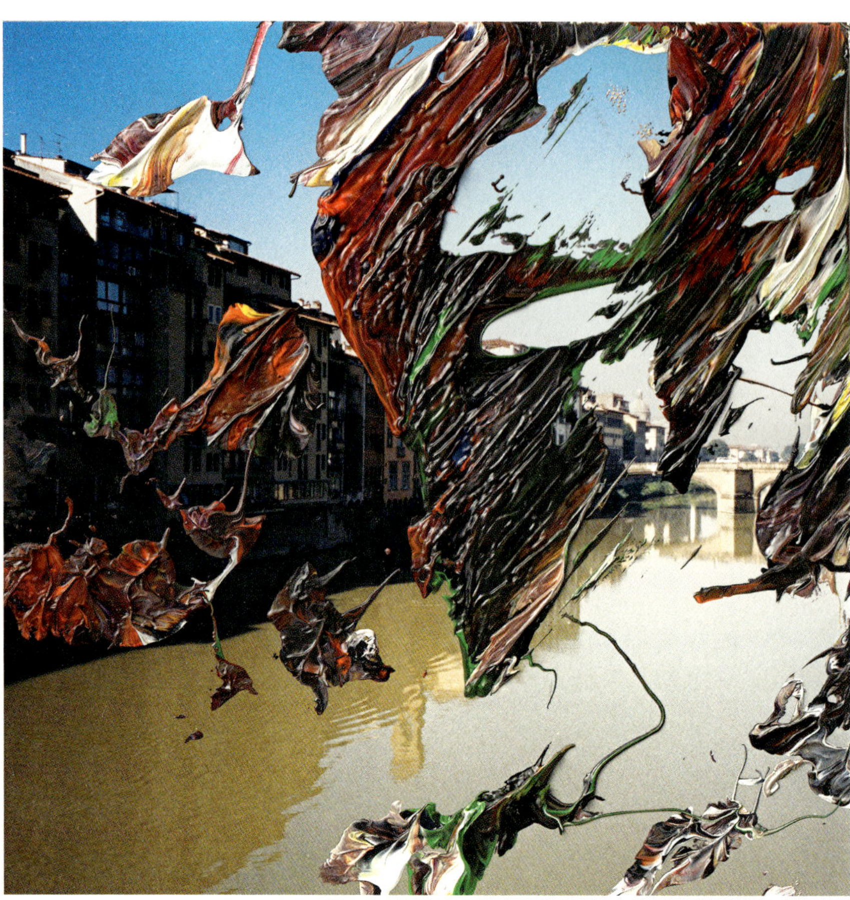

Firenze (29/99), 2000 (EDITION CR 110)
Oil on color photograph,
12 x 12 cm (4¾ x 4¾ in.)

modern abstract painting; not in the way abstraction was practiced by Wassily Kandinsky and Piet Mondrian, nor in the context of the geometric constructivism that followed World War I, nor in Frank Stella's mode of defining the image as a pictorial object. Kandinsky and Mondrian had abstracted from figurative, visual impressions and underlaid their images with esoteric and idealistic theories in order to dress them in a halo of spirituality.

In this respect, they become illustrations for the dubiously divine.[57] Richter's color chart pictures, on the other hand, are parodies of "spiritual" abstraction. The artist would never have hit on the idea of declaring them a reflection of cosmological coherences. Yet, "parody is basically *the* form of a break by means of continuity. Through which, as Victor Šklovskij has shown, innovators free themselves from their predecessors."[58] Hence, *Black, Red, Gold* may be an image in the form of an object, but undermines the doctrinaire power of Frank Stella's statement that "what you see is what you see."

Richter's photo paintings already exhibited a dazzling ambivalence. Are the abstracts more abstract than the photographic? According to artistic convention, they are, because abstracts disregard both photographic templates and the reality they represent. Richter's abstract pictures are linked neither to photography's operative image system, nor to our visual perception habits as regards visible reality. Rather, they create an independent, self-determined reality in which the artist approaches a view of abstraction that is pragmatic and based on experience, while at the same time exploring a new field of

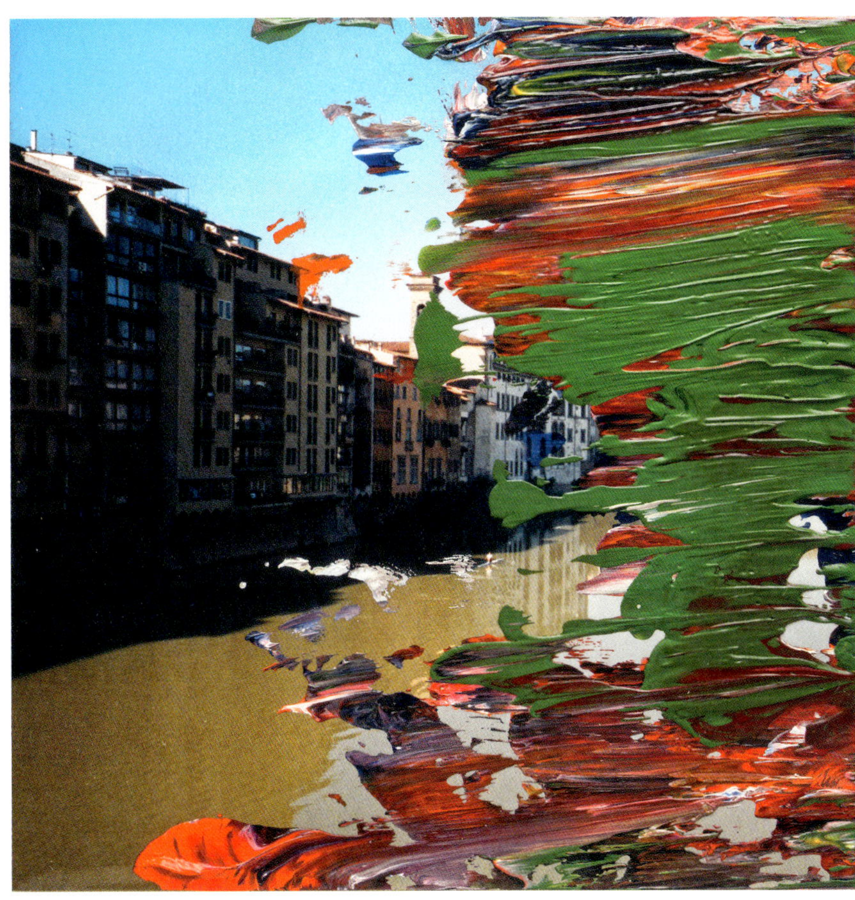

Firenze (94/99), 2000 (EDITION CR 110)
Oil on color photograph,
12 x 12 cm (4¾ x 4¾ in.)

artistic endeavor with his abstract images. It orbits the manifold forms and mechanisms of visual perception, thereby respecting the viewer's usual way of dealing with abstraction in art, unafraid to spin it out further. "The paintings only work because of people's desire to see something in them. Every aspect of them resembles something that's real, but the similarity only goes so far. … The fact that paintings come to life through this strange mechanism isn't appreciated nearly enough. Paintings present us with similarities that we attempt to categorize. They always remind us of something—otherwise they wouldn't be paintings."[59] The artist scratches at the assumption of the abstract image's autonomy and awards it with mimetic qualities. In doing so, he upgrades viewers to co-authors, asking them to discover the "similarities" that are hidden (to him as well).

Richter set out on the track of the "strange mechanism" of the desire to recognize what crystallizes before our eyes but is still without name or notion. He concretized his search with a plethora of painting techniques, both common and unusual. His techniques include layering, blurring, squeegeeing, scraping, overpainting, and the use of a variety of tools such as small and large brushes, brooms, blades, squeegees, and oversized spatulas. The last of these are often adapted to fit the format of large canvases and facilitate an even distribution of paint. When used without paint, they can tear into earlier coatings to reveal underlying layers of paint. Every process stems from practical considerations of the painterly process, and is suggested or forced by the unfinished state of each painting.

September, 2005 (CR 891-5)
Oil on canvas, 52 x 72 cm (20½ x 28⅜ in.)
New York, The Museum of Modern Art

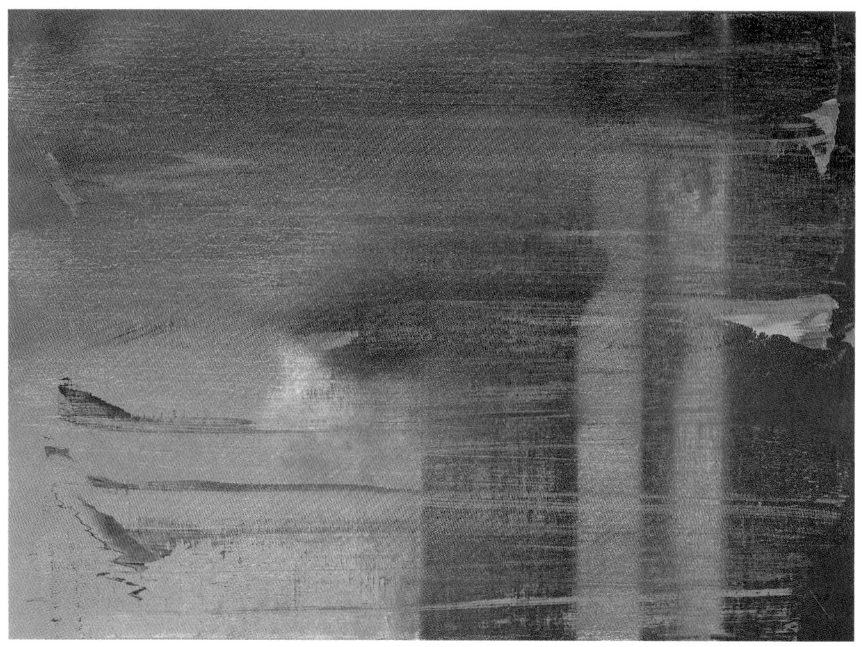

"Each picture has to evolve out of a painterly or visual logic: it has to emerge as if inevitably. And by not planning the outcome, I hope to achieve the same coherence and objectivity that a random slice of nature (or a readymade) always possesses."[60] Richter's abstract pictures literally emerge, but the apparent independence of the operation behind his abstract paintings is not a natural, but an artistic process—however much the artist at times laments his own helplessness in the face of painting's autonomy. The result is a synthesis between "having-made" and "having-become,"[61] filtered through the painter's cultural and artistic experiences. He has internalized the process to such an extent that it is now second nature.

After the abstract pictures based on photographs (1978 onwards), the expressive gestures of the 1980s, with their radiant reds and yellows, are a declaration of sovereignty within the realm of abstraction. Congruent or contrasting, with subdued green and ocher, they unfold their captivating power whose source is not only in the bright colors, but also in the violent conflict of the open color forms. They are fleeting, barely solidifying—as if occupied in a constant state of becoming. Unlike photographic snapshots, the forms retain their vitality as the intense vertical and horizontal paint trajectories invoke imaginary pictorial spaces in which the perspective order of classical painting collapses.

The fluid form entities in subsequent pictures seem to fragment at times in compact or loose formations, other times sharply, and then softly contoured while the colors grow darker. In *A B, Brick Tower* (1987), the spatial illusion of gestural images reduces in favor of an impression of a flat plane in which the painting's grounding and surface interweave. The movements of the vertical paint columns intersect with horizontal countermovements. There are color-splinter flashes and streaks of paint. The painting, with its loose, quieter all-over structure without formal or color hierarchies, is a precursor of the works created in the 1990s.

Silicate, 2003 (CR 885-1)
Oil on canvas, 290 x 290 cm (114¼ x 114¼ in.)
Düsseldorf, Kunstsammlung
Nordrhein-Westfalen

The situation is similar for making paintings, and the artist works on several simultaneously. Starting with a bucket of paint, he applies unruffled

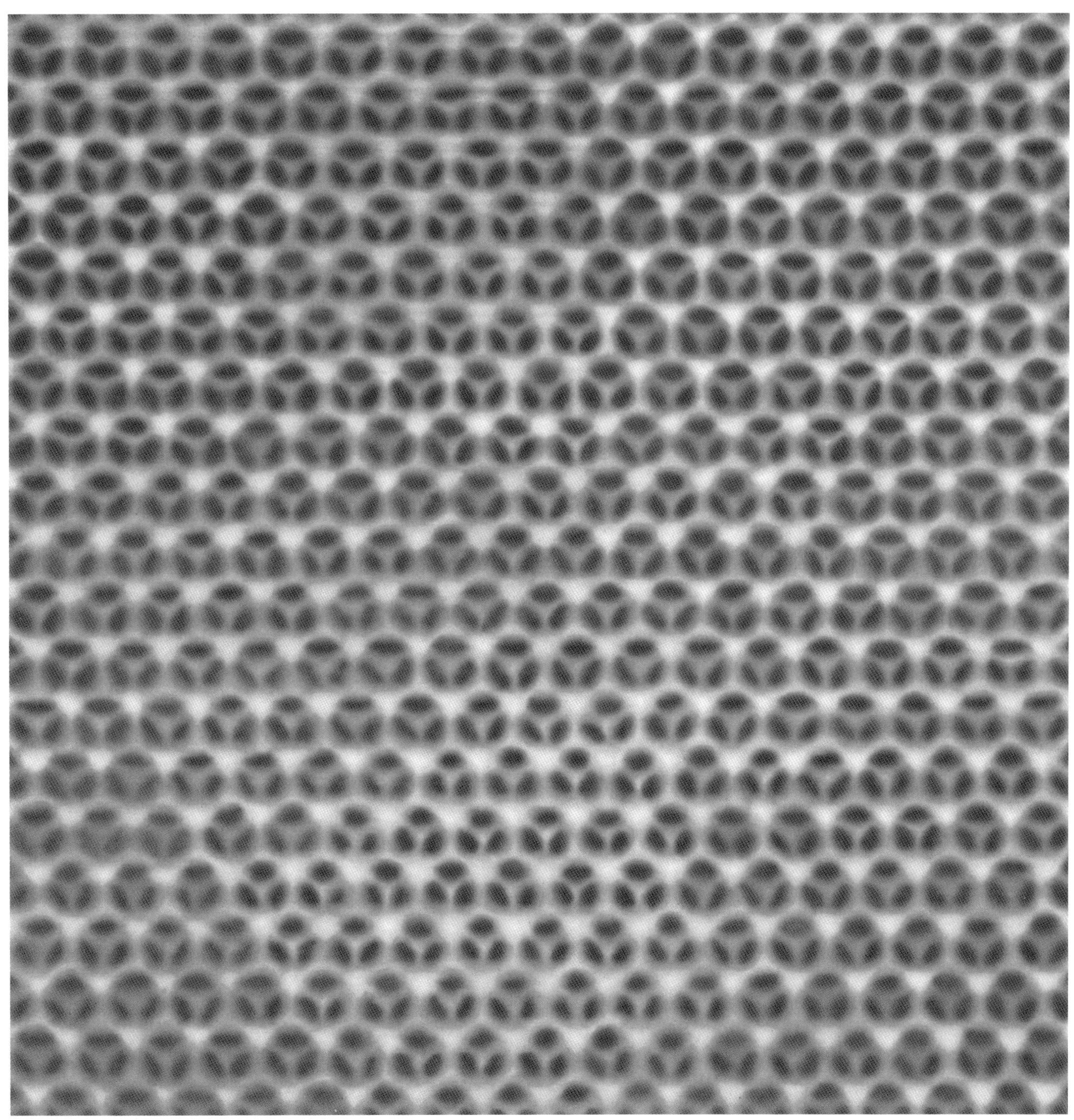

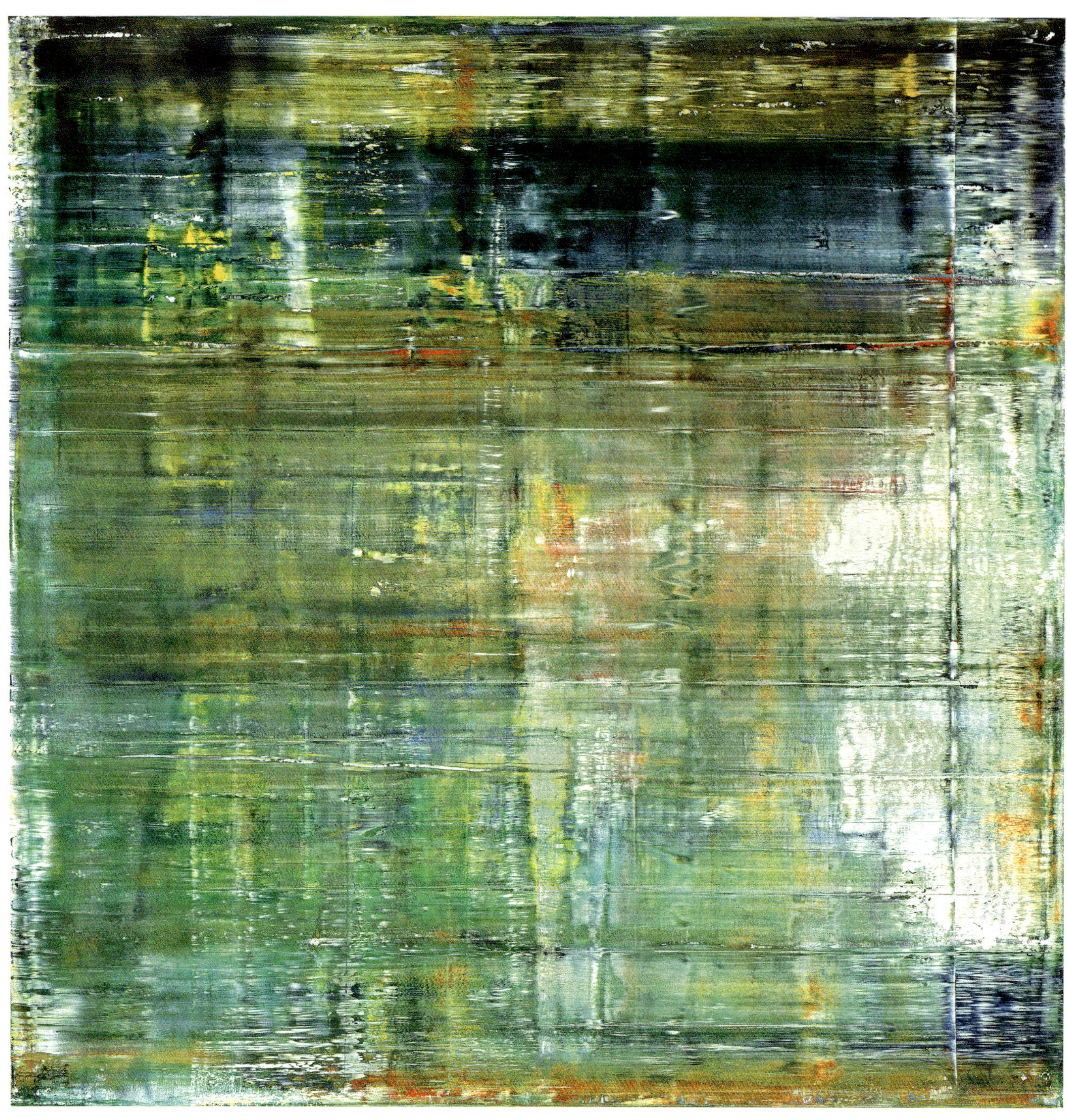

Cage 1, 2006 (CR 897-1)
Oil on canvas, 290 x 290 cm (114¼ x 114¼ in.)
London, Tate Modern
(loan from a private collection)

sweeps of paint over the prepared canvas using a broad brush. Other colors are added sparingly until there emerges a pictorial structure that superficially resembles a work of Abstract Expressionism. But this is only the basis for a subsequent and decisive artistic intervention. As soon as the foundation is complete, a process begins that rejects any form of control.

It is also this moment that a tool of Richter's own devising comes into use: the oversized squeegee-spatula hybrid. The tool is always cut to the outer dimensions of the canvas, and he uses two: one to fit the height, the other for the width. Consisting of a 20 to 30 cm-wide (8 to 12 in.) piece of Perspex, used either with or without paint, the squeegee is fitted with a grip along

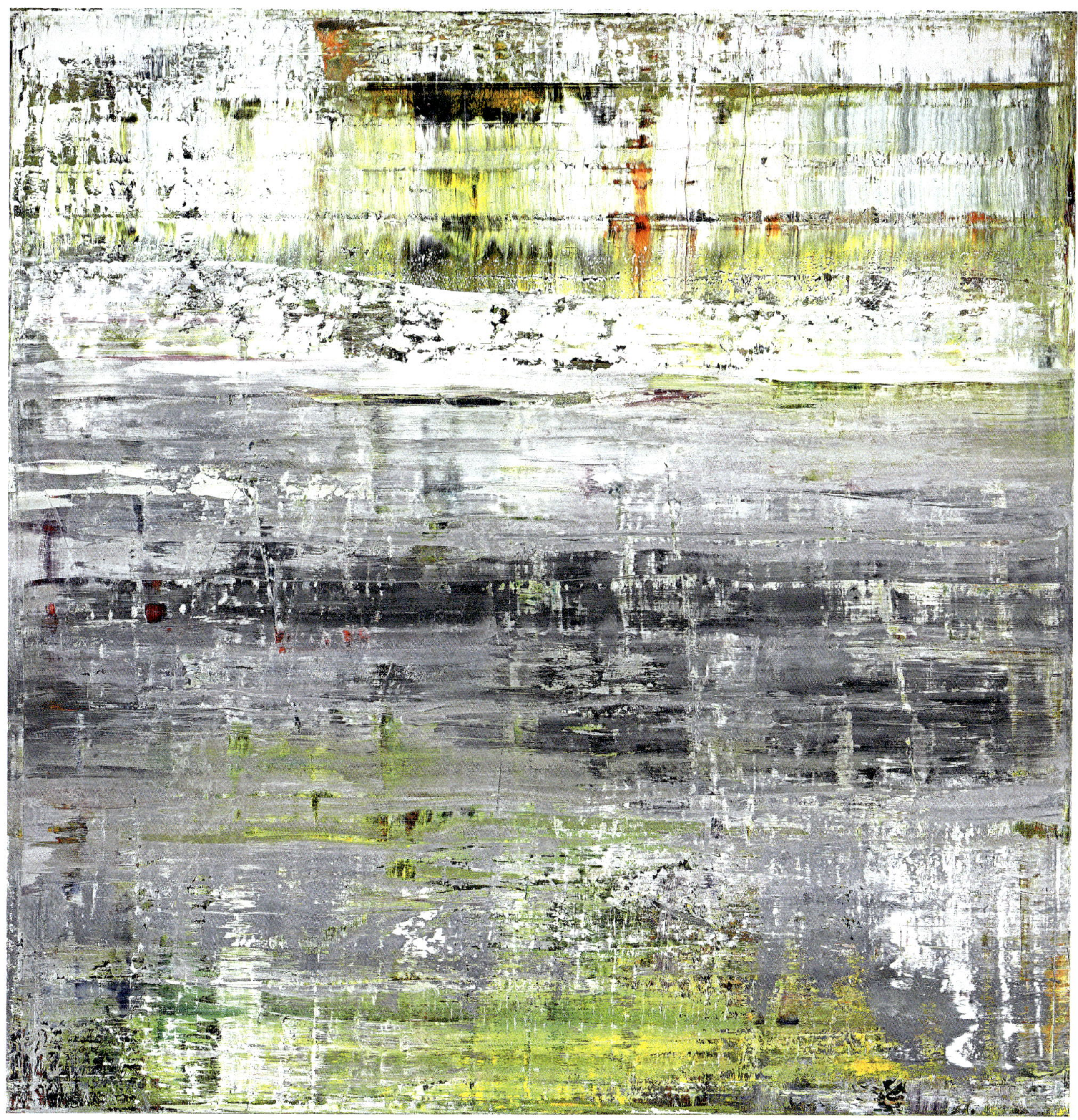

Cage 2, 2006 (CR 897-2)
Oil on canvas, 300 x 300 cm (118⅛ x 118⅛ in.)
London, Tate Modern
(loan from a private collection)

the tool's full length to make it easier to handle. The artist presses the bulky tool onto the far left or top of the wet canvas, pushing or pulling paint across the canvas with varying degrees of pressure. At the end of this exhausting procedure, the canvas is radically transformed. Instead of the sweeping surge of paint, distinct horizontal or vertical trails now dominate the work. They combine to make an extraordinarily differentiated image, the colors and spaces of which permeate each other and defy localization.

"The image," states Gaston Bachelard, "is no longer under the domination of things, nor is it subject to the pressures of the unconscious. It floats and soars, immense, in the free atmosphere of a great poem."[62] Richter favors

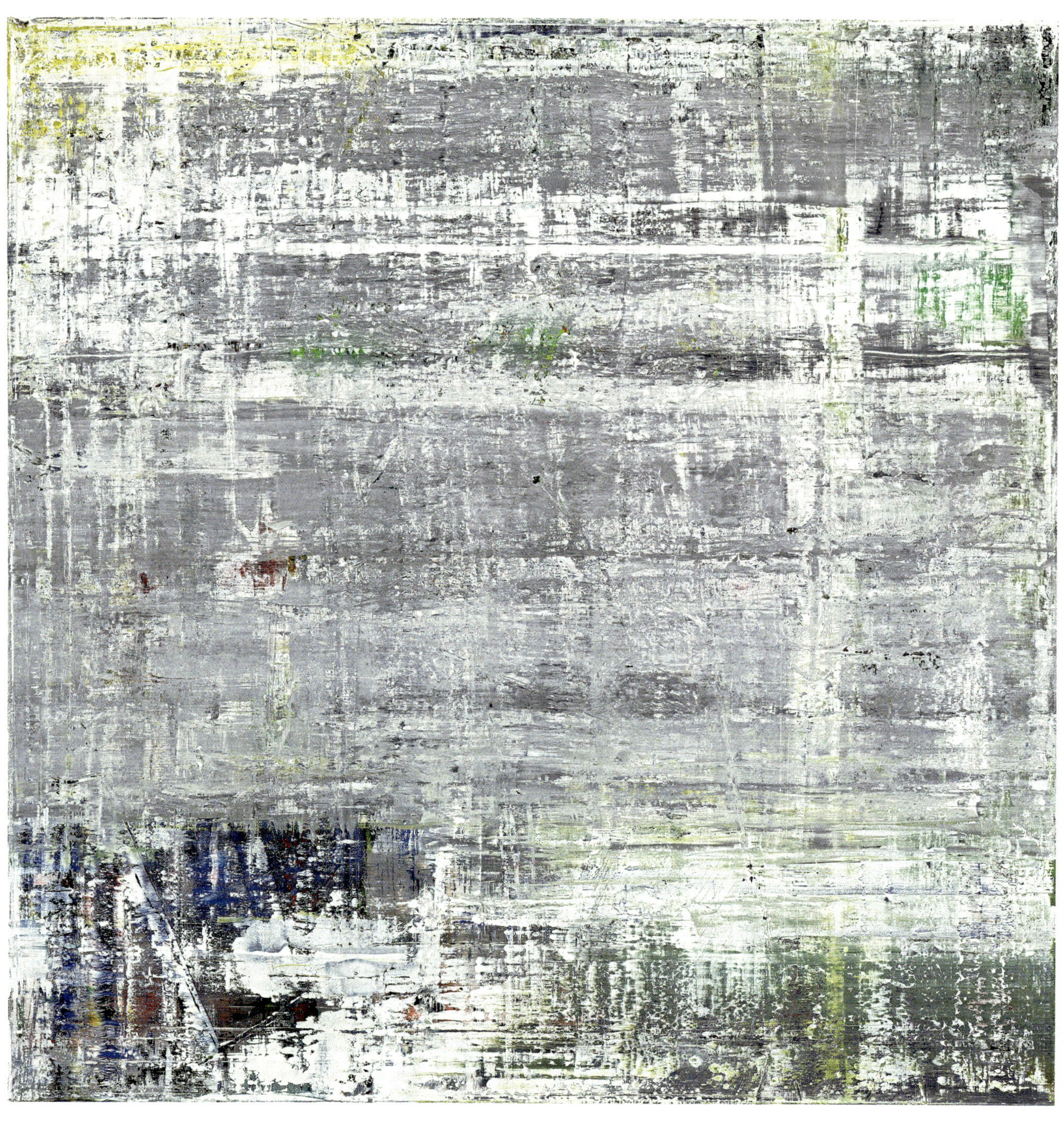

Cage 3, 2006 (CR 897-3)
Oil on canvas, 290 x 290 cm (114¼ x 114¼ in.)
London, Tate Modern
(loan from a private collection)

comparisons with music and often names paintings after composers, as in *Bach 1* and *Bach 2* (1992) or his masterful *Cage 1–6* (2006) cycle.

If successful, it would be difficult to express the effect of these images more vividly than with Bachelard's words. However, their success is not always certain. The artist's vast experience allows him to take precautionary measures, but at the crucial stage, as soon as Richter applies his spatula, he relinquishes all control, opening the door to coincidence and arbitrariness in the actual making of the painting. Or, to be more precise: to an unwieldy tool that foils almost any kind of organization, which he can push back and forth across the canvas, parallel to the painting's boundaries, to spread the paint or to scrape

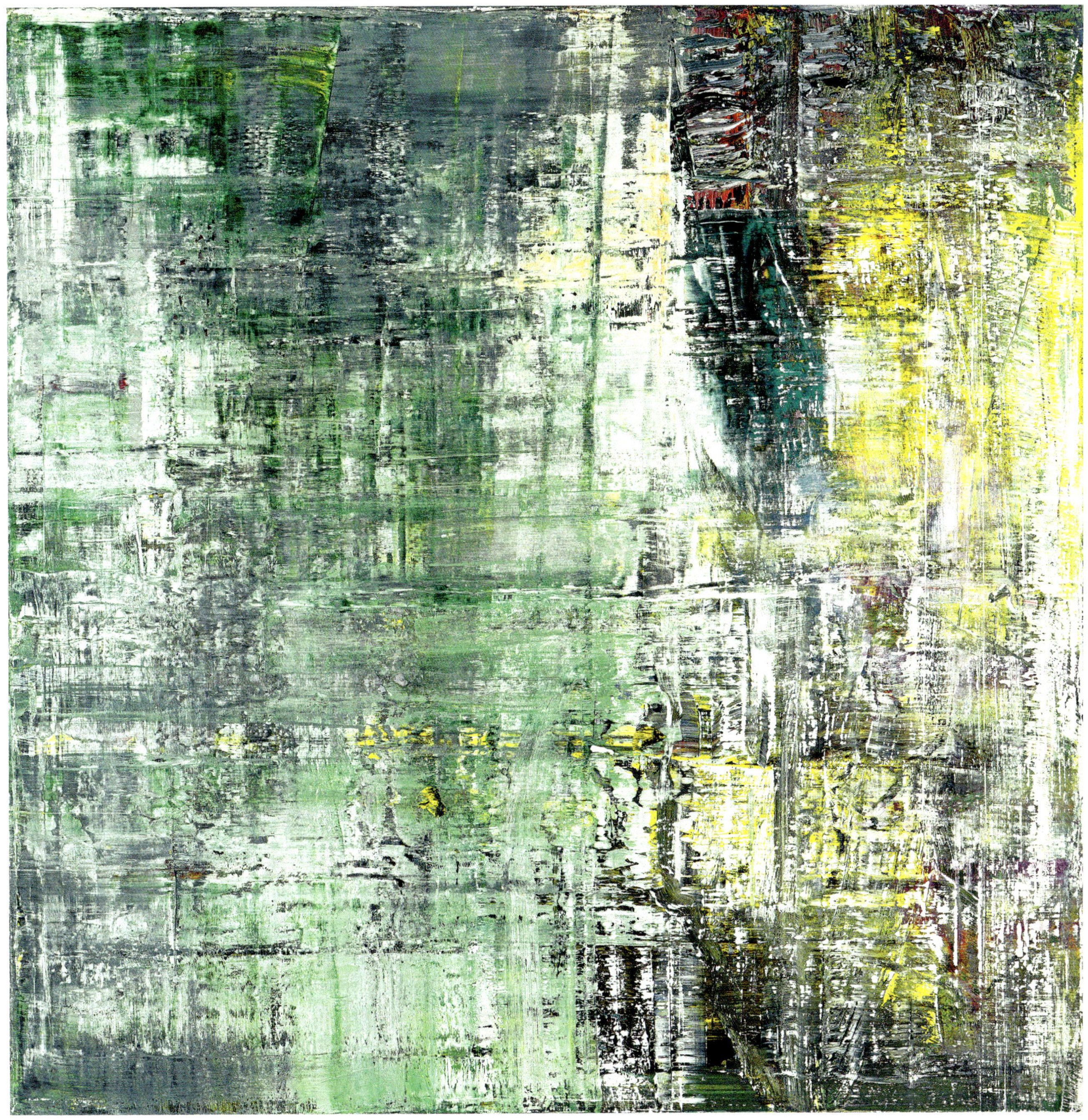

Cage 6, 2006 (CR 897-6)
Oil on canvas, 290 x 290 cm (114¼ x 114¼ in.)
London, Tate Modern
(loan from a private collection)

up earlier layers of paint. Richter says he has no particular picture in mind as he approaches a canvas, seeking to produce a picture he had not planned: "This method of arbitrary choice, chance, inspiration and destruction may produce a specific type of picture, but it never produces a predetermined picture."[63]

This tendency for destruction, with its inherent seductiveness, evidently reached the limits of obsession. On September 22, 1992, Richter noted: "Scraping off. For about a year now, I have been unable to do anything in my painting but scrape off, pile on and then remove again."[64] In some of the pictures, lower layers have re-emerged; in others, they are completely overpainted. "In this process I don't actually reveal what was beneath. …

The process of applying, destroying and layering serves only to achieve a more varied technical repertoire in picture-making."[65] This results in enormously varied surface textures. Thanks to the abrading technique, they are relatively uniform despite the many interventions.

Essentially, our eyes have to feel the surface of these pictures for us to be fully aware of them. This visual touch mixes with the desire to trace the pictures with our fingertips as visual and tactile experiences "go hand in hand." Aristotle understood the connection: "Perception is something ... that a living being actively pursues, not something that happens to it. The philosopher Alva Noë concluded that our model should be touch, as a skillful activity of the body, and not the customary model of the more passive mode of perception."[66] This is what Richter's pictures invite us to do. Diaphanous and opaque traces of blurring become structurally apparent horizontals and verticals in addition to streaks of paint, all of which provide indications of their origin while slipping away from neat descriptions. Descriptive language is not sufficiently smooth to make the grade.

One of the objectives of Richter's semi-mechanical technique is to achieve something approaching objectivity. To maximize this, Richter reduced his opportunities for influence to a minimum. His idea of objectivity is free of any geometric order as it is underpinned by central perspective. Instead, coolly, deliberately, and pragmatically, he takes a position that is far removed from the quasi-divine artistic genius imagined in the pre-modern era. Richter may have a penchant for romantic landscapes, but his artistic practice, although hugely sensitive, is not romantic.

In fact, he often created paintings as groups of works, thereby illustrating his attitude to art, which he saw as a working process. The serial production principle that governed the color canvases, whose juxtaposition of colors was left to chance in the later versions, he now applied, in a more systematic form, to his working method. To meet its requirements, he divided the studio in the house he designed in 1996 into two separate "aggregate" rooms: one for the manual production of pictures and another in which the completed works were hung, as in a gallery, where they were left a while to prove their visual worth. Those that didn't work were sent back to the work room.

In 1993, Richter and Isa Genzken separated. A year later he met the artist Sabine Moritz; they fell in love, were married, and settled in Hahnwald, a suburban neighborhood south of Cologne. The birth of three children heralded a chapter in his life that can be described as happy and it was underpinned by an extraordinarily fruitful period of creativity. A major touring exhibition was launched in 1993 at the Musée d'Art Moderne de la Ville de Paris, and cemented Richter's reputation as an outstanding painter. Furthermore, at the end of the millennium the German Bundestag commissioned Richter to produce a work of art for the Reichstag's foyer.

Nevertheless, cursory accounts suggest Richter's work did not progress as continuously as the above. The years were extremely labor intensive, and distinguished by constant experimentation. The artist tried out new artistic devices and fields of endeavor. This was a period of verifying, checking, auditing, and tireless new starts. Richter produced masterpieces such as *Reader* (1994), a shining tribute to Jean Siméon Chardin and Vermeer, as well as the composer cycles—milestones in an increasingly perplexing artistic world.

Around the turn of the millennium, the long-term consequences of the radical upheavals that had shaken the Western art world some four decades ago

Cologne Cathedral Window, 2007 (CR 900)
Genuine, handblown antique glass,
2,300 x 900 cm (905⅝ x 354⅜ in.)
South transept, Cologne Cathedral

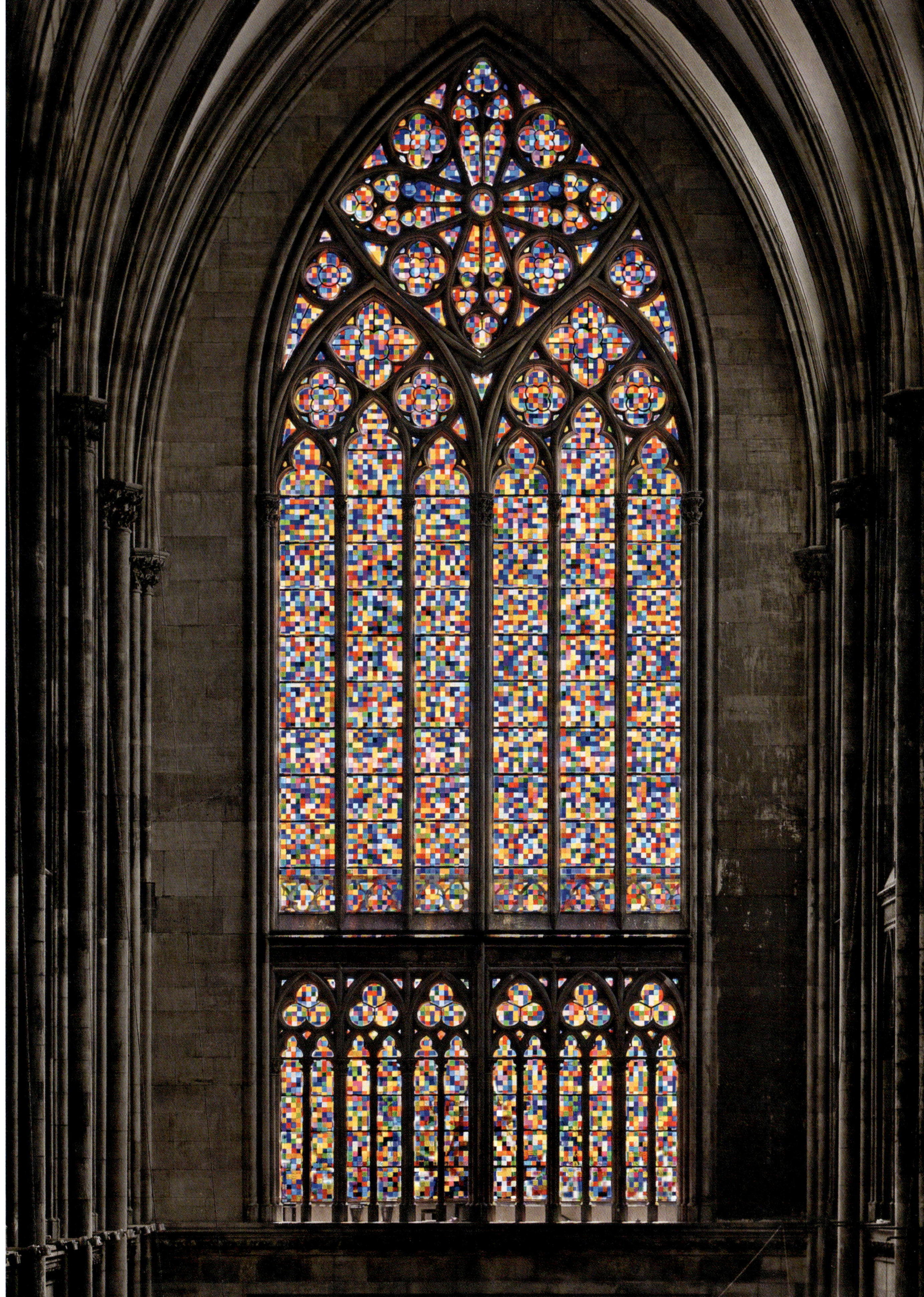

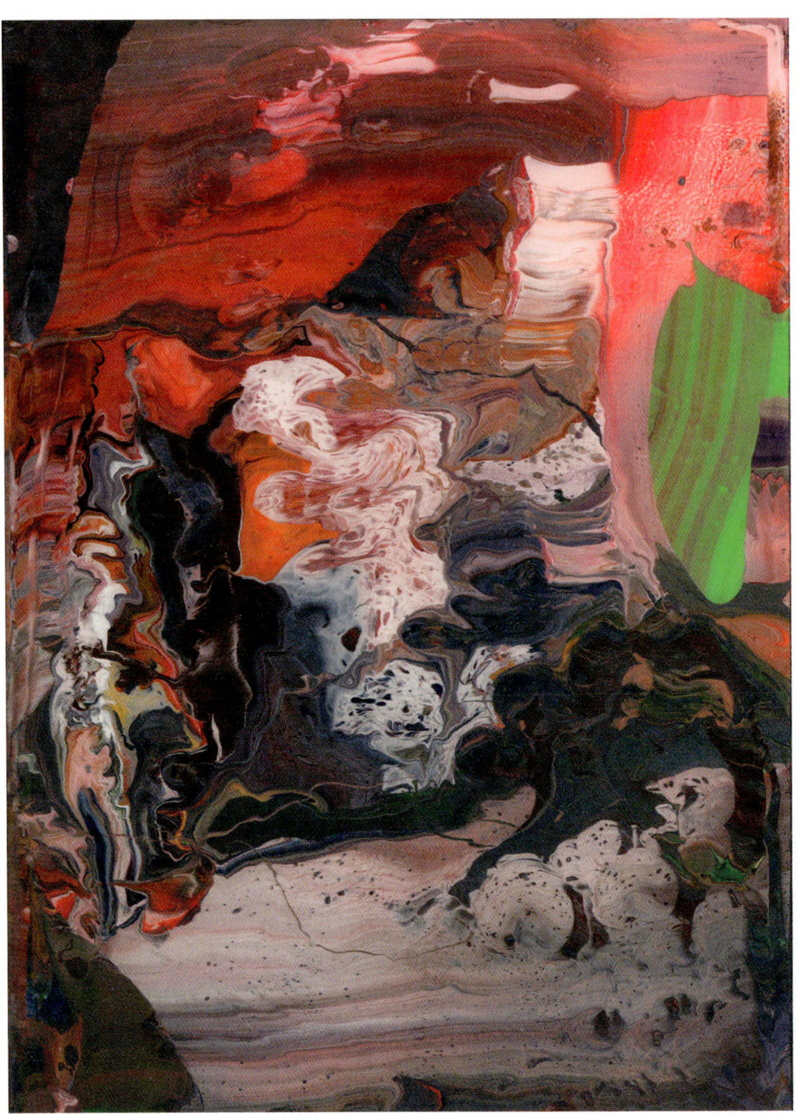

Aladdin, 2010 (CR 913-3)
Lacquer on back of glass,
50 x 37 cm (19¾ x 14⅝ in.)
Germany, private collection

became apparent. Such are comparable to the upheavals that led from medieval art to the Renaissance. They relate to the materials and supporters of art no less than to their criteria, categories, and reception. The familiar yardsticks of aesthetic judgment became progressively impoverished, their replacements vague outlines at best. The first generation that had grown up with computers, smartphones, and the Internet looked at the world with different eyes and emotions than their predecessors. They now entered the universities and the professions.

Step by step, contemporary art split into two camps: one, politically and socially engaged with either a journalistic or scientific methodology, and another that operated in the wake of traditional notions of artistic practice and sought to expand its terms. Film, video, Internet, performance, installation, and language are the main devices of one, craftsmanship the foundation of the other. Photography builds a bridge between the two. "Political art" also stepped out of the concept of art that had been dominant since the Renaissance. It proclaimed a targeted intervention into the entire realm of

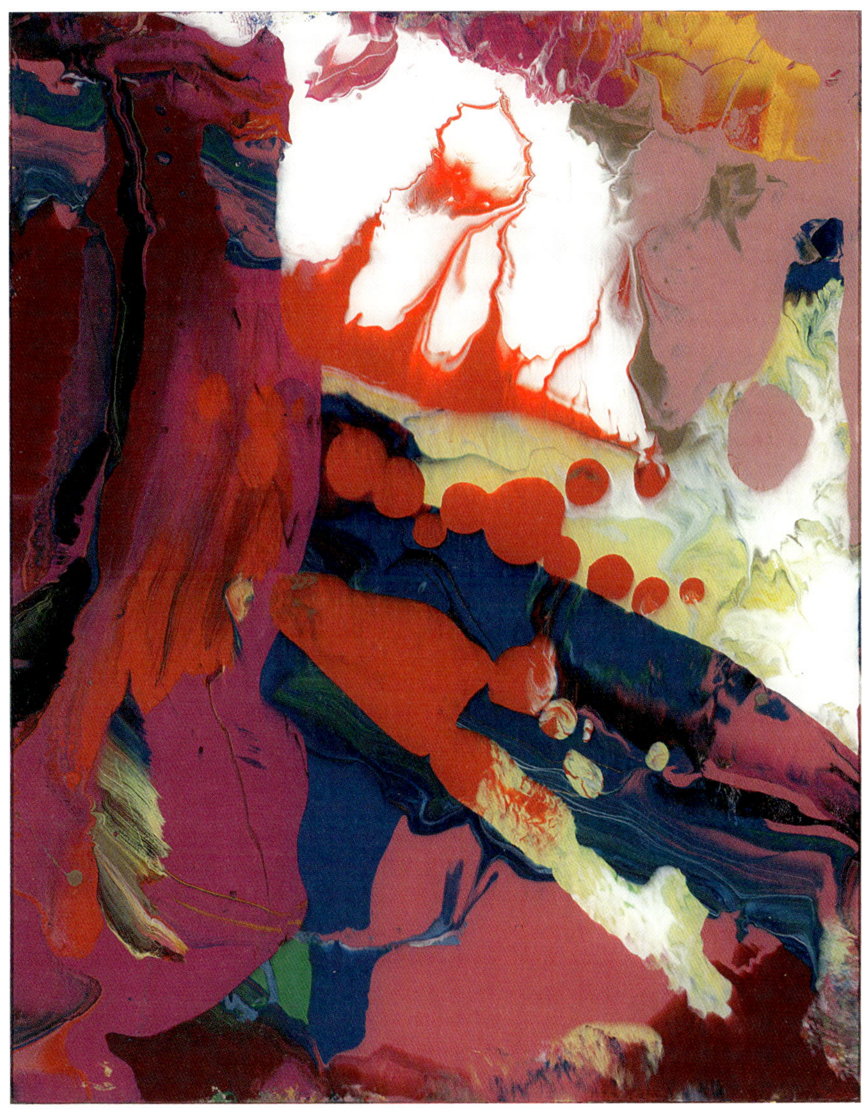

Sindbad, 2008 (CR 905-5)
Lacquer on back of glass,
30 x 24 cm (11⅞ x 9½ in.)
New York, The FLAG Art Foundation

experience. However, "artistic art" did not abandon the claim of autonomy and insisted on the "aesthetic difference" between art and politics. Major international exhibitions such as *documenta* in Kassel became forums of political and sociocultural art, whereas the art trade looked after the terrain of evolutionary art.

The successful global integration of economic and political relations after the end of the Cold War accelerated cultural upheavals and the Internet transformed the world into an unstructured, virtual village. The barriers between artistic disciplines crumbled, as did those between continental cultures. This relativized the legitimacy of art, but also added fresh impetus. On the other hand, it was inevitable that artistic and cultural characteristics would rapidly flatten under the mercantile pressures of a global art trade whose most powerful galleries settled in the world's financial centers and monopolized art dealing.

As well as noting artists' neglect of the question of form in pictorial art, Richter observed the art market's excesses and turbulent side effects with

PAGES 82/83
Strip, 2011 (CR 920-4)
Digital print on paper between
Alu Dibond and Perspex (Diasec),
160 x 300 cm (63 x 118⅛ in.)
New York, private collection

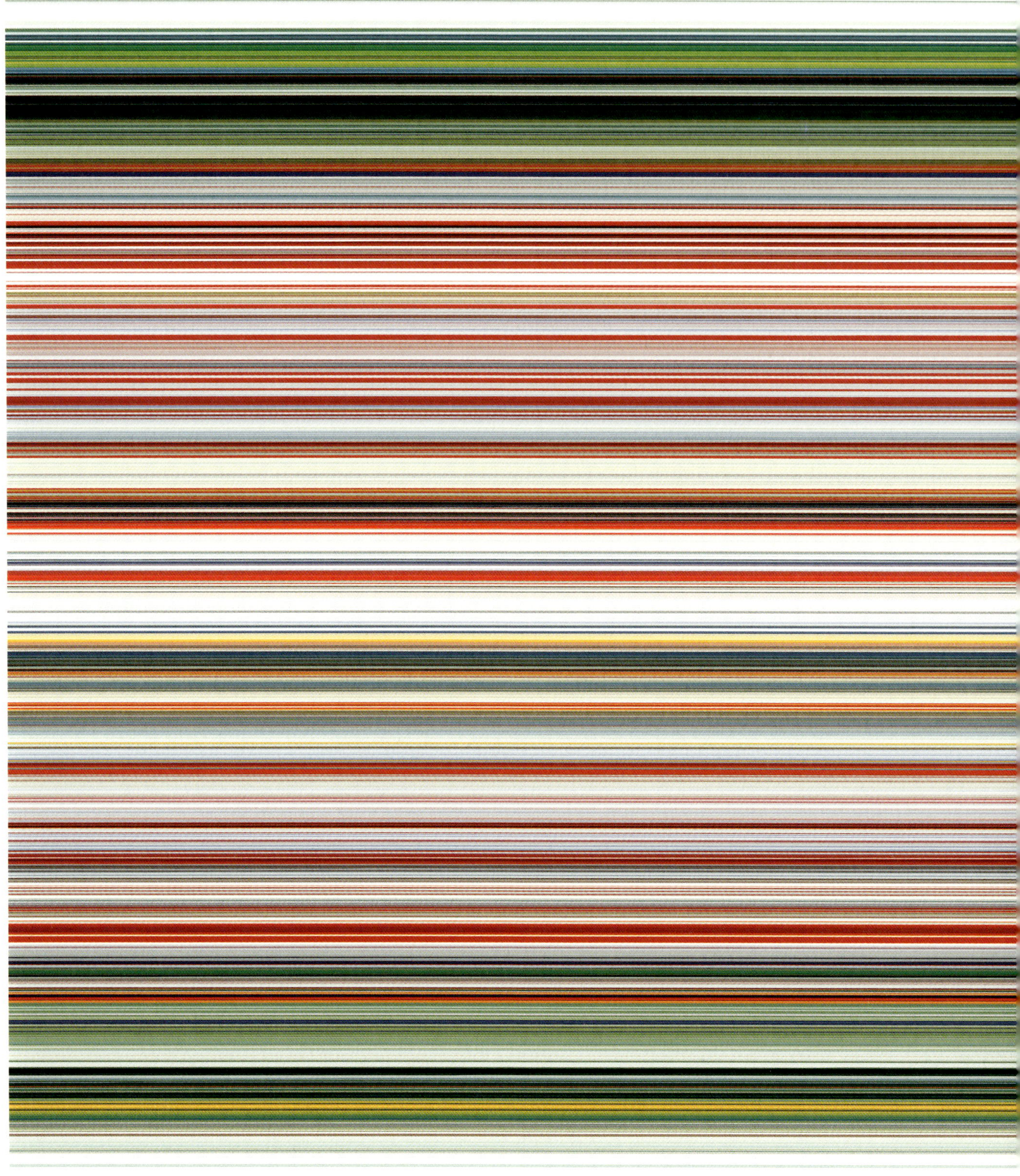

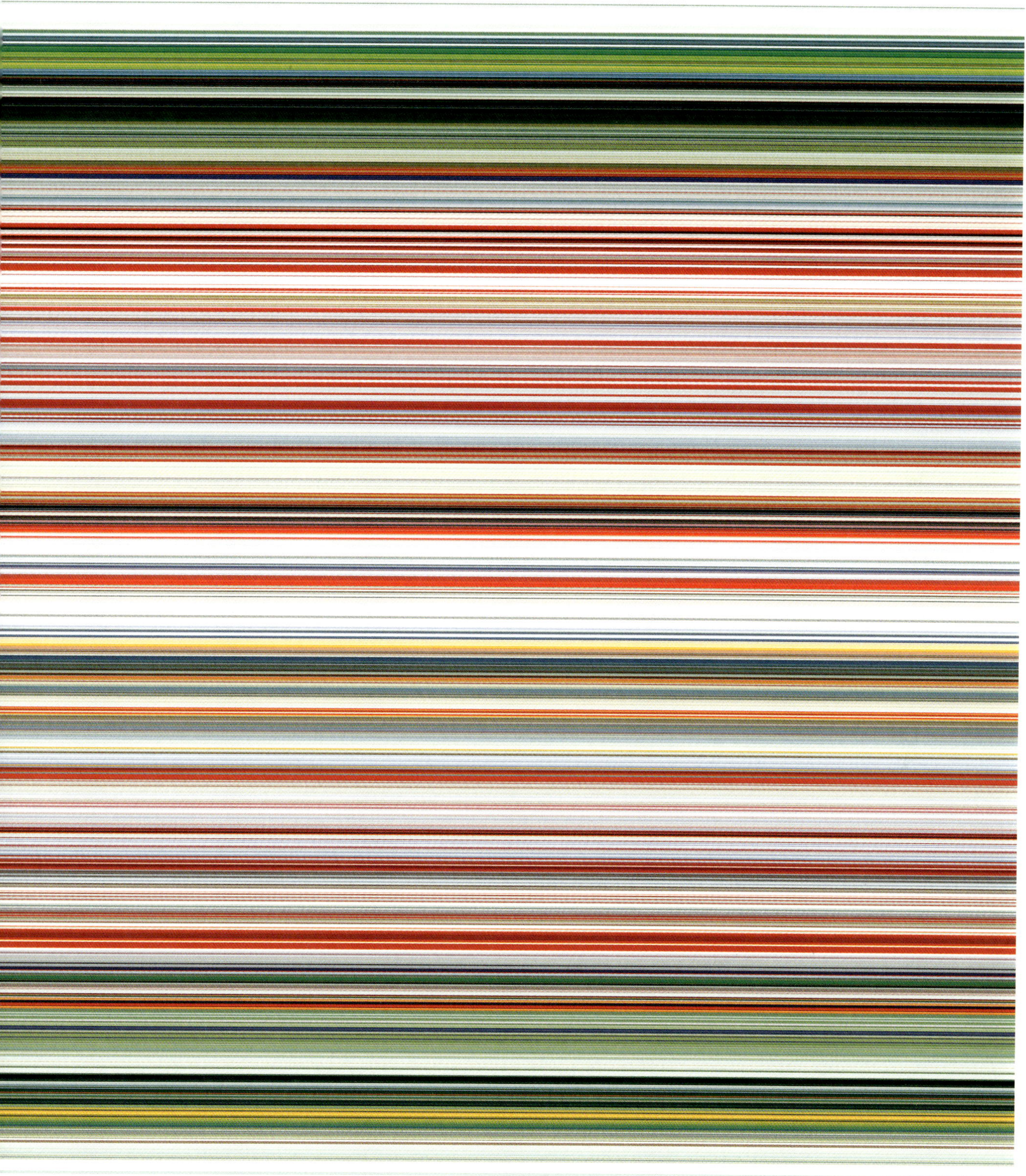

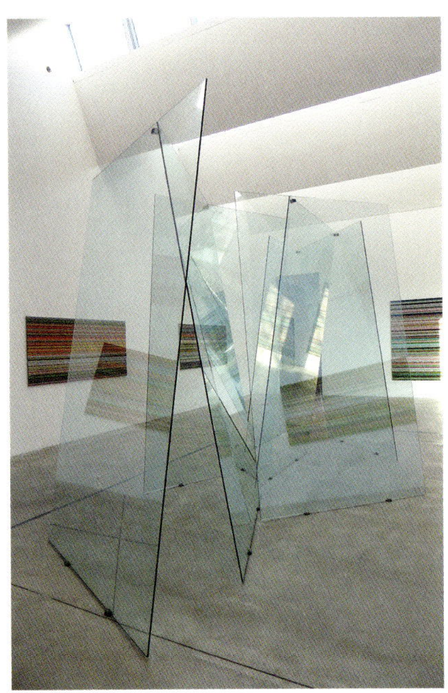

7 Panes (House of Cards), 2013 (CR 932)
Glass and steel construction,
257 x 650 x 360 cm (101¼ x 256 x 141¾ in.)
Private collection

undisguised skepticism—despite their favorable effect on the pricing of his work. In the interest of social balance, he privately donated many pictures, with the proceeds going to housing projects for Cologne's homeless population. In 2002, New York's Museum of Modern Art honored Richter with a prestigious retrospective, *Forty Years of Painting*, for which curator Robert Storr assembled 190 of his works. It was most the extensive show of Richter's works ever staged—a unique record of painting and its unrestricted vitality against the backdrop of mass electronic picture production. With regard to public recognition, it was the triumph of his artistic work.

What looks like a contest between the figurative and the abstract in the Firenze edition (2000), which interrupts a long period of abstract painting, is in fact Richter's silent and probably unintentional farewell to photography. From then on, the artist's use of photography for his work became infrequent. Like a storm, scraps of compact, coordinated agglomerations of color break into the color photograph of a tranquil, sunny street in Florence, threatening—or destroying, depending on the viewer's perception—its billboard prettiness, and replacing it with an exciting aesthetic beauty. Abstraction versus representation, painting versus photography; the passionate confrontations of modern art have long become obsolete and distinctions are superficial. In the *Firenze* edition, they exist side by side, proportionally and equally.

However, when Richter caught sight of a fuzzy photograph of the inside of an atom made with a scanning tunneling microscope that had been published in the scientific pages of a major German daily newspaper, he was riveted. "I was fascinated by the motif, because while imaging technology in microscopes has advanced to the point where you can really see an atom, you can never see it sharp. I find that important, because it sets a limit."[67] No wonder. Didn't this scientific photograph prove, in retrospect, that the blurriness of his photographic paintings corresponds with the inner nature of the real; because its component, the atom, cannot be defined? And that therefore the visual perception of visible reality as a fixed quantity is, in truth, an illusion? What seems, from a scientific point of view, considerably more complicated, Richter's work broke down to a plausible visual level. The small photograph depicting the electron clouds of a silicon atom inspired him to make four giant, almost 3-square-meter (32-sq-feet) pictures: *Silicate* (2003). Richter combined the blurring technique in familiar shades of gray with the visual realization of the mechanical principle of serial production. He repeated, as accurately as he could using stencils, a light-colored, blurred Y within a dark circle on a brighter ground in twenty horizontal lines.

The pictures' radiance is overwhelming and dizzying. Their dimension makes the pictures difficult to view. To get the full effect, it is necessary to step back, but this can never be completely successful. Although the blurring gradually seems to clear, the pictures slip away from the gaze, galvanizing an uncanny dynamic in contradiction to their serial structure: they behave like atoms. Science and art greet each other across their borders without enlisting each other's service.

It is as though, for the new millennium, Richter had set himself a task of overcoming both the limits of the visible and the imaginable in his paintings, engaging only observation and an exceptional painterly practice. He touches on metaphysical connections, but only coincidentally. His largest and most ambitious commission was for the design of a window for the south transept of Cologne Cathedral to replace the one destroyed during World War II.

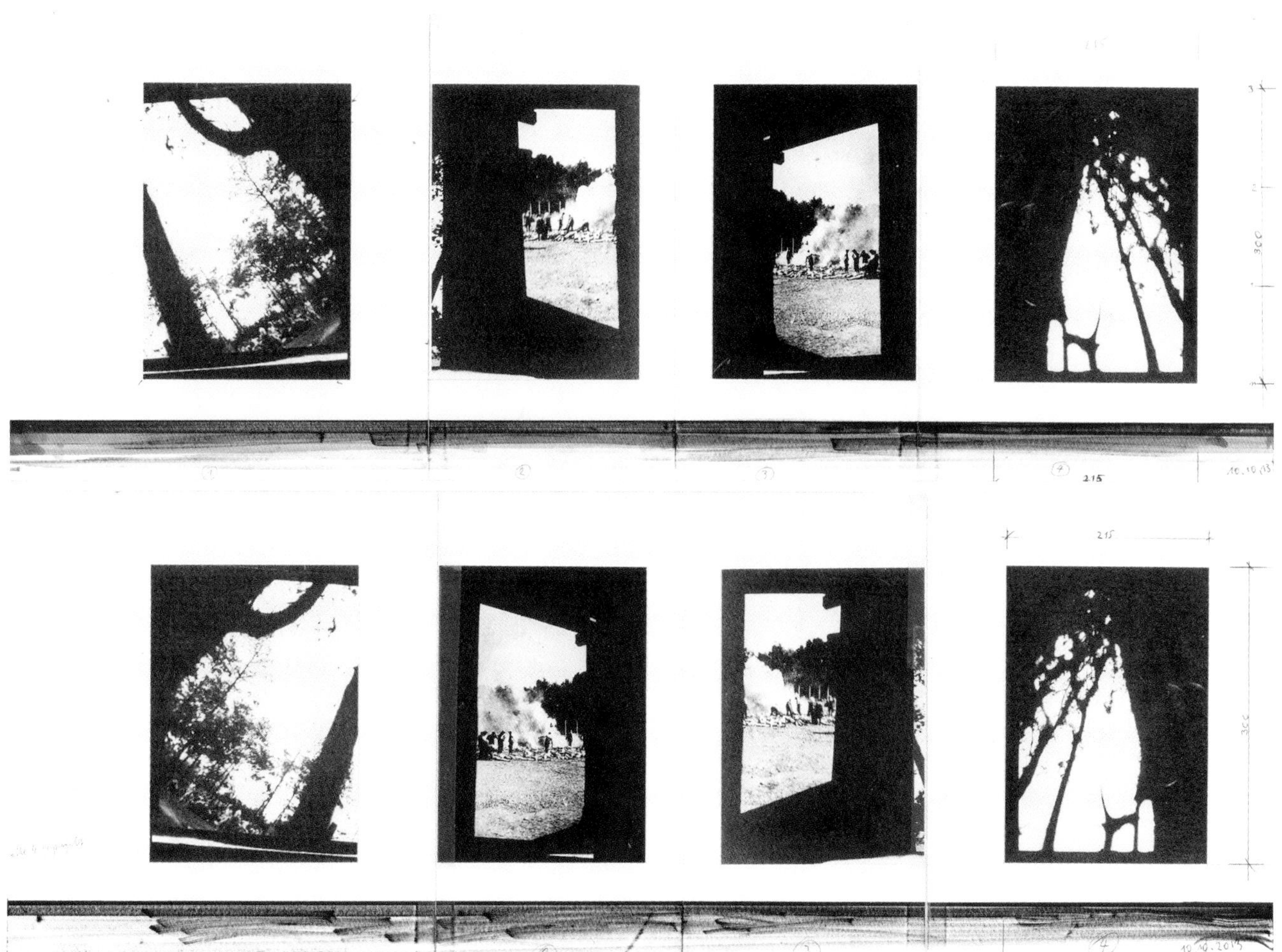

The artist had been asked to design a glass window depicting six contemporary martyrs. After many unsuccessful attempts, and close to giving up the commission, a casual glance at his *4096 Colors*, dating back to 1974, ignited a spark. "I put the template for the window design over it and saw that this was the only possibility,"[68] the artist noted in preparation for a press conference in July 2006. Realized in 2007, the window consists of 11,263 antique, handblown square glass segments (96 x 96 mm / 3¾ x 3¾ in.) in 72 colors and covering a total area of 23 x 9 meters (75½ x 29½ feet). A computer program determined the order of one half of the segments based on the laws of chance, and this was then mirrored by the other half.

With *Cologne Cathedral Window*, Richter moved "definitely inside of art history," as he had claimed to Robert Storr he was a few years earlier. An art that mocks all time-bound restrictions and will survive the institution of the museum. Even more powerful in its effect than his XXL-format images—from the *Silicate* series to *Strips* (2011), large-format digital prints on paper sandwiched between Alu Dibond and Perspex that are painful to look at even when viewed diffusely—*Cologne Cathedral Window* affects body and mind equally. Variously refracted, colored light interacts with Gothic architecture to create a reality that pushes the boundaries of modern humanity's familiar experiences. Seeing becomes experiencing. Even when the sky is gray, the

Studies for Birkenau, 2013 (ATLAS SHEET 807)
6 prints (copied and reworked with felt-tip pen and ballpoint pen), 50 x 70 cm (19¾ x 27⅝ in.)
Munich, Städtische Galerie im Lenbachhaus und Kunstbau

PAGE 86
Birkenau, 2014 (CR 937-1)
Oil on canvas, 260 x 200 cm (102⅜ x 78¾ in.)
Cologne, private collection

PAGE 87
Birkenau, 2014 (CR 937-2)
Oil on canvas, 260 x 200 cm (102⅜ x 78¾ in.)
Cologne, private collection

PAGE 88
Birkenau, 2014 (CR 937-3)
Oil on canvas, 260 x 200 cm (102⅜ x 78¾ in.)
Cologne, private collection

PAGE 89
Birkenau, 2014 (CR 937-4)
Oil on canvas, 260 x 200 cm (102⅜ x 78¾ in.)
Cologne, private collection

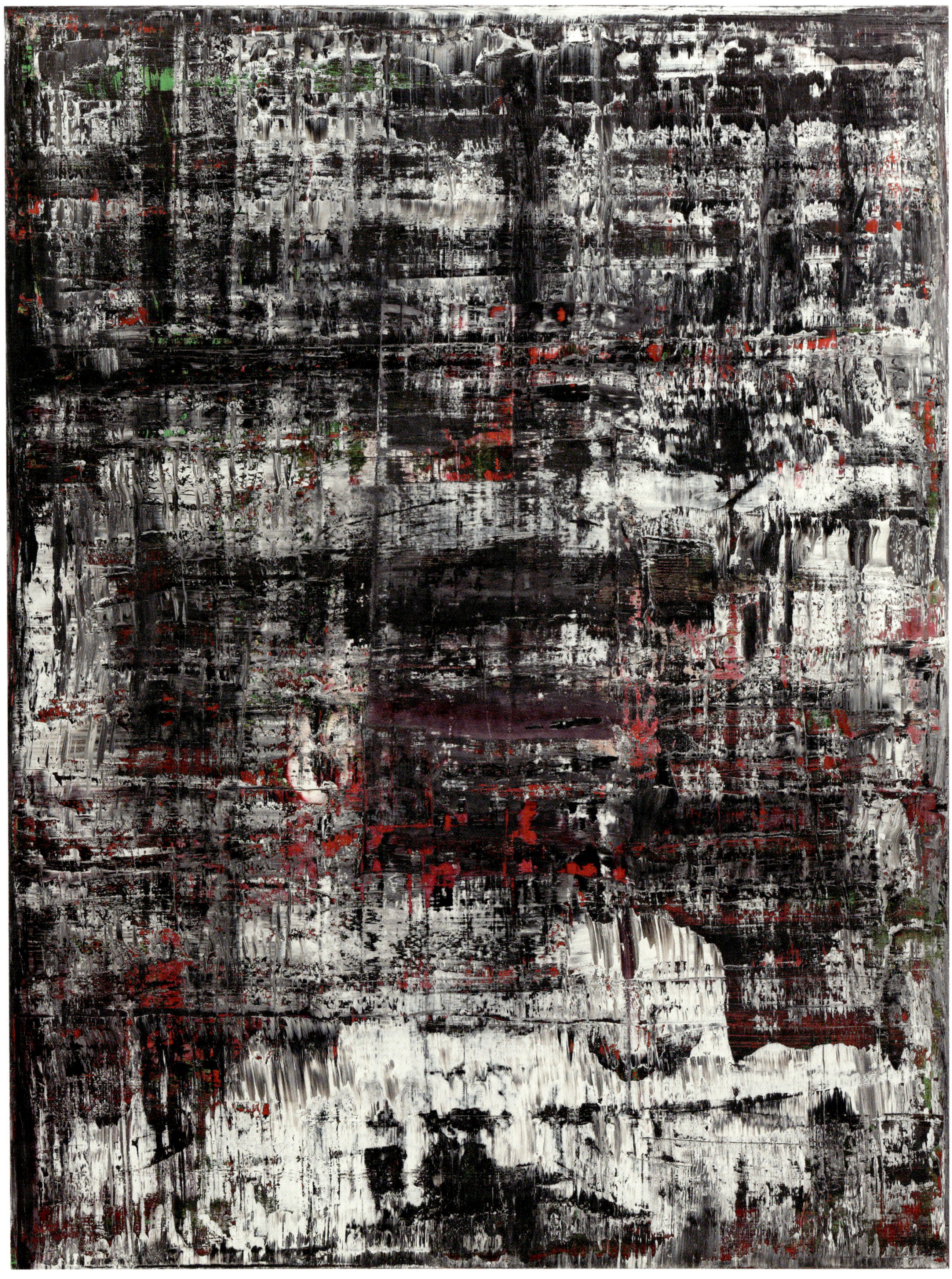

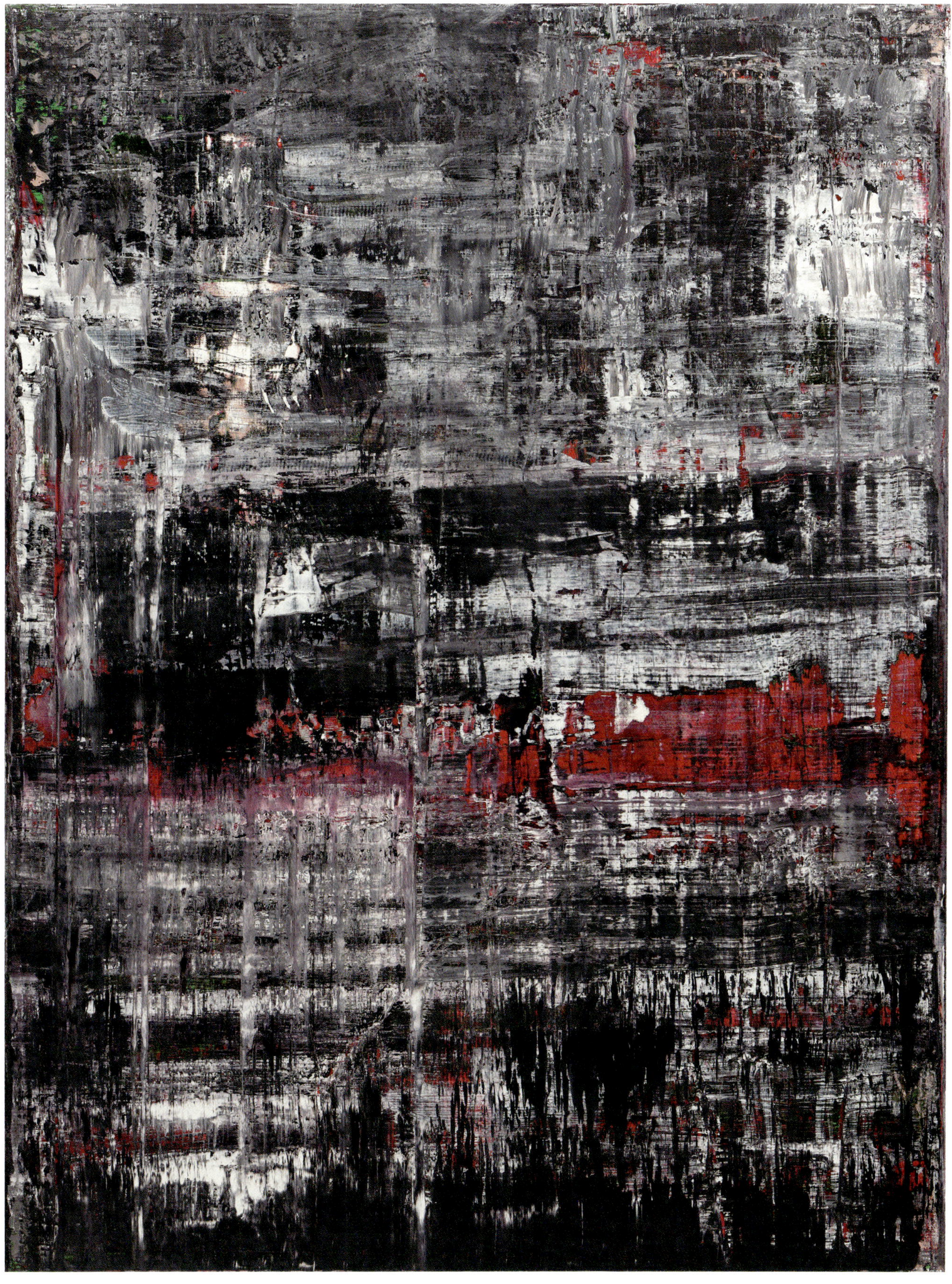

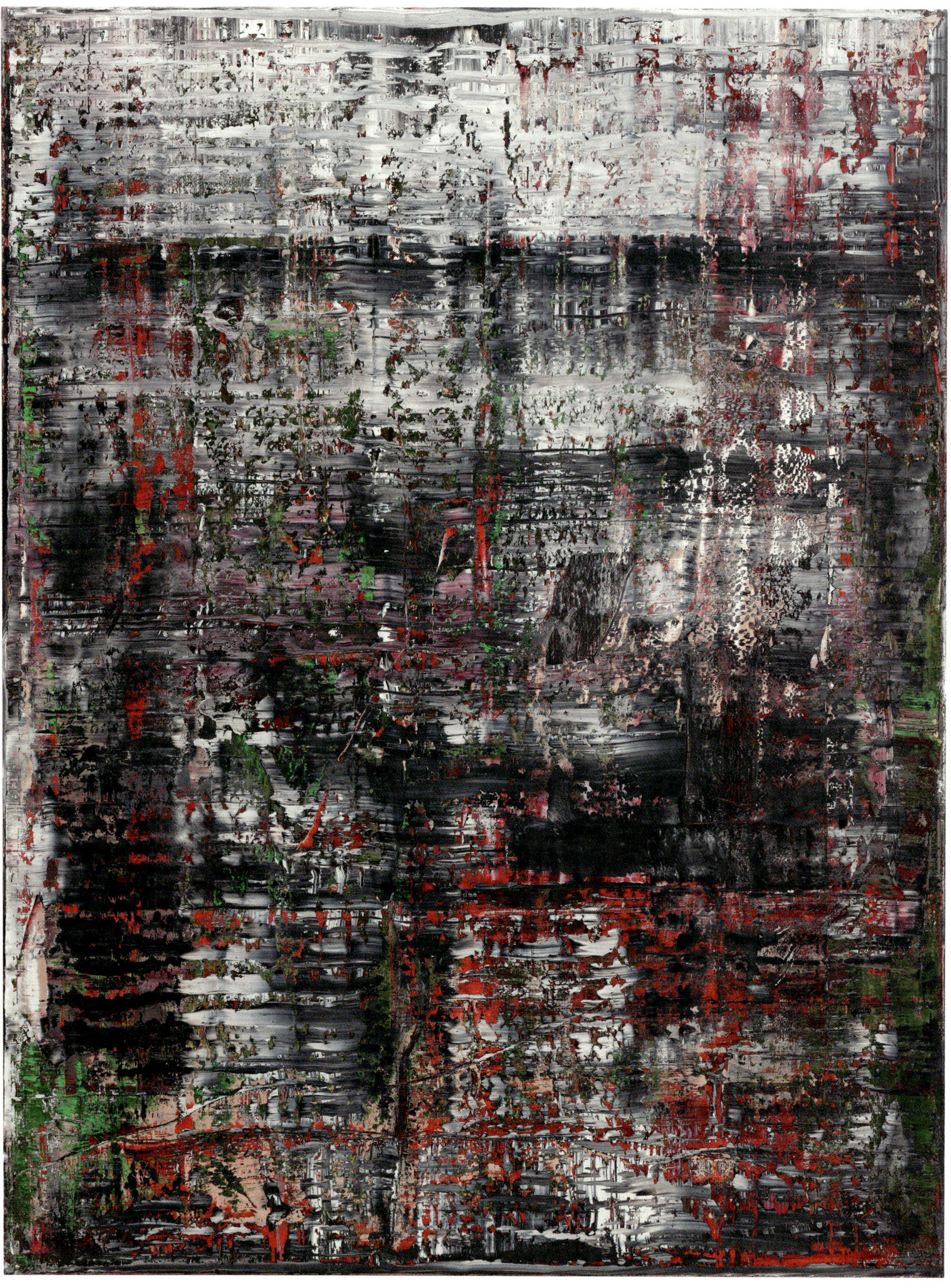

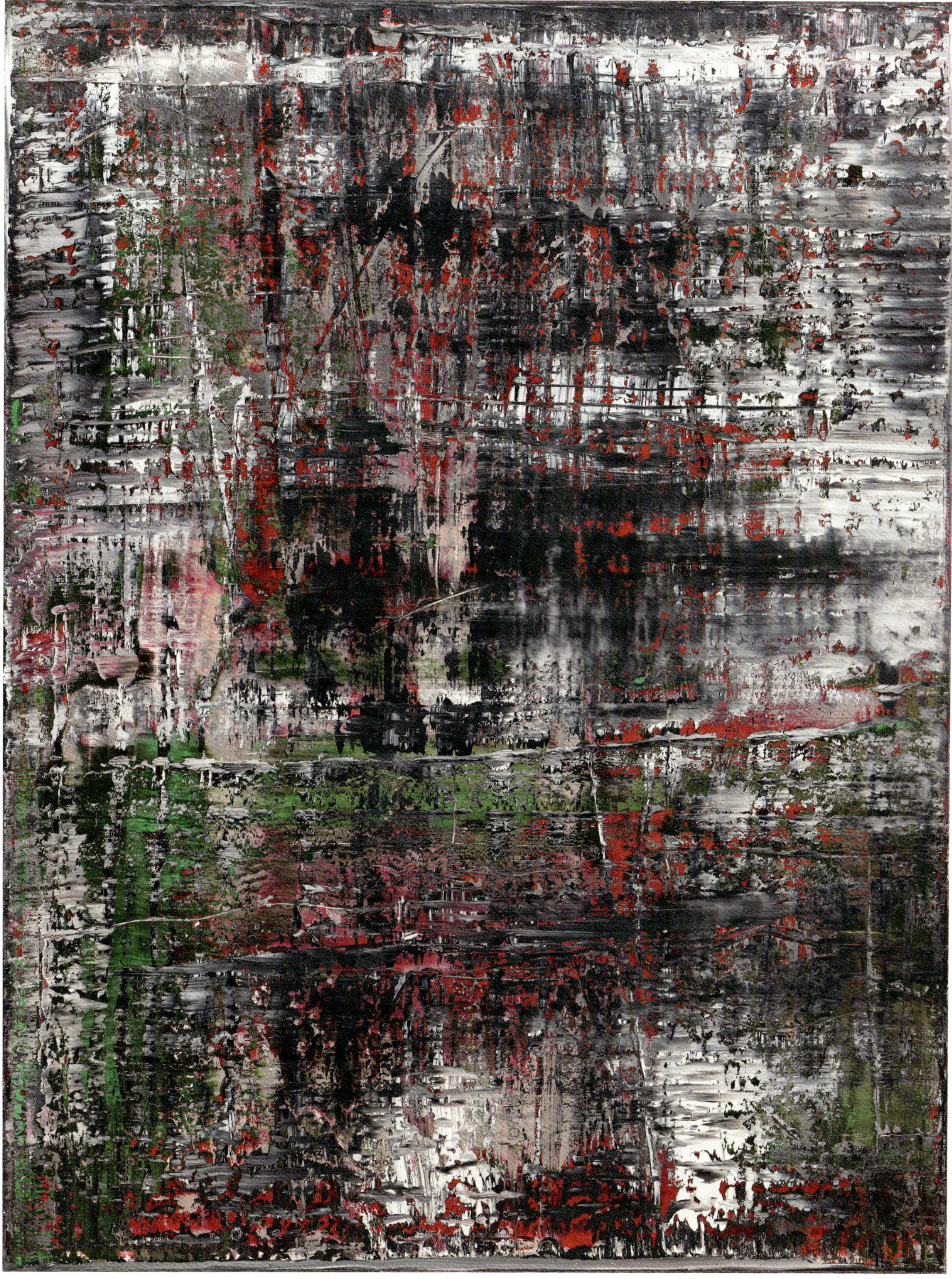

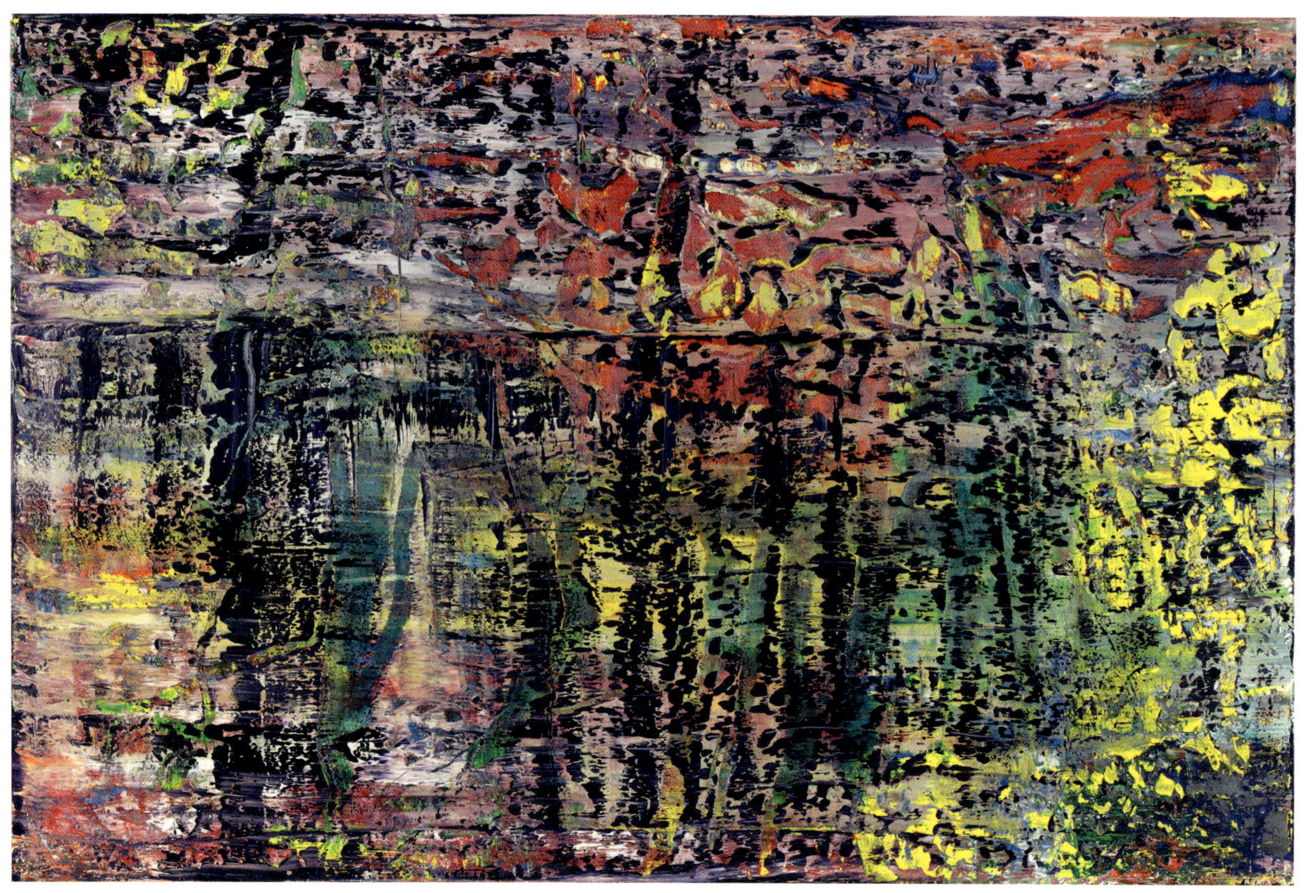

Abstract Painting, 2016 (CR 943-1)
Oil on canvas, 144 x 220 cm (56¾ x 86⅝ in.)
Private collection

window creates a wondrous luminosity. The colors chosen for the modern glass window were based on the preferred hues of the Middle Ages: red, blue, yellow, green, black, and white. It transports the cathedral's southern transept into the color universe of old, echoing both a sense of artistic loss and a new departure.

Opaque and transparent, concrete and abstract, linear and flat, as well as expressively silent—the half-dozen large square oil paintings that Richter made in 2006 for the Venice Biennale while preparing the cathedral window illustrate both the path and the outcome of his artistic work. They were supposed to be based on photographs: "photos of various atomic structures comparable to the silicate series."[69] When Richter began with the first painting, he changed his plan, and destroyed it. "And I just kept on painting like this somehow. This peculiar state of hopelessness, perplexity, and high spirits kept on long enough for me to finish all six paintings."[70] These pictures, that continuously coagulate and dissolve in the viewer's gaze, took three months to complete, and Richter dedicated the cycle to John Cage. Maybe this was because he unconsciously created it as a visual counterpoint to Cage's compositional approach—a mixture of coincidence and work discipline. Coincidences are only useful, says the artist, "because they've been worked out—that means either eliminated or allowed or emphasized; in short, brought into a particular form."[71]

Perhaps the complex experience of painting the *Cage* cycle paved the way for Richter finally tackling his most difficult project, one that has bothered

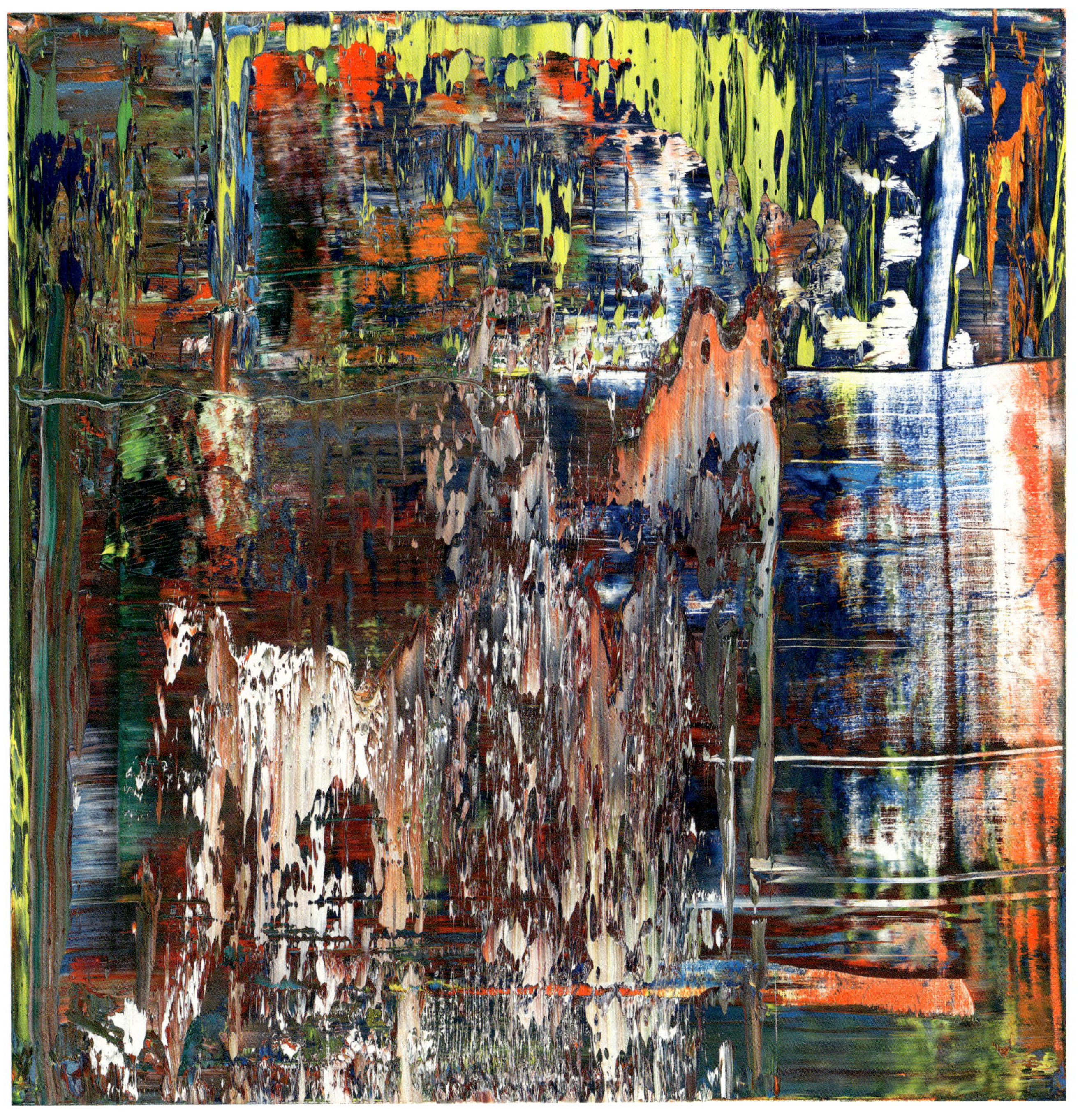

Abstract Painting, 2015 (CR 939-7)
Oil on canvas, 71.5 x 71.5 cm (28¼ x 28¼ in.)
Private collection

him for years: the Nazi genocide. Photographs of the Holocaust can be found early in the *Atlas*. Richter's aversion to the Nazi regime and its fellow travelers is in no doubt. He was also familiar with the less-well-known photographs of women walking into a Birkenau gas chamber and the cremation of gassing victims. Unnamed citizens risked their lives to document these events at the request of the Polish Resistance, paradoxically protected by the gas chambers and at a distance from the mass disposal of bodies. The acute sense of threat is emblazoned in the photographs. The unimaginable becomes irrefutable, irrespective of technical imperfection. These solitary, *in flagrante* pictorial testimonies of the genocide were shown to the supreme Western commanders, but failed to convince the Allies to bomb the extermination camps or their access roads.

Despite formal deficiencies, the photographs from the Auschwitz-Birkenau extermination camp have historical incontestability on their side. And yet, to paint them? Wouldn't that transgress a socially binding taboo? A taboo, according to which introducing unimaginable horror into pictures would mean relativizing the monstrous, and transforming it into voyeurism? Georges Didi-Huberman's profound study of these images, their history and their consequences, in the book *Images in Spite of All* (2007), prompted the artist to rise to the challenge. "In the fall of 2014, I began to transfer these four photographs to canvas, and quickly realized that it was not possible. So I scraped off and repainted until I had four abstract images."[72]

Once again, an artistic challenge turns out to be impossible. Poems based on Auschwitz are possible, but pictures? Yes—pictures too. So long as they impart the impossibility of success. Without images, the horror would have no grounding. Since Richter's *Birkenau* paintings (2014) give an allegorical meaning to the "how" of the technical process of scraping and overpainting, there is at least a glimmer of the unimaginable. It stirs the imagination just as the pictures' titles, *Birkenau*, point the way. "The fact that you cannot recognize a picture of Auschwitz simply follows from the fact that you cannot see Auschwitz, not even in Auschwitz."[73] Scratching rips open the substratum and repainting covers it: a metaphor for the course of history. However, genocide can neither be scratched away nor painted over. It festers beneath the surface of Germany's political and social events like the hidden canvas beneath the surface of the *Birkenau* paintings. After completing them, Richter sent them to his archive in Dresden. A photographic version of the group hangs in the Reichstag, across from *Black, Red, Gold*—and is reflected in it. This perpetual encounter expresses the indivisibility of German history.

With *Two Gray Double Mirrors for a Pendulum* (2018), a room-height installation in the abandoned Dominikanerkirche in Münster, Richter offers visitors a cosmological perspective. The 48-kilogram (106-lb) ball of the Foucault pendulum swings on a 29-meter-long (95-feet) rope through the former church space and seems to circulate continuously to the day's rhythm, around its suspension point above a massive stone disk. In reality, the pendulum does not move but the viewers are moved; they are moved by the rotation of Earth, even if they believe themselves to be stationary, while the pendulum keeps swinging in the same direction. The unimaginable becomes visible but somehow escapes us. Just as Richter's work constantly evades our grasp.

Two Gray Double Mirrors for a Pendulum, 2018 (CR 953)
Magnetic microprocessor, metal sphere, steel chain, Charron ring, stone plate, mirror
Each 600 x 134 x 1 cm (236¼ x 52⅞ in.)
Floor panel: diameter 400/560 cm (157½ in./220½ in.), steel cable (length): 28.75 m (1132 in.)
Münster, Dominikanerkirche

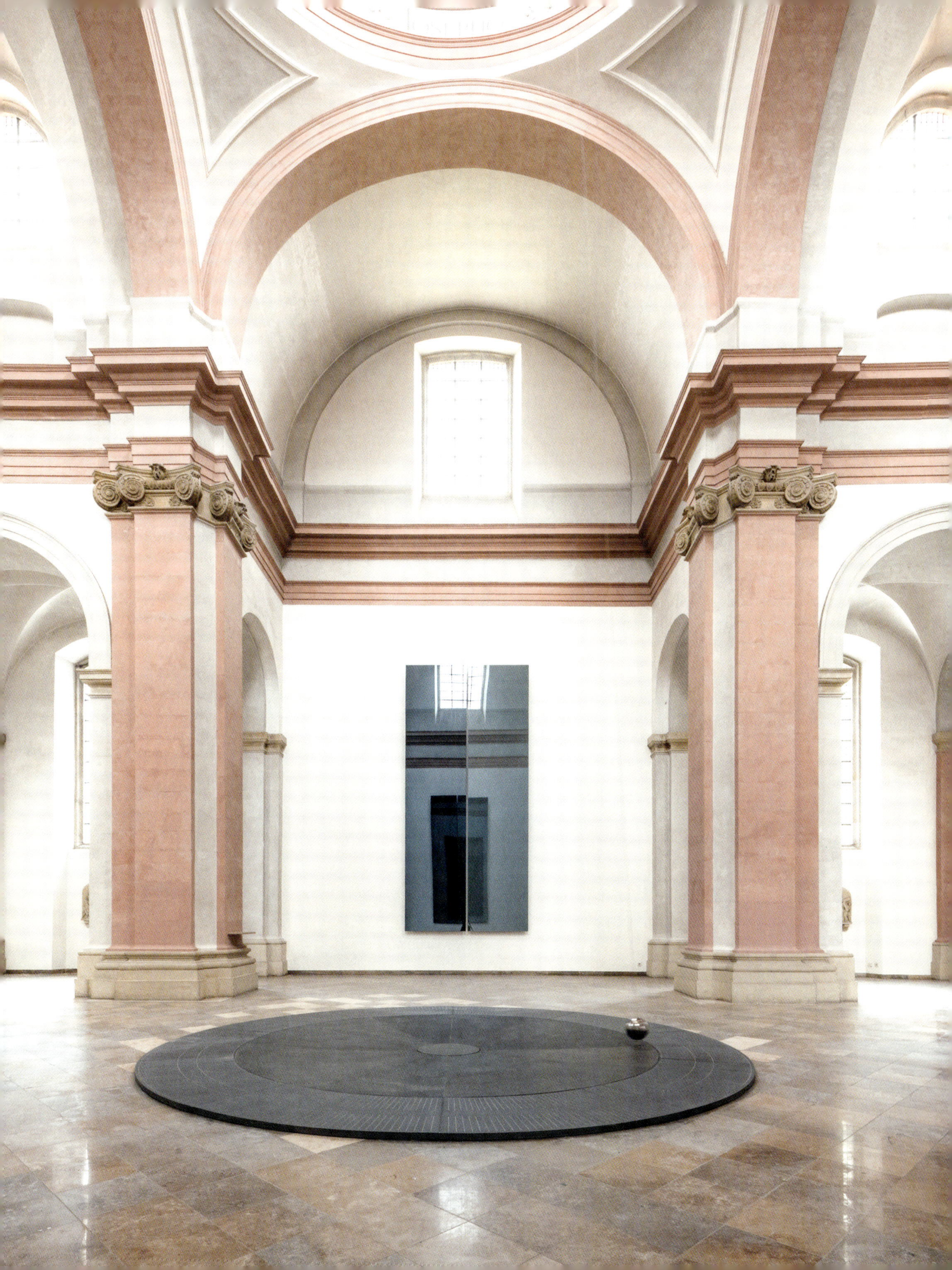

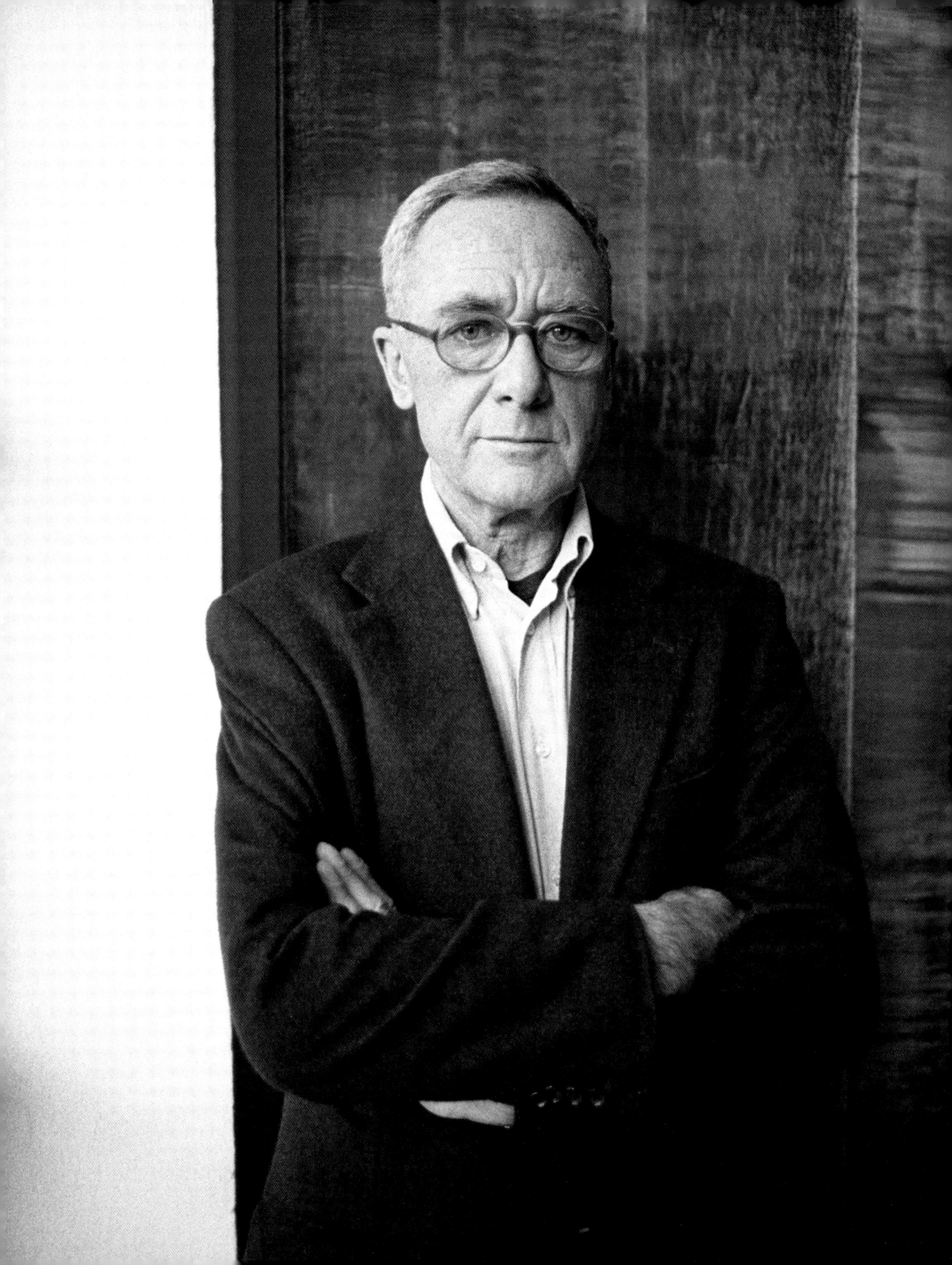

Gerhard Richter
Life and Work

1932 Born on February 9 in Dresden · **1948** Completes commercial school diploma in Zittau · **1949** Assistant in an advertising office in Zittau · **1950** Paint shop assistant at the municipal theater in Zittau. Working artist at DEWAG, the only East German advertising agency · **1951** Studies at the Academy of Fine Arts, Dresden · **1953** Studies mural painting with Heinz Lohmar · **1956** Graduates and completes the *Joy of Life* mural, German Hygiene Museum, Dresden · **1957** Three-year apprenticeship and studio at the Academy of Fine Arts, Dresden · **1959** Visits *documenta 2* in Kassel.

1961 March 30, defects to West Germany. Moves to Düsseldorf. Studies at Düsseldorf's Art Academy under Ferdinand Macketanz · **1962** Beginning of friendships with Konrad Lueg (later Konrad Fischer), Sigmar Polke, and Blinky Palermo · **1963** Exhibition of work by Richter, Lueg, and Polke at Kaiserstraße 31 A, Düsseldorf, an abandoned shop. Performance and exhibition *Living with Pop—A Demonstration for Capitalist Realism*, with Lueg, at Möbelhaus Berges furniture store, Düsseldorf · **1964** Leaves the Academy. Exhibition at Galerie Friedrich and Dahlem (with Peter Klasen) in Munich. First solo exhibitions: Gallery Schmela, Düsseldorf; Gallery René Block, Berlin. Exhibition with Lueg and Polke, Galerie Parnass, Wuppertal · **1966** Exhibition with Polke in galerie h, Hannover.

1967 Visiting professorship at the University of Fine Arts Hamburg. Wins the *Junger Westen* art prize awarded by the city of Recklinghausen **1969** Solo exhibition in Gegenverkehr e.V. Zentrum für aktuelle Kunst, Aachen · **1970** Travels to New York with Palermo.

1971 Professorship at the Düsseldorf Art Academy. Exhibition at the Kunstverein für die Rheinlande und Westfalen, Düsseldorf · **1972** Richter exhibits in the German Pavilion at the 36th Venice Biennale. First time his works are exhibited at *documenta 5* in Kassel · **1973** First solo exhibition in New York at the Onnasch Gallery · **1975** Exhibition at the Kunsthalle Bremen and at the Palais des Beaux-Arts, Brussels · **1977** Solo exhibition at the Musée National d'Art Moderne, Centre Pompidou, Paris · **1978** Visiting professorship at the Nova Scotia College of Art and Design in Halifax · **1982** Receives Arnold Bode Prize in Kassel. *Gerhard Richter: Abstract Paintings* exhibition at Kunsthalle Bielefeld and Mannheimer Kunstverein.

Gerhard Richter, 1992
Photo: Benjamin Katz

1983 Moves from Düsseldorf to Cologne · **1985** Awarded the Oskar Kokoschka Prize in Vienna **1986** Touring retrospective, Städtische Kunsthalle Düsseldorf, Neue Nationalgalerie, Berlin; Kunsthalle Bern; Museum of the 20th Century, Vienna · **1988** *Paintings*, Art Gallery of Ontario, Toronto; Museum of Contemporary Art, Chicago; Hirshhorn Museum and Sculpture Garden, Washington, D.C.; guest professorship, Städelschule Frankfurt am Main. Awarded the Kaiserring der Stadt Goslar art prize. Creation of *October 18, 1977*, a cycle of 15 paintings · **1989** Solo exhibition, Museum Boijmans Van Beuningen, Rotterdam; *Paintings*, San Francisco Museum of Modern Art · **1991** Retrospective at the Tate Gallery, London · **1993** Retrospective, Musée d'Art Moderne de la Ville de Paris, Kunst- und Ausstellungshalle der Bundesrepublik Deutschland, Bonn; Moderna Museet, Stockholm; Museo Nacional Centro de Arte Reina Sofía, Madrid.

1994 Richter resigns from the Düsseldorf Art Academy · **1995** Receives Wolf Prize in Arts, Jerusalem · **1996** New studio on the outskirts of Cologne · **1997** Receives Golden Lion at the 47th Venice Biennale and Praemium Imperiale, Tokyo · **1998** *Landscapes* at the Sprengel Museum Hannover. Wexner Prize, Columbus, Ohio · **1999** *Works on Paper* in Winterthur, Dresden, Krefeld, and Tilburg. *Black, Red, Gold* installed in the Reichstag building · **2000** Awarded North Rhine-Westphalia's State Prize · **2001** Awarded honorary doctorate by the University of Leuven.

2002 *Forty Years of Painting*, Museum of Modern Art, New York; Art Institute of Chicago, San Francisco Museum of Modern Art · **2003** *Forty Years of Painting*, Hirshhorn Museum and Sculpture Garden, Washington, D.C.

2004 The Albertinum, Staatliche Kunstsammlungen, Dresden, opens three rooms dedicated to Richter's work · **2005** *Gerhard Richter*, K20 Kunstsammlung Nordrhein-Westfalen, Düsseldorf; Städtische Galerie im Lenbachhaus; Kunstbau, Munich; 21st Century Museum of Contemporary Art, Kanazawa; Kawamura Memorial Museum of Art, Sakura · **2007** Becomes honorary citizen of Cologne. Dedication of *Cologne Cathedral Window* in the south transept · **2008** *Paintings from Private Collections*, Museum Frieder Burda, Baden-Baden; National Galleries of Scotland, Edinburgh; National Art Museum of China, Beijing. *Overpainted Photographs*, Museum Morsbroich, Leverkusen. *Abstract Paintings*, Museum Ludwig, Cologne; Haus der Kunst, Munich · **2009** *Portraits*, National Portrait Gallery, London. *Paintings from Private Collections*, Vienna and Duisburg. *Overpainted Photographs*, Centre de la Photographie, Geneva; Fundacion Telefonica, Madrid.

2010 The Albertinum, Staatliche Kunstsammlungen Dresden, is reopened with two rooms dedicated to works by Gerhard Richter · **2011** *Panorama*, Tate Gallery, London · **2012** Exhibition of *Atlas*, Kunsthalle im Lipsiusbau, Dresden. *Panorama*, Neue Nationalgalerie Berlin; Musée National d'Art Moderne, Centre Pompidou, Paris. *Dessins et Aquarelles* 1957–2008, Musée du Louvre, Paris · **2013** *Stripes and Glass*, Albertinum, Staatliche Kunstsammlungen Dresden. *Atlas* at the Lenbachhaus Kunstbau, Munich · **2014** *Stripes and Glass*, Kunstmuseum Winterthur. *Pictures/Series*, Fondation Beyeler, Basel-Riehen

2015 *Birkenau* is exhibited for the first time at the Albertinum, Staatliche Kunstsammlungen, Dresden. *New Abstract Paintings*, Wako Works of Art, Tokyo · **2016** Pavilion with the permanent installation of *14 Panes of Glass for Toyoshima, Dedicated to Futility*, opens on Toyoshima Island, Japan. *Paintings and Drawings*, Marian Goodman Gallery, New York.

2017 Exhibitions held on the occasion of Richter's 85th birthday at Museum Ludwig, Cologne; Albertinum Dresden. First solo exhibitions in the Czech Republic: National Gallery Prague, and Australia: Queensland Art Gallery, Brisbane. Presentation of the *Birkenau* cycle to the Reichstag building · **2018** Installation of *Two Gray Double Mirrors for a Pendulum* in Dominikanerkirche Münster. *Abstraction*, Museum Barberini, Potsdam.

Gerhard Richter lives and works in Cologne.

Notes

Chapter 1

1 Notes, 1962–93, trans. in: *Gerhard Richter Text: Writings, Interviews and Letters 1961–2007*, edited by Dietmar Elger and Hans Ulrich Obrist, 2009, p. 15 · **2** Interview with Robert Storr, 2002, in: *Gerhard Richter: Text 1961 bis 2007, Schriften, Interviews, Briefe*, edited by Dietmar Elger and Hans Ulrich Obrist, Cologne 2008, p. 400 · **3** Ibid. · **4** Notes, 1962, as note 1, p. 15 · **5** Pierre Bourdieu. *Manet. A Symbolic Revolution*, Berlin 2015, p. 166 · **6** Ibid., p. 167 · **7** Interview with Dorothea Dietrich, 1985, in: *Gerhard Richter* as note 1, p. 151 · **8** Roland Barthes. *The Death of the Author, in: Texte zur Theorie der Autorschaft*, edited and with commentary by Fotis Jannidis, Gerhard Lauer, Matias Martinez and Simone Winko, Stuttgart 2000, p. 189 · **9** Notes, 1964 (–1967), in: *Gerhard Richter* as note 1, p. 22 · **10** Notes, 1962, as note 1, p. 14 · **11** Ibid. · **12** Gerhard Richter cited by: Jürgen Harten. *Gerhard Richter. Bilder 1962–1985*, Cologne 1986, p. 57, note 10 **13** *Gerhard Richter. Atlas*, edited by Helmut Friedel, Cologne 2006 · **14** Interview with Wolf Schön, 1972, in: *Gerhard Richter* as note 1, p. 60 **15** Notes, 1964–1965, in: *Gerhard Richter* as note 1, p. 32 · **16** Ibid., p. 33 · **17** Letter to Benjamin H.D. Buchloh, 30 August 1979, in: *Gerhard Richter* as note 1, p. 114

Chapter 2

18 Interview with Babette Richter, 2002, in: *Gerhard Richter* as note 1, p. 453 · **19** Interview with Jonas Storsve, 1991, in: *Gerhard Richter* as note 1, p. 276 · **20** Interview with Babette Richter 2002, as note 1, p. 453 · **21** Ibid. · **22** *Ludwig Goes Pop*, edited by Stephan Diederich and Luise Pilz, Cologne 2014 · **23** Interview with Jonas Storsve, 1991, in: *Gerhard Richter* as note 1, p. 276 · **24** Pierre Bourdieu. *Manet: A Symbolic Revolution*, Berlin 2015, p. 812 · **25** Conversation with Jan Thorn-Prikker concerning the *18 October 1977* cycle, 1989, in: *Gerhard Richter* as note 1, p. 245 **26** Jürgen Harten. *Gerhard Richter: Bilder 1962–1985*, Cologne 1986, p. 47 · **27** Sol LeWitt. *Paragraphs on Conceptual Art, Artforum* 5, no. 10 (June 1967) pp. 79–83 · **28** Klaus Honnef. *Concept Art*, Cologne 1971, p. 30 · **29** Notes, 1966, in: *Gerhard Richter* as note 1, p. 46 · **30** Interview with Jonas Storsve, 1991, in: *Gerhard Richter* as note 1, p. 277 · **31** Interview with Irmeline Lebeer, 1973, in: *Gerhard Richter* as note 1, p. 83 · **32** From a letter to Edy de Wilde, 23 February 1975, in: *Gerhard Richter* as note 1, p. 91 · **33** Ibid., p. 92

Chapter 3

34 Interview with Amine Haase, 1977, in: *Gerhard Richter* as note 1, p. 96 · **35** Interview with Gislind Nabakowski, 1974, in: *Gerhard Richter* as note 1, pp. 85–90 · **36** Ibid., p. 85 **37** Ibid., p. 89 · **38** Ibid., p. 86 · **39** Ibid. · **40** Dietmar Elger. *Gerhard Richter, Maler*, Cologne 2002, p. 265 and p. 411 · **41** Gerhard Richter cited by: *Der Spiegel*, 38/1993, p. 248 · **42** Interview with Rolf-Gunter Dienst, 1970, in: *Gerhard Richter* as note 1, p. 56 · **43** Klaus Honnef: *Schwierigkeiten beim Beschreiben der Realität: Richters Malerei zwischen Kunst und Wirklichkeit*, in: Gerhard Richter, Catalogue 3/69, Aachen 1969 · **44** Dietmar Elger, as note 7, p. 206 **45** Conversation with Mathias Schreiber, 1972, in: *Gerhard Richter* as note 1, p. 62 · **46** Ibid., p. 63 · **47** Interview with Dorothea Dietrich, 1985, in: *Gerhard Richter* as note 1, p. 157 · **48** Interview with Irmeline Lebeer, 1973, in: *Gerhard Richter* as note 1, p. 82 · **49** Conversation with Jan Thorn-Prikker concerning the *18 October 1977* cycle, 1989, in: *Gerhard Richter* as note 1, p. 232 · **50** Ibid. · **51** Interview with Gregori Magnani 1989, in: *Gerhard Richter* as note 1, p.226

Chapter 4

52 Interview with Bruno Corà, 2000, in: *Gerhard Richter* as note 1, p. 369 · **53** Interview with Stefan Koldehoff, 1999, in: *Gerhard Richter* as note 1, p. 359 · **54** Ibid. · **55** *Es geht nur noch um den Preis.* Interview: Hanno Rauterberg and Gerhard Richter, in: Die Zeit, no. 10/2015, 5 March 2015 · **56** Interview with Babette Richter, in: *Gerhard Richter* as note 1, p. 454 · **57** Beat Wyss. *Der Wille zur Kunst: Zur ästhetischen Mentalität der Moderne*, Cologne 1996, pp. 157–172 · **58** Pierre Bourdieu. *Manet: A Symbolic Revolution*, Berlin 2015, p. 727 · **59** *Gerhard Richter* as note 1, p. 360 and p. 365 · **60** Interview with Sabine Schütz, 1990, in: *Gerhard Richter* as note 1, p. 262 · **61** Pierre Bourdieu. *Zur Soziologie der symbolischen Formen*, Frankfurt 1970, p. 194 · **62** Gaston Bachelard. *Poetik des Raumes*, Frankfurt 1975, p. 99 · **63** Interview with Sabine Schütz, 1990, as note 9, p. 262 · **64** Notes, 1992, in: *Gerhard Richter* as note 1, p. 283 · **65** Ibid. **66** Manuela Lenzen. *Warum Kaffeetassen ergriffen werden wollen: Der Körper denkt mit: Die Kognitionswissenschaft erweitert ihren Begriff von Geist und Wahrnehmung*, in: *Frankfurter Allgemeine Zeitung*, March 6, 2019 **67** Interview with Hans Ulrich Obrist, November 2006, in: *Gerhard Richter* as note 1, p. 539 · **68** Notes for a press conference, July 28, 2006, in: *Gerhard Richter* as note 1, p. 527 · **69** Interview with Hans Ulrich Obrist, 2007, in: *Gerhard Richter* as note 1, p. 541 · **70** Ibid., p. 542 **71** Ibid., p. 543 · **72** Julia Voss and Peter Geimer: *Gespräch mit Gerhard Richter: Man kann Auschwitz nicht abmalen*, in: *Frankfurter Allgemeine Zeitung*, 25 February 2016 · **73** Karlheinz Lüdeking. "Was heißt hier 'Abstraktion'?" in *Frankfurter Allgemeine Zeitung*, July 7, 2018

The author

Klaus Honnef was honorary professor of photography theory at the Kassel Art Academy. He was one of the organizers of documenta 5 and documenta 6 in Kassel, and has been the curator of more than 500 exhibitions in Germany and abroad. He has written numerous books, including TASCHEN's *Contemporary Art*, *Andy Warhol*, and *Pop Art*.

FRONT COVER
Abstract Painting, 2017 (CR 952-4, detail)
Oil on canvas, 200 x 250 cm (78¾ x 98½ in.)
Cologne, private collection

BACK COVER
Gerhard Richter, 2010
Photo: Anton Corbijn

Imprint

EACH AND EVERY TASCHEN BOOK PLANTS A SEED!
Each year, we offset our annual carbon emissions with carbon credits at the Instituto Terra, a reforestation program in Minas Gerais, Brazil, founded by Lélia and Sebastião Salgado. To find out more about this ecological partnership, please check: www.taschen.com/institutoterra.
Inspiration: unlimited.
Carbon footprint: (almost) zero

Want to see more? Visit *taschen.com* to view our current publications, browse our latest magazine, and subscribe to our newsletter.

Hohenzollernring 53, D–50672 Köln
www.taschen.com

English translation: Karen Waloschek for Grapevine Publishing Services, London

Printed in Bosnia-Herzegovina
ISBN 978–3–8365–7523–2

The publisher and the author are grateful to Konstanze Ell, Atelier Gerhard Richter, Dr. Dietmar Elger and Kerstin Küster, Gerhard Richter Archive Dresden, as well as Gabriele Honnef-Harling for their kind support.

In addition to the collections and institutions mentioned in the captions, we would like to mention the following photographers: Hohe Domkirche Köln, Dombauhütte Köln, Matz and Schenk: 79; Benjamin Katz: 94; Michael C. Moeller: 93.
All other photographs in this book were provided by Atelier Gerhard Richter, Cologne.